Spiritual Masters of the World's Religions

Spiritual Masters of the World's Religions

Edited by
Victoria Kennick and Arvind Sharma

SUNY PRESS

Cover art:

Moon Reflections on Rice Paddies at the Foot of Kyodai Mountain, Shinano Province
From the series *Famous Places of the Sixty Odd Provinces*
Hiroshige Utagawa
Color woodblock print, 1853
Gift of Louis W. Hill, Jr.
Courtesy of the Minneapolis Institute of Arts

eight moons: seven masters
every one whole
reflecting the Reflection
—V. Kennick

Published by State University of New York Press, Albany

Printed in the United States of America

For information, contact State University of New York Press, Albany, NY
www.sunypress.edu

Production by Eileen Nizer
Marketing by Michael Campochiaro

Library of Congress Cataloging-in-Publication Data

Spiritual masters of the world's religions / edited by Victoria Kennick and Arvind Sharma.
p. cm.
Includes bibliographical references and index.
ISBN 978-1-4384-4497-0 (hc : alk. paper)—978-1-4384-4498-7 (pbk : alk. paper)
1. Religious leaders. 2. Religions. 3. Leadership—Religious aspects.
I. Kennick, Victoria. II. Sharma, Arvind.

BL72.S695 2012
206'.1—dc23 2012003672

10 9 8 7 6 5 4 3 2 1

This book is dedicated to all for whom
an "obligation of obedience" is a possibility.

Contents

Preface ix
Arvind Sharma

Introduction: Defining *Spiritual Master* 1
Victoria Kennick

1 Jewish Spiritual Masters 55
Harold Kasimow

2 Christian Spiritual Masters 73
James A. Wiseman

3 Muslim Spiritual Masters 91
Osman Bakar

4 Hindu Spiritual Masters 111
Arvind Sharma

5 Sikh Spiritual Masters 127
Mary Pat Fisher

6 Buddhist Spiritual Masters 155
Victoria Kennick

7 Confucian Spiritual Masters 189
Simon Man Ho Wong

8 Daoist Spiritual Masters 225
Eva Wong

Preface

Arvind Sharma

If the ultimate reality is infinite and eternal then it must be present right here. Why then do we need a master to gain access to it? The answer to this question is provided by another question: If gravity is one of the four forces that constitute the universe of matter-energy—then it must be present right here under our feet, since we are also a part of this universe. Then why do we need a Newton or an Einstein to tell us what it is or what it is not? This is because nothing is more difficult to know than that with which we are intimately familiar. Spirituality is the process by which we become ultimately familiar with what we have been intimately familiar.

A spiritual master is one who sets this process in motion.

Introduction

Defining *Spiritual Master*

Victoria Kennick

The Procrustean Bed

A Greek myth tells of Procrustes,[1] who invited strangers to spend the night on his marvelous bed. They were enticed by the promise of a bed that exactly fit the size of every guest. The unknown terror of the bed was that Procrustes stretched short guests, and severed the feet of tall ones to make each guest fit the bed. Needless to say, all guests died on Procrustes's bed. A definition is like a procrustean bed when the subject is stretched or cut to "fit" its dimensions. Yet definitions by nature require acts of stretching through abstraction, and cutting through specification. The conceptual challenge in fabricating an intelligent definition is to perform these acts of generalization and abbreviation with the least feasible amount of distortion that stems from bias and ignorance. This introductory chapter fabricates a definition of *spiritual master* that should accommodate, but not constrain, the exemplars discussed in this book. We say *fabricate* to connote artifice, as well as falsehood, because definitions are conceptual "constructs" that necessarily "lie."

The Task

To avoid creating a procrustean bed for the spiritual masters presented in this book, its contributors worked from a set of questions designed to allow each tradition to speak for itself, in both descriptive and critical ways. They examined such matters as the qualities, qualifications, role, and contributions of specific spiritual masters, with attention to critiques provided by the tradition for determining the authenticity of a spiritual master. The inquiry was set up as *one way to begin* probing issues relative to spiritual masters across religious traditions. Contributors were not asked to survey the history of spiritual masters in their tradition—nor were they discouraged from doing so. They were to wrestle with the topic of *spiritual master* from the ground of their own expertise, as the topic made most sense to them, using classic and modern exemplars.

Contributors introduced readers to terms specific to the tradition at hand,[2] using those most pertinent to the context of their inquiry, along with the trope *spiritual master* when suitable. They understood that their work was meant—at once—to broaden our knowledge about a particular religion, and to deepen our thinking about a certain type of figure in the history of religions. Those involved in the project expected that parameters of the subject matter would be shrunken and stretched from one chapter to the next. But this was to be like shrinking and stretching a bed to fit the guest—not the guest to fit a bed. Because contributors made efforts to evince the specific outlook on spiritual masters of the tradition for which they were responsible, we wound up with a variety of orientations. Indeed, paying attention to these orientations is instructive. The approach of each contributor gives a sense of the cultural values attached to spiritual masters in that particular tradition.

The first chapter opens with perplexity where Harold Kasimow begins: "When I recently told a rabbi that I was writing an essay on Jewish saints, he was somewhat puzzled. I am not surprised." By contrast, the term *spiritual master* was a natural for James A.Wiseman writing on Christianity, as his discussion gravitated to the Roman Catholic tradition where the very roots of the words *spiritual* and *master* are sunk in Latin, the language of its classic liturgy. Osman Bakar stressed the Ṣūfī fight for survival—an issue that beset Muslim mystics from its early days, and thus heavily impacted the role of spiritual masters across the centuries. Arvind Sharma surveyed the evolving role of Hindu spiritual masters, as Hindus often make sense of their massive set of traditions by identifying layers of thought. Our Sikh chapter centered on narrative portraits of spiritual masters, as Mary Pat Fisher saw "*Gurū*" as the key symbol to elucidate. Victoria Kennick geographically delineated the Buddhist world to account for the cultural impact on representative spiritual masters. For Simon Man Ho Wong, a corrective to the mistaken notion of "no spiritual masters among Confucians" was of key import, as his focus on exemplary Chinese sages showed otherwise. Eva Wong categorized spiritual masters, telling stories to subtly convey the spontaneity and hidden wisdom that characterize Daoist literature.

The Definition

In the Christian chapter, Wiseman reduces the trope *spiritual master* to its Latin roots. *Spiritual* comes from *spirare,* which means "to breathe." *Spirare* is associated with staying alive, thus the adjective *spiritualis* could mean simply "belonging to breathing" or "belonging to air." *Master* is based on *magister,* meaning "master" or "authority." The root of *magister* is *mag,* whose adjectival form *magnus* means great or large; thus *master* in English connotes leadership, authority, and mastery. Naturally, the term *spiritual master*, stemming from the language still used by the Roman Catholic Church for official liturgical texts, is well suited to Roman Catholicism. Despite this specific linguistic connection, the basic sense of the words can be adapted to cross cultures. Using these connotations, spiritual master should be understood as a subset of the more generic category of religious leader.

In English, the word *spiritual* picked up the sense of otherworldliness. Yet for cross-cultural application its basic meaning of "breath of life" or "staying alive" is more versatile, because not every religious tradition concerns itself with a transcendent otherworld. And though *master* can reference the more powerful figure in a hierarchical relationship, for our purpose its basic meaning of "authority" and "master of oneself" is best retained. In no way should *master* be restricted to connote only the masculine gender. Excising the trope *spiritual master* from superfluous associations with things otherworldly, hierarchical, and gender specific, it becomes suited to a wide spectrum of religious traditions. Thus, even in nontheist traditions, the word *spiritual* is applicable. Indeed, Simon Man Ho Wong devotes his entire chapter to the *immanent* character of Confucian spirituality.

Here follows our definition of *spiritual master,* based on the Latin etymology: A SPIRITUAL MASTER IS A CHARISMATIC MEDIATOR WHO AUTHORITATIVELY TEACHES TRADITIONS, PERSONALLY SUPPORTING RELIGIOUS VITALITY. The term *charismatic mediator* indicates one who transmits a "gift of grace."[3] It carries the sense of *spirare,* to breathe—as a charismatic mediator is enthused by the sacred (inspiration) and conveys it into the profane (expiration). The phrase *authoritatively teaches traditions* affirms the fact of mastery, as the charismatic mediator is a *magister,* master or authority. The word *personally* indicates that one who authoritatively teaches traditions does so through intimate contact. The term *religious vitality* relates to the experience of what is *spiritualis*—a term from the Greek *zōtikos,* associated with *vitalis,* meaning "vital."[4] The word *supporting* indicates that the spiritual master, in some manner or other, contributes to the flourishing of religion.

Religionist and Reductionist Approaches to the Data of Religions

We just noted that the words *spiritual* and *master* picked up the aggravating connotations of otherworldly and hierarchical. What is more, in the course of history some religious leaders capitalized on such connotations to abuse their authority, politically elevating themselves above and beyond the reach of reasoned critique. To account for both the healing and the harming power exercised by religious leaders, scholars of the history of religions developed two basic approaches to their subject: religionist and reductionist. The view of a spiritual master changes radically depending on which of these is taken, and one view acts as a corrective to the other.

The religionist approach takes religion as *sui generis* (in a class by itself), positing that *experience of the sacred* makes religion unique. It calls for the study of religion *as religion*—not as a subset of another academic discipline. The key religionist question is: What do the data of religions mean? By contrast, the reductionist approach posits that religion is a thoroughly human creation. Claiming that nothing is inherently *religious,* reductionists tend to enlist questions from the social sciences, particularly sociology, to bolster their analyses. The key reductionist question is: How do the data of religions serve human interests? Below we will see how religionist and reductionist approaches are complementary.

The Religionist Approach

Mircea Eliade (1907–1986), a founding scholar of the history of religions, articulated a classic religionist approach in saying,

> The work of deciphering the deep meaning of religious phenomena rightfully falls to the historian of religions. Certainly, the psychologist, the sociologist, the ethnologist, and even the philosopher or the theologian will have their comment to make, each from the viewpoint and in the perspective that are properly his. But it is the historian of religions who will make the greatest number of valid statements on a religious phenomenon *as a religious phenomenon*—and not as a psychological, social, ethnic, philosophical, or even theological phenomenon.[5]

Eliade balanced this focus on religious phenomena, *sui generis,* insisting that they be seen in historical context. He studied the morphology (structure) of religious phenomena, as part of a two-pronged method, and cautioned against the use of typologies in the absence of historical context.

> The historian of religions will not confine himself merely to a typology or morphology of religious data; he knows that "history" does not exhaust the content of a religious phenomenon, but neither does he forget that it is always in History—in the broadest sense of the term—that a religious datum develops all its aspects and reveals all its meanings. In other words, the historian of religions makes use of all the *historical* manifestations of a religious phenomenon in order to discover what such a phenomenon "has to say"; on the one hand, he holds to the historically concrete, but on the other, he attempts to decipher whatever transhistorical content a religious datum reveals through history.[6]

A prime example of the religionist approach to *spirituality* is seen in Ewert Cousins's comment on problems faced by the editors of *World Spirituality: An Encyclopedic History of the Religious Quest*:

> In the planning of the project, no attempt was made to arrive at a common definition of spirituality that would be accepted by all in precisely the same way. The term "spirituality," or an equivalent, is not found in a number of the traditions. Yet from the outset, there was a consensus among the editors about what was in general intended by the term. It was left to each tradition to clarify its own understanding of this meaning. . . . As a working

hypothesis, the following description was used to launch the project:

> The series focuses on that inner dimension of the person called by certain traditions "the spirit." This spiritual core is the deepest center of the person. It is here that the person is open to the transcendent dimension; it is here that the person experiences ultimate reality. The series explores the discovery of this core, the dynamics of its development, and its journey to the ultimate goal. It deals with prayer, spiritual direction, the various maps of the spiritual journey, and the methods of advancement in the spiritual ascent.[7]

Despite their historical awareness, the religionist editors leaned into the domain of theological inquiry through presumptions about the reality of a spiritual core, transcendent dimension, and ultimate reality. Whether or not these exist as such, a historian of religions, taking either a religionist or a reductionist approach, does not engage in truth claims about the data of religions.

The Reductionist Approach

The reductionist focus on religion as a human creation serves to check and balance the religionist treatment of religion as *sui generis,* which easily slips into theological truth claims. For instance, when religionists begin to speak theologically of "the spirit" as a unique and irreducible aspect of reality by which the person opens to the transcendent dimension, reductionists look with healthy suspicion on words explicitly relating to the divine, such as *spiritual, sacred,* and *transcendent.*

Sometimes, reductionists even use the word *religion* with reluctance. Consider this view of the defining characteristic of religion, articulated by the contemporary historian of religions, Bruce Lincoln:

> Of particular interest, I think, is the way religion connects to the other domains of culture [i.e., ethics and aesthetics]: specifically, the capacity of religious discourse to articulate ethical and aesthetic positions in a uniquely stabilizing fashion. What religion does—and this, I submit, is its defining characteristic—is to invest specific human preferences with transcendent status by misrepresenting them as revealed

> truths, primordial traditions, divine commandments and so forth. In this way, it insulates them against most forms of debate and critique, assisting their transmission from one generation to another as part of a sacred canon.[8]

From Lincoln's definition of *religion,* we infer the key role of spiritual masters to be "investing specific human preferences with transcendent status by misrepresenting them as revealed truths, primordial traditions, divine commandments and so forth." Thus, what a religionist may think of as a "spiritual core [that] is the deepest center of the person," a reductionist may regard as a fiction created by "investing specific human preferences with transcendent status" through propagandistic means. However, a religionist approach need not become so idealistic with regard to spiritual masters; nor a reductionist, so suspicious.

Our definition of *spiritual master* accounts for both religionist and reductionist perspectives. It does not preclude the possibility of spiritual masters receiving authentic revelations, according to their own definitions; nor does it assert the reality of those revelations. It keeps the door open to discover the meaning of religious claims from the insider viewpoint of adherents, recognizing that religious authorities might either *represent* or *misrepresent* their putative wisdom as revealed truths, primordial traditions, and divine commandments. Yet, an inquiry based on the definition of a spiritual master as *a charismatic mediator who authoritatively teaches traditions, personally supporting religious vitality* invites scrutiny as to whether a religious leader creatively promotes religious teachings to foster human intelligence or insulates them "against most forms of debate and critique," as Lincoln cautioned. It should be obvious by now that not every religious leader should be counted as a spiritual master. Those who stifle religious vitality do not qualify.

The foregoing discussion of religionist and reductionist approaches is of key importance to our understanding of spiritual masters, because personal surrender to religious leaders historically has allowed uncritical acceptance of truth claims and abuses of power. We now turn to the work of Max Weber (1864–1920), who spoke of such surrender as the "obligation of obedience." Weber, the "father of sociology," examines the role of charismatic individuals in terms of the legitimation of their authority in society. His reductionist work contributes significantly to an understanding of the social function of spiritual masters. Subsequently, we examine the work of Daniel Gold, a contemporary historian of religions who built on Weber's sociology to develop important categories that accommodate a religionist perspective.

Max Weber and the Problem of Charismatic Authority

In Germany, Max Weber was most prolific in his writing from 1903 to 1920—a time spanning World War I and events leading up to it. He studied the means by which political authority became accepted as legitimate in societies, and classified *Herrschaft* (German for "rule" or "domination") into three types: legal, traditional, and charismatic. Knowing full well that typological analysis has its limits,[9] Weber further classified charismatic authority into three types: magician, priest, and prophet. Provisionally, we suggest that, spiritual master could be counted as a fourth type of charismatic authority

Charismatic Authority and the "Obligation of Obedience"

Weber posited three grounds upon which *Herrschaft* as social rule or domination rests: (1) rational grounds that rest on a belief in the legality of normative rules and the right of those elevated to authority under such rules to issue commands, (2) traditional grounds that rest on established belief in the sanctity of immemorial traditions and the legitimacy of the status of those exercising authority under them, and (3) charismatic grounds that rest on devotion to a sanctified, heroic, or otherwise exceptional or exemplary person, and of the normative order revealed or ordained by that person.[10] Domination or rule is accepted as legitimate when an "obligation of obedience" springs from such belief or devotion.

> In the case of legal authority, obedience is owed to the legally established impersonal order. It extends to the persons exercising the authority of office under it only by virtue of the formal legality of their commands and only within the scope of authority of the office. In the case of traditional authority, obedience is owed to the *person* of the chief who occupies the traditionally sanctioned position of authority and who is (within its sphere) bound by tradition. But here the obligation of obedience is not based on the impersonal order, but is a matter of personal loyalty within the area of accustomed obligations. In the case of charismatic authority, it is the charismatically qualified leader

> as such who is obeyed by virtue of personal trust in him and his revelation, his heroism or his exemplary qualities so far as they fall within the scope of the individual's belief in his charisma.[11]

Here we see the three substantive ways in which religious authority is exercised in society, namely through: (1) a charismatic individual who is unique, and is, in that sense, a revolutionary hero, (2) a person who stands in a traditional lineage of some sort, often exercising authority through an office established after a charismatic leader passes away, and (3) a set of normative rules, administered by an officeholder who does not personally command the authority owed to the legal entity.

Initially it is useful to think of a spiritual master as a charismatic individual who mediates a "dual relationship between men and the supernatural."[12] Many exemplars discussed in this book have charisma in the sense Weber that attaches to it here:

> The term "charisma" will be applied to a certain quality of an individual personality by virtue of which he is set apart from ordinary men and treated as endowed with supernatural, superhuman, or at least specifically exceptional powers or qualities. These are such as are not accessible to the ordinary person, but are regarded as of divine origin or as exemplary, and on the basis of them the individual concerned is treated as a leader. In primitive circumstances this peculiar kind of deference is paid to prophets, to people with a reputation for therapeutic or legal wisdom, to leaders in the hunt, and heroes in war. It is very often thought of as resting on magical powers. How the quality in question would be ultimately judged from any ethical, aesthetic, or other such point of view is naturally entirely indifferent for purposes of definition.[13]

The designation *spiritual master* as a charismatic individual might suit some of Weber's exemplars better than his categories of magician, priest, or prophet—the obvious example being Jesus. Weber classifies Jesus as a prophet; and though Jesus is recognized as a prophet by Muslims, *spiritual master* is a more religiously neutral term that circumvents the critical point of contention about Jesus that divides Christians and Muslims. Whether Jesus is identified as prophet or spiritual master, his qualities well illustrate a key aspect of the charismatic individual, namely, a self-reflective sense of possessing charisma. Weber reminds us:

> It must not be forgotten for an instant that the entire basis of Jesus' own legitimation, as well as his claim that he and only he knew the Father and that the way to God led through faith in him alone, was the magical charisma he felt within himself. It was doubtless this consciousness of power, more than anything else, that enabled him to traverse the road of the prophets. . . . There was always required of such prophets a proof of their possession of particular gifts of the spirit, or special magical or ecstatic abilities.[14]

Given the foregoing discussion of Weber's *Herrschaft*, charisma, and obligation of obedience, we suggest that spiritual masters are mediators of the sacred, obeyed by people who have developed personal trust in them based on their exceptional sanctity, heroism, or special qualities. This renders them charismatic and authoritative, according to Weber's understanding. People become devoted to spiritual masters after being impressed by their charisma, exhibited through putative gifts of the spirit, or special magical or ecstatic abilities. Moreover, the charisma has been felt by the spiritual masters themselves, giving them a sense of their own legitimacy. This produces in spiritual masters a sense of duty and confidence to exercise charismatic authority in promoting a normative social order—even with new and revolutionary patterns. Indeed, "within the sphere of its claims, charismatic authority repudiates the past, and is in this sense a specifically revolutionary force."[15]

The Routinization of Charismatic Authority

Weber questioned the extent to which the force of charisma—hence, the corresponding obligation of obedience—might diminish in the transfer of authority from a charismatic individual to a traditional authority established in a subsequent lineage, and further into an impersonal set of legal rules, whose caretaking officeholder defers to the legal framework. Weber posits that the exercise of authority by a traditional officeholder involves less charisma than the exercise of authority of a charismatic personality, per se. By definition, the charismatic personality is a unique, heroic, and revolutionary individual who embodies charisma. In contrast, a traditional officeholder's authority is limited within the sphere of tradition, and thus mediates through charisma that is more circumscribed. Further, according to the definition, legal authority is devoid of charisma, as there is no place for a *personal* set of rules to meditate charisma, and there is no allegiance due to the noncharismatic officeholder who administers the rules. Within this framework, Weber develops his theory of the "routinization" of charisma, which involves the diminution of charisma through three sociological stages in the exercise of authority.

Weber predicts a natural expiration date for every case of charismatic authority. Personal charisma is extraordinary; but when disciples lose confidence in its special character, the authority of the magician, priest, or prophet dissolves. Weber explains:

> Charismatic authority is thus specifically outside the realm of everyday routine and the profane sphere. . . . The only basis of legitimacy for it is personal charisma, so long as it is proved; that is, as long as it receives recognition and is able to satisfy the followers of disciples. But this lasts only so long as the belief in its charismatic inspiration remains.[16]

Once charismatic individuals fail to excite an obligation of obedience, their authority fails. Even when a magician, priest, or prophet maintains an obligation of obedience, the charismatic authority cannot continue in their absence. According to Weber, the charisma becomes "routinized," whereby the intensity of the charisma of a founding charismatic individual necessarily becomes depleted.

> In its pure form charismatic authority has a character specifically foreign to everyday routine structures. The social relationships directly involved are strictly personal, based on the validity and practice of charismatic personal qualities. If this is not to remain a purely transitory phenomenon, but to take on the character of a permanent relationship forming a stable community of disciples or a band of followers or a party organization or any sort of political or hierocratic organization, it is necessary for the character of charismatic authority to become radically changed. Indeed, in its pure form charismatic authority may be said to exist only in the process of originating. It cannot remain stable, but becomes either traditionalized or rationalized, or a combination of both.[17]

Weber provides the case of the dalai lamas as an instance of the routinization of charismatic authority, whereby a new charismatic leader is sought to replace a dalai lama that has passed away.[18] The routinization of charismatic authority of a dalai lama can occur

> on the basis of criteria of the qualities which will fit him for the position of authority; . . . by revelation manifest in oracles, lots, divine judgments, or other techniques of selection; . . . by the designation on the part of the original charismatic leader of his own successor and his recognition on the part of the followers; . . . [and by] designation of a successor by the charismatically qualified administrative staff and his recognition by the community.[19]

One can apply Weber's insights on routinization of charismatic authority to the lineage of Sikh *gurūs*, insofar as the ten historical charismatic leaders were maintained "by the designation on the part of the original charismatic leader of his own successor and his recognition on the part of the followers."[20] Every Sikh *gurū* is recognized as having charisma, technically known as *jot*, or divine light, of which each is a vessel. Certainly, Sikh *gurūs*, as well as Tibetan Buddhist dalai lamas, Roman Catholic popes, and other spiritual masters who belong to what we might call lineage offices have charisma that to some degree survives the process of routinization. With such examples in mind, we are reassured in the notion that spiritual master is a category commensurate with magician, priest, and prophet—insofar as it includes persons garnering an obligation of obedience, hence legitimacy, even into the routinized contexts of traditional and legal forms of authority. But there is a catch.

The Limits of the Person in Weber

If Weber's reductionist inquiry were sufficient for studies in the history of religions, his typology of *Herrschaft* would accommodate all cases of spiritual masters. However, for example, the case of the final Sikh *gurū*—a scripture called "Gurū Granth Sāhib"—drives Weber's typology to the breaking point. This scripture forces us to shift gears. Gurū Granth Sāhib fits into Weber's typology neither as a charismatic authority, nor as a traditional authority, because Weber defines both as personal. As a sociologist, he never asks how an object such as a holy scripture might function as a *person*. Moreover, Gurū Granth

Sāhib does not fit as a legal authority, because Weber defines legal authority as impersonal. So, where is the place for Gurū Granth Sāhib in Weber's typology of *Herrschaft*? The same question can be asked in connection with numerous other sacred texts in the history of the world's religions.

Gurū Granth Sāhib is a collection of hymns that provide an ethical foundation in Sikh tradition. As such, according to Weber's model, one would identify the document as a legal authority that is impersonal and devoid of charisma. However, Gurū Granth Sāhib is viewed not only as a collection of hymns, but also as a unique charismatic mediator. Gurū Granth Sāhib—having the outward appearance of a book—exhibits charismatic qualities and is treated by Sikhs as a person. The *gurū* is even retired at night in its home, the Golden Temple in Amritsar, India. Fisher says:

> Gurū Granth Sāhib [is] enshrined in the Golden Temple in Amritsar, the most revered Sikh holy place. At night, the scripture is closed, wrapped in fabrics, and carried on someone's head, with water sprinkled ahead of it to symbolically purify the way. It is then lovingly placed to rest for the night, as it were, on pillows in a specially constructed "bed." In the winter, it may be covered with a fine quilt so that the Gurū does not become cold. (151–52)

Indeed, there is a religious reason that Sikhs call their scripture *Gurū*: it embodies the divine light (*jot*), as did the preceding Ten Gurūs, who were human vessels of *jot*. There are many cases in the history of the world's religions where one finds special treatment given to sacred objects. They, too, can be seen in light of their personal impact on religious people.

Bearing in mind how Gurū Granth Sāhib is existentially experienced from a Sikh religious standpoint, *in a limited sense,* the scripture might be classified not only as a legal authority, but also as a charismatic authority and a traditional authority, both of which are personal. Gurū Granth Sāhib is treated as a charismatic living *gurū*; in this sense, the scripture is a charismatic authority. Gurū Granth Sāhib is part of the lineage of Sikh *gurūs* and makes available the sanctity of immemorial traditions; in this sense, it is a traditional authority. Gurū Granth Sāhib is also a revered document; in this sense, it is a legal authority—but, not the impersonal legal authority of Weber's typology. Moreover, following Weber, the First Gurū should have held charismatic authority, the Second Gurū through the Tenth Gurū should have held traditional authority, and Gurū Granth Sāhib should have held legal authority. But this does not explain everything.

From the Sikh point of view, an obligation of obedience is owed to Gurū Granth Sāhib, which is a vessel of the same the same *jot* as was Gurū Nānak and each of the intervening human Sikh *gurūs*. From the First Gurū to the Tenth Gurū, all have been called "Nānak," though they are each known by another name as well. Moreover, in reading Gurū Granth Sāhib, one comes into contact with Gurū Nānak through the *jot* of the hymns. Thus, the charisma of Nānak proceeds through all three types of *Herrschaft*, and nothing is lost to a process of routinization. Hence, we begin to see two limits of Weber's typology of *Herrschaft* for the context of the history of religions: (1) the process of routinization, or loss of charismatic authority over time, does not always apply, and (2) an authority can function in more than one category, as they function in a nonhierarchical relationship.

The Sikh case suggests that the charismatic authority of spiritual masters is not necessarily diminished according to the social process of routinization described by Weber in connection with magicians, priests, and prophets. Rather, spiritual masters might maintain a high level of personal charisma regardless of the context of authority through which they gain social legitimation: legal, traditional, or charismatic. Moreover, since all Sikh *gurūs* command an equal obligation of obedience based on identical charisma, they should all be counted as charismatic individuals that function sometimes in a heroic capacity, sometimes in the context of a traditional lineage, and sometimes as a legal authority. Thus the three types of *Herrschaft* cannot in this case be viewed as a hierarchy of discrete classes of authority. Weber's analysis of *Herrschaft* remains useful for a sociological study of spiritual masters. But one must realize with such a reductionist analysis, the religious meaning of numerous spiritual masters in the history of the world's religions is left unattended; and thus the complexity of the cultural dynamics surrounding them is overridden.

We could end here, and remain content with one theoretical context in which to understand spiritual masters. To limit ourselves to Weber's reductionist model, we would be obliged to omit troublesome examples of spiritual masters, such as the Sikh holy scripture and nine other Nānaks. But of what use is a definition that cannot account for all cases that call for admission and fit nowhere else? Accepting the challenge of fabricating a definition that can cogently accommodate outliers brings the boon of deeper understanding of all members of the class, here, specifically, *spiritual masters*. To fabricate such a definition requires the shift from a reductionist to a religionist approach to our data. There the import of the term *charisma* may come closer to the early meaning that Weber elaborated to serve his sociological agenda.[21] At this point, our provisional identification of spiritual master as a fourth type of charismatic individual in Weber's typology has reached its limit.

To open our minds to the full range of spiritual masters that our definition must serve, let us consider a conversation between Bhagavan Ramana Maharshi (1879–1950) and a disciple named Dilip. This passage, presented by Sharma in the Hindu chapter, challenges us to seriously consider the case of inanimate spiritual masters:

> *Dilip*: Sri Aurobindo often refers to you as having had no Guru.
>
> *B.*: That depends on what you call Guru. They need not necessarily be in human form. Dattatreya had twenty-four Gurus—the elements, etc. That means that any form in the world was his Guru. Guru is absolutely necessary. The Upanishads say that none but a Guru can take a man out of the jungle of mental and sense perceptions, so there must be a Guru.
>
> *Dilip*: I mean a human Guru. The Maharshi didn't have one.
>
> *B.*: I might have had at some time or other. And didn't I sing hymns to Arunachala? What is a Guru? Guru is God or the Self. (120–21)

How can we admit Dattatreya's twenty-four *gurūs* into our definition of *spiritual master*? Beyond Dattatreya's elements, etc., and Gurū Granth Sāhib, what should be done with other exemplars that would be problematic to Weber's model—including many sacred texts, members of spiritual lineages, and other existentially meaningful objects? To find a way to account for such spiritual masters in the history of the world's religions, we now move from the reductionist model.

Daniel Gold and the Categories of Religious Perception

As a sociologist, Weber focused on social institutions. As a reductionist, he did not provide as full a characterization of spiritual masters as that needed by historians of religions. Weber presented a typology of social authority exercised by religious leaders, but did not focus on the *existential meaning* leading to the obligation of obedience that grants that legitimacy. Building on Weber's insights, Daniel Gold developed a "grammar of religious perception" for the history of religions that did focus on such meaning. We will find largely that whatever can be said of Gold's *gurū,* can be said of *spiritual master.*

Toward a Grammar of Religious Perception

Gold developed his grammar first to comprehend the Hindu *gurū,* and then to offer a comparative framework. Consistent with Eliade's two-pronged method that includes phenomenology and history, Gold understood that

> *our* problem as historians of religion[s] is to understand problems of human beings struggling to comprehend their existence in the world. Our religio-historical constructs must then be able to make sense of the worlds that they conceive.[22]

Gold's grammar throws us into a religionist discussion of *religious meaning* that grew from Weber's reductionist discussion of *social processes.* He focused on "perhaps most intriguing [of problems that history of religions treats, namely] the complex relationships between outer tradition and inner life."[23]

Gold made three methodological moves that help unpack our definition of *spiritual master*: (1) he developed a nonhierarchical morphological frame, instead of a typology, to better accommodate the fluid and dynamic categories relative to the *gurū,* (2) he took an epistemological turn to see aspects of the *gurū*—four immanent foci of the divine, namely, holy man, singular personality, eternal heritage, and unifying truth—as categories of religious perception, rather than as external objects, and (3) he recognized a continuum between inner spiritual life and outer traditions, which he designated as esoteric and exoteric, or hidden and public (revealed).

Four Immanent Foci of the Divine

Earlier, we provisionally identified spiritual master as an additional type of charismatic individual, alongside Weber's magician, priest, and prophet. Gold's holy man could be considered in similar terms, as a type of charismatic individual—with all the benefits and limitations attending Weber's sociological context. In this limited, reductionist sense, spiritual master and holy man are equivalent to each other, but only insofar as they are defined as charismatic human individuals, the legitimation of whose authority derives from an obligation of obedience.

Now, we must break open the trope *spiritual master* in light of the full spectrum of the four immanent foci of the divine, to see that *spiritual master* is none other than the *gurū*. Gold's *gurū*—like our spiritual master—occupies a nonhierarchical morphological frame that encompasses all four charismatic mediators identified in the grammar, of which holy man is just one. As such, a spiritual master, like a *gurū*, can function not only as a holy man (e.g., a human), but also as a singular personality (e.g., a deity), an eternal heritage (e.g., a scripture or temple), and a unifying truth (e.g., an interreligious teaching). The *gurū* is all of these; and each is a source "through which divine grace, knowledge, and power are mediated to humankind."[24]

Gold emphasized the function of mediation, more than the substance of divine grace or charisma itself. Here we see how the first three foci function to mediate the divine:

> Mediation through the eternal heritage is perceived as the assimilation of the ageless wisdom underlying the accumulated tradition of a people. Mediation through the singular personality comes through participation in a universal fount of grace established on earth by a divine being, which is often accessible through a teaching and a sacrament he has left. Mediation through the holy man is experienced as a direct communication from a living person qualified to transmit the divine. Conceived according to different understandings of the way in which spiritual power finds a center on earth, each of these sources represents a particular perception of the *immanent focus* of the divine.[25]

Gold developed the concept of unifying truth less than he does the other three immanent foci of the divine, because "it does not support any large-scale religious tradition."[26] Accordingly, it does not appear in the above passage. However, for our understanding of *spiritual master*, all four foci are of equal import; and we occasionally reference them later in this chapter.

In Weber's model of routinization, charismatic authority stands in hierarchical relationship to traditional authority and legal authority—all within an exoteric, public context that Gold calls outer tradition. This hierarchical structure, and the lack of the esoteric dimension of inner life limits Weber to his sociological context, around which he developed an understanding of the generation and distribution of charismatic, traditional, and legal authority in society. Echoing Weber's view of self-recognized charisma and the garnering of authority in society through an obligation of obedience, Gold sees the potential for loss of charismatic authority of a holy man:

> The distinctive dynamic of the holy man, then, whether within established traditions or without, is to continually make hidden truths immediate, and mundane community divine. To do this effectively, the holy man must remain at once true to his own possibly changing realizations and sensitive to his devotees' probably changing needs. And should he begin to lose touch with his hidden sources of inspiration or fail to keep communicating convincing revelations to his disciples, his perceived position as holy man [read: Weber's charismatic magician, priest, or prophet] is likely first to become shaky and then to break down.[27]

Here, Gold's claim reflects Weber's sociological perspective. However, despite this affirmation of Weber's model, Gold goes further to permit charismatic authority to remain undiminished, free from the impact of what Weber called routinization. Methodologically, he got there by taking an epistemological turn.

The Epistemological Turn

Gold's epistemological turn transforms the four immanent foci of the divine into categories of religious perception. He releases *gurū* from the constraints of a substantive typology into a functional morphological frame to show how holy man, singular personality, eternal heritage, and unifying truth *existentially appear* along an interpenetrating continuum. In this fluid and dynamic model, Gold imposes no substantive restrictions relative to what might play the role of *gurū* within the four categories of religious perception. There is room in the morphological frame for Gurū Granth Sāhib, Dattatreya's twenty-four *gurū*s, and more.

Gold moved beyond reductionism when he realized that "to understand the dynamics of relationship among the foci we must look to some uncharted depths of religious perception."[28] This was outside of Weber's mandate as a sociologist. In his grammar, Gold found an alternative to Weber's routinization. Weber posited that whenever magicians, priests, or prophets die or are discredited, their charismatic authority inevitably fades or disappears. Gold created a seismic shift by recalibrating types of authority as *categories of religious perception*. His understanding of charismatic mediation and the exercise of authority, in the morphological frame of the *gurū*, complements Weber's sociological perspective, but is not limited by it.

> The same collectively recognized spiritual image can appear as a different type of immanent focus to different religious individuals. A figure taken respectively by one individual as a guru, a holy man, may be glorified by another as an avatar—who is at least a very special personage, more likely a singular personality. A deity to whom one individual can relate as a magnificent, complex personality is seen by another as merely belonging to a class of rather manipulable godlings in a heritage. *The immanent foci, then, do not refer directly to external objects.* Certainly, people in the same tradition have similar experiences of their common objects of faith, which may then attain constant local values. *The immanent foci, however, are here offered explicitly as categories of religious perception.* And as categories of religious perception, the immanent foci reveal the divine in distinctive conceptual dimensions. (emphasis supplied)[29]

Nothing by way of charisma or charismatic authority need be lost in the transition from one sociological center of spiritual power to the next—provided that there is a vitality of inner life associated with the obligation of obedience.

Weber's view of routinization does not account for the existential meaning of inner life. That is to say, the reductionist model recognizes no esoteric category of religious perception in which outer tradition gains enhanced personal meaning. It does not theoretically account for the degree to which charisma is or is not lost in the routinized social transfer from a magician, priest, or prophet to a traditional authority (e.g. a lineage holder) or a legal authority (e.g. a set of laws). Although the sociological model can say whether or not the obligation of obedience has collapsed, it does not account for the interplay of inner tradition and outer tradition. When one detects from a sociological perspective that charismatic authority has been diminished, there is a possibility of understanding the loss in connection with the degree of vitality of existential meaning of the inner life. Thus, with Gold's model we can utilize Weber's model, and go still deeper into cultural dynamics.

We can understand Gold's move away from sociology into the history of religions in terms of two axes: an esoteric-exoteric vertical axis, and a horizontal axis of the four immanent foci of the divine. In Gold's model of the *gurū*, no charisma need be lost in a disciple's religious perceptions of any of the four foci. This is because they function along an interpenetrating continuum of the four foci along what we call a horizontal axis. The image of horizontal here is meant to indicate nonhierarchical structural relationship. This horizontal axis of the four foci intersects with the vertical axis of esoteric and exoteric categories of religious perception. The image of vertical here is meant to indicate two complementary poles that become sources for a disciple's existential meaning. In other words, each focus of the divine generates existential meaning for disciples through both their inner life and their outer tradition. The *gurū* is thus religiously perceived according to specific intersections of the horizontal and vertical epistemological axes.

Esoteric and Exoteric Categories of Religious Perception

Weber's notion that charismatic authority weakens through routinization as it becomes traditional or legal, holds within a methodological model that is focused on society, recognizing only what Gold labels as an outer tradition that is exoteric or public. Gold's observations are consistent with Weber's observations, as long as one assumes that the hidden, esoteric dimension of religious perception has weakened:

> What seems to distinguish a successful transformation from a breakdown of tradition is the continuing balance it keeps between the hidden and revealed aspects of the divine that it makes manifest. In a *progression*, our term for a successful transformation, the forms of religious expression available through a tradition change along with the tradition's dominant focus: as new hidden meaning is seen in a focus, the tradition develops revealed forms that reflect it adequately. In *breakdowns*, on the other hand, a serious gap occurs between the revealed forms of a tradition and the hidden ideals that these forms are supposed to represent. Neither the theoretical nor the practical forms of religious expression offered by the tradition lead any longer to a potent appreciation of the immanent divine. For a large

> portion of its members the tradition appears to be presenting something meaningless, or even false.[30]

Charismatic authority in society cannot be maintained in the absence of a vital hidden, esoteric dimension of religious experience. Gold emphasizes the dynamic relationship between the exoteric or public dimensions, and the esoteric or hidden dimensions of religious experience:

> As bases of both personal salvation and communal solidarity, these three immanent foci demonstrate revealed aspects—visible to all—and hidden ones, which only the wise can see. The holy man is revealed visibly in his discourses and commands, the singular personality in a scripture and church, and the eternal heritage through the mythic and legal tradition of a venerable culture. The other, more esoteric qualities of the foci are made known only to those fit to understand: the holy man offers hidden help for his disciples and a particular cosmic mission for the universe; the singular personality presents hidden saving grace to the true church of the elect; and the complex lore of the eternal heritage holds deep meanings and teaches hidden precepts.[31]

This dual mode of private and public religious perception is activated in connection with the charismatic mediation of the *gurū* as holy man, singular personality, eternal heritage, and unifying truth. Together this esoteric-exoteric vertical axis and the horizontal axis of the four foci that intersects it constitute a fluid and dynamic nonhierarchical morphological frame of the *gurū*.

The obligation of obedience to a *gurū*—hence the social legitimacy of the *gurū*'s authority—gains strength to the degree that both categories of religious perception are vital. This is because they reinforce each other. Moreover, we suggest that when all categories of religious perception of the four foci are active, existential meaning is enhanced and culture is enriched. The exoteric religious forms of a culture's public outer tradition give shape to the existential meaning in a disciple's esoteric inner life experience. On the other hand, the intensity of inner meaning generates enthusiasm for the outer cultural forms. This enthusiasm excites an obligation of obedience that accepts charismatic authority as legitimate. From the dynamic of the two axes, we can see "the complex relationships between outer tradition and inner life" that Gold found to be "perhaps the most intriguing" of problems treated by historians of religions. Gold was able to bring complex cultural and epistemological relationships into cogent view with his morphological frame of the *gurū* in which the horizontal four foci dynamically propel the interaction between inner life and outer tradition.

A Morphological Frame

In building his nonhierarchical morphological frame with its six categories of religious perception along two axes, Gold dispensed not only with hierarchy, but also with typology. Both Weber and Gold recognized permeable boundaries that exist between the pure types of social authority. However, while Weber worked with a typology, Gold set up a nonhierarchical morphological frame in which the *gurū* appears in an epistemological context of categories of religious perception.[32] Four permutations of the *gurū* move along the interpenetrating continuum from one focus to the other depending on circumstances of the inner life of the disciple and outer circumstances of the disciple's culture.

The form of the *gurū* in outer tradition can take on different existential meanings along the vertical axis of inner life and outer tradition, for "every component of this configuration of foci around the *gurū* has its own role, each can in fact turn out to be crucial for different individuals in different circumstances."[33] Thus, a *gurū* is perceived as one or another focus, depending on which category of religious perception is central at that moment. Here follow some examples that allow us to see the nonhierarchical character of Gold's morphological frame. Clearly, the morphological frame is not a *typology* in the expected sense that one pure type is distinct from another. Fluid boundaries are expected in any typology, as there are no pure types. However, here we see a concomitant—rather than a hierarchical—relationship among the categories of religious perception.

A *Gurū* Weaves through the Immanent Foci of the Divine

The *gurū* can appear as predominately one immanent focus of the divine, but weave through the other categories of religious perception as befits circumstances:

> The mission of the holy man and the meaning of the help he offers is given definition through the greater context

> in which he stands. Within an eternal heritage, the holy man finds a place as a conduit of ancient hidden wisdom, revealing the true relationship between customary tradition and the natural order of the divine. In a wider religious context focused on a singular personality the holy man may be understood to carry on that personality's mission in the world at present. His esoteric help is then taken as a concrete manifestation of the personality's saving power. Holy men proclaiming highly inclusive unifying truths, finally, are understood to know the mysteries of all the world's religions.[34]

Here we see the holy man as the central target that transforms as occasions arise. Any of the other three foci could also function as the central target. The Hindu story of Lord Kṛṣṇa on the battlefield with the warrior Arjuna, as told in the *Bhagavadgītā* comes to mind as a good illustration of the singular personality undergoing the three other permutations: As Arjuna's cousin who drives the chariot, Kṛṣṇa humanly functions as a holy man; when Kṛṣṇa outlines details of the dharma (law, duty) to Arjuna, he embodies the eternal heritage of the Hindus; when Kṛṣṇa bestows the divine eye on Arjuna, he functions in the category of unifying truth; and when Arjuna emerges from the *mysterium tremendum* (terrifying mystery) of experiencing Kṛṣṇa as Time Itself, the disciple realizes that his cousin is a divine singular personality. Here follow some examples from Gold's work.

Holy Man and Singular Personality

We noted that the *gurū* can function as any of the four immanent foci of the divine. Here is a case that shows how disciples perceived two Hindu yogis in an Indian hermitage. One *gurū* was perceived as a holy man; the other, as a singular personality.

> Jītā Dās as living holy man presents a figure offering marked contrasts to Govind conceived as singular personality. Jītā Dās projects his divine presence unexpectedly into people's lives—intimately through their sleep and their service to him—in ways they do not particularly seek. The unusual events that occur in his wake may be understood, at least by the outsider, less as inexplicable miracles than as coincidence, perspective, and psychological suggestion. . . . Perceived subjectively by devotees, his is a hidden divine

> presence known only to the wise. By contrast, when Govind brings the Saryū [River] down from Ayodhyā, he is seen to have performed a concrete physical miracle on a grand scale. . . . He is a superhuman fount of grace and power, not, like Jītā Dās, an enigmatic divine presence.[35]

Jītā Dās and Govind were both human *gurūs*. Yet, disciples saw one functioning as a holy man, and the other, as singular personality who was perceived as the symbol of a deity. Thus, the two human *gurūs* were not equivalent in their function at that time.

Singular Personality and Eternal Heritage

The physical form of a holy book can function as eternal heritage, and simultaneously as singular personality:

> The singular personality, for example, normally offers a basis of salvation in a specific communication from the divine, a definite teaching. The essence of this teaching is frequently revealed in a single holy book that presents the personality's holy life and words: the Rāmāyaṇa, the Gospels. But through their saving power, Rām, Jesus, and the Buddha may also remain accessible in a hidden form, continuing to communicate divine truths and to hear the prayers of devotees.[36]

Both the singular personality (e.g., Rām, Jesus, the Buddha) and the eternal heritage (e.g., *Rāmāyaṇa,* the Gospels) are immanent foci of the divine. This example of the *gurū* functioning interchangeably along the interpenetrating continuum of the horizontal axis reminds us of Gurū Granth Sāhib, the Sikh holy scripture whose *person* was difficult to fit into a Weberian typology.

The plot thickens as we look more deeply at the category of eternal heritage. It proves to be more diffuse than its simple manifestation in a holy book. This immanent focal point of the divine involves "an eternal mythic nexus." Thus, for example, temples and bathing ghats also stand as the eternal heritage, and function as *gurū* concomitant with other foci of the divine.

> The bathing ghats on the river Saryū, the temples by the ghats, and the priests in the temples all derive meaning from the significance of King Rām's story in the entire complex of Indian lore. To the extent that he is experienced

> within the whole of the cultural tradition, Rām the singular personality stands in the eternal heritage of Hinduism. And to the extent that the living brahmin priest uses ritual means to link the individual to this mythic reality, he is more of a focal point in the heritage than an independent holy man.[37]

In this example, the singular personality (Rām) is religiously perceived along an interpenetrating continuum with the eternal heritage, which is part of a mythic nexus that includes both the *Rāmāyaṇa* story and the bathing *ghaṭs*. Moreover, the brahmin priest through the performance of ritual serves as an additional layer of eternal heritage.

Holy Man and Unifying Truth

A *gurū* whose teaching transcends cultural constraints might function simultaneously as a holy man and a unifying truth. Gold notes:

> During times of interaction among different traditions, the holy man may arise to play a more crucial revelatory role. Here he works not out of a single accepted set of revealed traditions, but out of a grand unifying truth. Yet the one saving truth revealed in all the world's scriptures demands a correct interpretation—and this the holy man reveals through his revealed discourse and example. . . . When a holy man presents a grand unifying truth, he usually reveals it in our technical sense. That is, he gives this amorphous truth some specific working dimensions through the revealed bases of faith that he characteristically offers.[38]

Exoterically, the holy man functions in a cultural context. Esoterically, the teachings can be perceived through various forms—or through formlessness. The unifying truth is an amorphous truth that takes form through the chosen outer tradition of the holy man, and accrues a private existential meaning within a disciple's inner life.

> A vision of a unifying truth thus provides a fertile context for the holy man, since it is he who knows the hidden meaning of diverse scriptures and can initiate disciples into the select brotherhood of the wise.[39]

As with the other immanent foci of the divine, unifying truth can be religiously perceived from both esoteric and exoteric perspectives. However, in the case of unifying truth, the esoteric category of religious perception implodes and explodes to obliterate microcosmic and macrocosmic boundaries along the vertical esoteric-exoteric axis. Outer tradition takes on a radical new existential meaning, as impacted by a profound revolution of inner life. Gold quotes a Hindu song of *gurū* devotion in which the *gurū* shows up in a hidden place of the disciple's body. Here, the *gurū* moves from the focus of holy man to the focus of unifying truth as his image overspreads the disciple's heart in a formless hierophany (manifestation of the sacred in the profane).

> I won't worship Brahma,Viṣṇu, or Maheśa,
> Nor fix my attention on a god of stone.
> The object of my love resides within my body;
> To him alone I'll bow my head. . . .
> The guru's image overspreads my heart
> And gets all my attention.
> When he obliterates our separateness
> What's left I'll call the Formless.
> The world within the sky will be our Kingdom
> And with fanfare I will call out, "I am He."[40]

The above song of *gurū* devotion illustrates a specific case of esoteric religious perception, namely, the coincidence of microcosm and macrocosm. As the *gurū*'s image overspread the heart, the disciple perceived unifying truth in the microcosm of the body. But the concomitant utterance, "I am He," signals a macrocosmic religious perception, as well. The *gurū* manifests as unifying truth beyond all specific religious traditions obliterates the boundaries between oneself and the universe. Thus, the *gurū* as unifying truth might be each thing (microcosm) or everything (macrocosm) in the universe. This spells a dynamic tension of the all-tiny and the all-pervasive, which unifies the disciple with the universe, in the temporary dissolution of cultural packaging, as well as the distinction between inner and outer.

The Sikh Gurū, Revisited

Let us return to our Sikh example to see what we learn from Weber's and Gold's models. In Weber's sociological terms, one would count Gurū Nānak as the charismatic individual who founded the Sikh religion. Nānak inaugurated a lineage in passing religious leadership to the Second Gurū, who thereby became a traditional authority. Subsequently, the office of Sikh Gurū was occupied by the Third Gurū through to the Tenth Gurū, all of whom were human beings commanding the highest Sikh authority—presumably with diminished charisma. When the Tenth Gurū appointed Gurū Granth Sāhib as the final Sikh *gurū,* the book of hymns became the preeminent Sikh legal authority, presumably with no intrinsic charisma.

The strength of Weber's model is the clarity with which one can trace the transfer of power in Sikh history and understand its social dynamics. However, as we discussed earlier, this reductionist perspective accounts neither for the existential sense that all Sikh *gurūs,* human or not, have identical charisma, nor for the obligation of obedience that legitimates the charismatic authority of all eleven *gurūs*, ten human beings and a holy scripture. At this point, we can shed new light on the case by recalling Gold's openness to a religionist perspective as he declared that "*our* problem as historians of religion[s] is to understand problems of human beings struggling to comprehend their existence in the world. Our religio-historical constructs must then be able to make sense of the worlds that they conceive" (16).

In Gold's morphological frame, any of the Sikh *gurūs* might function as any of the immanent foci of the divine, with identical charismatic authority. The Sikh *gurū*—and here we might speak in the singular—functions along an interpenetrating continuum, at times manifesting as holy man, singular personality, eternal heritage, or unifying truth. Gurū Granth Sāhib bears similarity to the *Rāmāyaṇa* of Gold's example above: both *gurūs* function as an eternal heritage. Further, as Rām manifests as singular personality through the *Rāmāyaṇa,* Nānak and other poets whose hymns are contained in the Sikh scripture, manifest as singular personalities through Gurū Granth Sāhib. Full charismatic authority is exercised, regardless of whether a Sikh *gurū* is the charismatic founder of a religion (Gurū Nānak), or a subsequent traditional lineage holder (the Second Gurū through Tenth Gurū), or an inanimate embodiment of normative rules (Gurū Granth Sāhib).

In the context of sociology, we can say that the spiritual master is a charismatic individual similar to magicians, priests, and prophets, in Weber's sense of the terms. Moreover, in the context of history of religions, we can say that the spiritual master is a *gurū* that functions through the four immanent foci of the divine, in Gold's sense of the terms. Weber's notions of charisma, obligation of obedience, and routinization are key to our study because they help us understand that spiritual masters garner legitimacy through the charisma that inspires an obligation of obedience, and their authority diminishes if the charisma is not continually renewed. Gold's grammar of religious perception allows us to consider spiritual master as a category of religious perception, rather than as an external object. His nonhierarchical morphological frame provides the requisite flexibility for defining *spiritual master* in a way that can accommodate a full spectrum of exemplars found in the history of the world's religions. Gold's study of the Hindu *gurū* and its application to a broader context in the history of religions built upon, but did not annul, Weber's sociological insights. Accordingly, our understanding of spiritual master deepens in light of the work of both Weber and Gold.

Consolidating Our Working Definition of Spiritual Master

In this chapter we have proposed neither a new typology, nor a new morphological frame. We simply fabricated a definition to delimit the object of inquiry—spiritual master—to accommodate the wide spectrum of exemplars discussed in the rest of this book. Weber's and Gold's interpretive models are sufficient to account for all instances of spiritual masters covered by the definition.[41] Our discussion of *spiritual master* accounts for both religionist and reductionist perspectives. It does not preclude the possibility of spiritual masters receiving authentic revelations, according to their own cultural categories; it does not assert or deny the reality of those revelations. It keeps the door open to discover the meaning of religious claims from the insider viewpoint of adherents, recognizing that religious leaders might either *represent* or *misrepresent* their putative wisdom as revealed truths, primordial traditions, or divine commandments. Terms from both religionist and reductionist camps are used in the following expansion of our definition of *spiritual master*. Religionist terms, such as *sacred* and *profane*, are not to carry ontological implications; following Gold, they are to be counted as categories of religious perception. Reductionist questions, such as those pertaining to moral exhaustion, stand as a corrective to run-away assumptions about what might be right or wrong, good or bad, virtuous or evil, and so forth.

We now parse the definition of *spiritual master* into three portions: A CHARISMATIC MEDIATOR / WHO AUTHORITATIVELY TEACHES TRADITIONS / PERSONALLY SUPPORTING RELIGIOUS VITALITY. A Venn diagram with the following three intersecting circles describes the discussion: (1) those who are charismatic mediators, (2) those who authoritatively teach traditions, and (3) those who personally support religious vitality. The center portion—where the three circles intersect—represents spiritual masters. Existentially meaningful objects qualify as spiritual masters when understood as "persons" in dependence on an esoteric category of religious perception. As such, they are experienced as charismatic, religiously vital, authoritative teachers. The example of Sikh scripture has been given, and the following discussion is geared largely toward anthropomorphic beings.

The Spiritual Master as a Charismatic Mediator

The first portion of our definition of *spiritual master* states the nominal form of the person: A SPIRITUAL MASTER IS A CHARISMATIC MEDIATOR. Weber defined *charisma* as "a certain quality of an individual personality by virtue of which he is set apart from ordinary men and treated as endowed with supernatural, superhuman, or at least specifically exceptional powers or qualities."[42] *Mediator* identifies the charismatic person's ability to manage hierophanies—that is, brings forth the sacred into a profane body of people's experience, according to their available categories of esoteric and exoteric religious perception. As a manager of hierophany, the spiritual master exhibits both a symbolic body and symbolic conduct. These give the impression that the spiritual master is charismatic. A crafty use of symbols, rituals, sacred narratives, and political persuasion might also generate an impression that a religious leader is charismatic.

Symbolic Body

Gross physical characteristics of people vary depending on such factors as ethnicity, cultural habits, and personal history. By contrast, symbolic body features belie a connection with hierophany. True to the function of religious symbols, the symbolic features of a spiritual master's body mediate the sacred. They also advertise—to those with consonant categories of religious perception—the fact that the bearer is a liminal being, betwixt-and-between the sacred and profane. The advertisement can be exoteric or esoteric. Two ways that symbolic features manifest on the body of a spiritual master are: atypical marks and subtle auras.

Atypical Marks

The connection of spiritual masters to the sacred shows itself in a symbolic body that has atypical marks. For example, second-century Christians argued over whether or not Jesus was beautiful, based on apparently contradictory verses of the Hebrew Bible. Justin Martyr, Clement of Alexandria, Tertullian, Cyril of Alexandria, and Irenaeus depended on this verse from Isaiah to claim that Jesus was neither beautiful, nor majestic:

> Who has believed our message and to whom has the arm of the LORD been revealed? He grew up before him like a tender shoot, and like a root out of dry ground. He had no beauty or majesty to attract us to him, nothing in his appearance that we should desire him. (Is 53:1–3 NIV)

Insisting the opposite, Gregory of Nyssa, Ambrose of Milan, John Chrysostom, Jerome, and Origen said that Christ was physically beautiful on account of this biblical line: "You are the most excellent of men and your lips have been anointed with grace, since God has blessed you forever" (Ps 45:2). The Syrian "golden mouthed" monk John of Damascus (d. 749 CE) determined that the radiance of Christ transcended ordinary notions of beauty or homeliness. To this day, traditional Christian Orthodox icon painters render Jesus and various saints as flawed by worldly standards. Facial features appear deformed with clipped ears, mottled nose, and sunken eyes that symbolize a link from the profane to the sacred dimension of existence. Icons of Jesus in the Byzantine tradition are supposed to serve as windows to the divine.

> The unnatural details of appearance which we see in the icon—in particular the sense organs: the eyes without brilliance, the ears which are sometimes strangely shaped—are represented in a non-naturalistic manner not because the iconographer was unable to do otherwise, but because their natural state was not what he wanted to represent. The icon's role is not to bring us closer to what we see in nature, but to show us a body which perceives what usually escapes man's perception, *i.e.*, the perception of the spiritual world.[43]

Other examples of atypical physical marks on a spiritual master include: the auspicious mark between Muḥammad's shoulder blades, noted by a Christian monk when the future Prophet of Islam at age twelve went to a Syrian monastery; the body features of Christian saints, whose stigmata or holy marks resemble the wounds on the sacred body of Jesus from his crucifixion; and Gautama Buddha's thirty-two major and eighty minor marks of a *mahāpuruṣa* (great person), including long earlobes, and webbed fingers.

Subtle Auras

An extension of the symbolic body is the subtle aura or energy field. The subtle aura said to surround some spiritual masters can be divine light, mystic sound, or the warmth of loving-kindness. Here are three examples:

Aura of divine light. The Christian Gospel according to Mark says that John the son of Zacharias baptized his cousin Jesus in the Jordan River, and "as Jesus was coming up out of the water, he saw heaven being torn open and the Spirit descending on him like a dove" (Mk 1:10). Such energy is indicated symbolically in Christian art by the halo.

Aura of mystic sound. A divine sound (*divya-dhvani*) is said to emanate from the bodies of Jain spiritual masters. This reportedly happened to the Tīrthaṅkara Mahāvīra (d. 500s BCE) after he attained the highest knowledge (*kevala-jñāna*). His body became pure as crystal, and gifted disciples could hear a sound like a booming drum surrounding him.

Aura of loving-kindness. Gautama Buddha is said to have calmed a rutting elephant coming toward him on a rampage. He did this by emanating an aura of loving-kindness (Pali: *metta*).

A study of personality cults would be instructive to show how a supernatural aura is manufactured around a charismatic figure through ritual ceremonies, such as those that capitalize on fire symbolism in the midst of darkness, and so forth. All manner of propaganda has been used to excite an obligation of obedience to legitimize the authority of a charismatic individual, in the course of history; but use of such manipulative means for self-serving ends would disqualify a religious leader from the rank of spiritual master.

Symbolic Conduct

The conduct of a spiritual master belies contact with something extraordinary. The charismatic mediator is a manager of hierophany, bringing what is counted as sacred into the profane world. Thus, their conduct is symbolic. It pertains to two categories of religious experience that represent the poles through which the sacred manifests in hierophany: *mysterium tremendum* and *mysterium fascinans*. On one hand, spiritual masters exhibit the majesty of the *mysterium tremendum*, acting with the tenor of a tremendous, terrific mystery that prompts people to run away. On the other hand, they exhibit the grace of the *mysterium fascinans*, acting with the tenor of a fascinating, felicitous mystery that draws others to them.

The Majestic Conduct of the *Mysterium Tremendum*

Weber noted that charismatic individuals tend to have a revolutionary quality, and we see that spiritual masters often stir up social resistance due to their majestic and daunting behavior. This exhibition of the *mysterium tremendum* can manifest as a direct challenge to the status quo. For example, the Hebrew prophet Jeremiah (fl. seventh century BCE) was reviled and attacked by angry mobs for his outspoken social criticisms; Gautama Buddha (fl. sixth century BCE) saw the ire of his cousin Devadatta, an arch conservative, made two attempts to kill him; and Confucius (sixth-fifth centuries BCE) was repeatedly denied influential government positions, due to his radical thinking. In other cases, spiritual masters act less overtly political, but still evoke a sense of the *mysterium tremendum* by chafing at the sense of complacency that comes with social conformism. When Jesus of Nazareth (fl. first century CE) overturned the tables of the money changers at the Temple in Jerusalem, he showed the majesty of the *mysterium tremendum*.

The Graceful Conduct of the *Mysterium Fascinans*

Some spiritual masters are recognized for their graceful demeanor. Examples of this *mysterium fascinans* include, Francis of Assisi (twelfth-thirteenth century CE), the Christian saint known for preaching to birds; Prophet Muḥammad (sixth-seventh century CE), the "praiseworthy one," who earned his reputation as an upright, honest, person of exceptional grace. In the history of religious art, one can see representations of charismatic individuals with a sacred aura of light, the halo, around them. This is a visual way to represent the graceful, edifying conduct that evokes an experience of the *mysterium fascinans*.

The *mysterium fascinans* complements the *mysterium tremendum*. Spiritual masters can show both fierce and comforting conduct, depending on circumstances and the categories of religious perception available to the disciple. For example, Jesus of Nazareth was fiercely demanding, majestic, and daunting at times; yet, he is well known for his comforting, graceful displays of love and mercy. Indeed, the evocative combination of edifying and daunting conduct seems to enrich a spiritual master's charisma.

Rudolf Otto, who set forth what has become our classic understanding of the *mysterium tremendum* and *mysterium fascinans,* remarks on the existential impact of these two forms through which the content of numinous experience comes. Here we get a sense of the power of a charismatic individual:

> These two qualities, the daunting and the fascinating, now combine in a strange harmony of contrasts, and the resultant dual character of the numinous consciousness . . . is at once the strangest and most noteworthy phenomenon in the whole history of religion. The daemonic-divine object may appear to the mind as an object of horror and dread, but at the same time it is no less something that allures with a potent charm, and the creature, who trembles before it, utterly cowed and cast down, has always at the same time the impulse to turn to it, nay even to make it somehow his own. The "mystery" is for him not merely something to be wondered at but something that entrances him; and beside that in it which bewilders and confounds, he feels a something that captivates and transports him with a strange ravishment, rising often enough to the pitch of dizzy intoxication.[44]

From Otto's observation, we get a hint at how religious leaders might, under carefully engineered circumstances, press unwitting bystanders into a dizzying obligation of obedience. Beset by the power of what Otto calls nonrational factors, disciples may be uncritically convinced of the putative exceptional powers or supernatural qualities embodied by the aspirant to charismatic authority. Whether exhibiting the frightening *mysterium tremendum* or the attractive *mysterium fascinans,* the symbolic conduct of spiritual masters is linked to what Weber identified in Jesus, namely "the magical charisma he felt within himself" that incites them to override social norms of conduct.

The Spiritual Master Authoritatively Teaches Traditions

The second portion of our definition of *spiritual master* states the social function of the charismatic mediator. A spiritual master is one who AUTHORITATIVELY TEACHES TRADITIONS. *Authoritative* is understood in Weber's sense of commanding an obligation of obedience. *Teaches* echoes the sense of *mediator,* and admits a wide spectrum of means, both esoteric and exoteric, by which traditions are transmitted. *Traditions* refers to a variety of texts—including not only written documents, but also customs, arts, religious rituals, and living oral bodies of knowledge. To define the authority that becomes legitimate, we must keep in mind that the teacher of traditions has the additional requirement of personally supporting religious vitality. Thus, the authority should be moral authority. The moral authority that gives legitimacy to a spiritual master derives from two complementary sources: disciplined attainment and religious inheritance.

Moral Authority Based on Disciplined Attainment

Moral authority based on disciplined attainment is derived from personal effort exerted by a spiritual master. This effort involves mastery of traditional texts (in the broad sense of the term) in three areas: study, contemplation, and personal relationships. In practice, these overlap, and can be combined. However, a spiritual master tends to build a reputation as a specialist in one of the three areas, and thereby gain moral authority based on its mastery.

Master of Study

Suppose a spiritual master is accomplished in more than one area of specialization? In such cases, we gain some cultural understanding by considering the value system in which the teacher of traditional texts operates. Traditional Hindu teachings provide a strong example of the premium placed on mastery of study, over mastery of contemplation. Sharma notes that Hindu *gurūs* are to be both well versed in revealed scripture (*śrotriya*), and "firmly established in the experience of the ultimate reality" (*brahmaniṣṭha*). Yet, the former is deemed to be more critical:

> The traditional discussion of requirements for qualification as a spiritual master contains an interesting wrinkle. The question is asked: Suppose a *gurū* possesses only one of the two qualifications—then what does one do? Curiously, the answer has been that a *gurū* who is a *śrotriya,* but not a *brahmaniṣṭha* should be preferred to one who is *brahmaniṣṭha,* but not a *śrotriya*. This is because the *śrotriya* will at least

> be able to pass on the tradition to the disciple even if not realized oneself. On the other hand, the *brahmaniṣṭha* may have had the experience of the ultimate reality, but would not possess the vocabulary to communicate it, due to lack of acquaintance with the Vedas. (113)

Keeping in mind Gold's insights on the relationship between outer tradition and inner life, we should recognize that the body of material studied by a spiritual master is anchored in both esoteric and exoteric categories of religious perception. This Hindu case names a preference regarding what gives authority. Here we see a cultural priority placed on the exoteric category of outer tradition; this is done to ultimately safeguard the inner life.

Master of Contemplation

Authoritative teachers of traditions can specialize in mastery of contemplation. Their contemplative discipline might produce mystical experience, or meditative insights. Exemplars of spiritual masters who gained moral authority through mastery of contemplation include: the early Daoists, who underplayed the value of written words, stating that people must discover the Dao (Way) themselves in association with the natural world; and Gautama Buddha, who told his disciples to discover the nature of reality for themselves—regardless of the putative authority of any religious text. Naturally, contemplative methods and goals vary according to the religious context and individual proclivities of the spiritual masters. Likewise, the obligation of obedience would be proportional to the extent to which a teacher of contemplative traditions is considered an authority.

Master of Personal Relationships

Some spiritual masters are known more for their good hearts than for mastery of either study or contemplation. Their mastery of personal relationships includes love of God, as well as kindness and compassion for living beings; and while such spiritual affection can be cultivated through study and contemplation, it is accessible through the basic heroism of everyday life.

In his chapter on Jewish spiritual masters, Kasimow underscores the tension between two views of what it takes to "love the Lord your God with all your heart and with all your soul and with all your might," as commanded in the Torah (Dt 6:4). Must a spiritual master be an expert in Torah, or is a personal relationship with God in everyday life enough?

> Some Jews who are not great scholars may also be considered saints. They may be recognized as saints because of their intense love of God or their humility or because they may be blessed with divine inspiration, which gives them special power to influence God. The greatest challenge to the classical conception of a Jewish saint was the Baal Shem Tov (1700–1760), the founder of the Ḥasidic movement, who did not come from the ranks of the *talmid hakhamim* and was not known for his extraordinary knowledge of the Torah. (56)

The traditions taught by a spiritual master can derive from religions in any stage of social transformation—identified by Bruce Lincoln as religions of the status quo, religions of resistance, and religions of revolution.[45] A spiritual master is not necessarily a political or social revolutionary, despite what Weber posited as the intrinsically revolutionary character of a charismatic authority. The revolutionary impact of a spiritual master's teachings can be revolutionary for the disciple's inner life and approach to the world.

Moral Authority Based on Religious Inheritance

In the case of moral authority based on religious inheritance, the charisma of a spiritual master literally fits its denotation as "a gift of grace." Indeed, the charismatic mediator might be highly accomplished through personal discipline, but the foundational source of charisma that earns them an obligation of obedience is a religious inheritance through incarnation, revelation, or lineage transmission. Each of these represents a different level of charismatic intensity, and its consequent degree of legitimate authority.

Incarnation

Incarnations are full embodiments of the divine. As such, spiritual masters who are incarnations carry the highest degree of legitimate charismatic authority. The authority of an incarnation appears to be immune from routinization in the history of the world's religions: either it is not transferrable (e.g., Jesus in the Christian tradition) or it manifests through the proper channels without discrimination (e.g., the Hindu *avatāras* of Viṣṇu, such as Kṛṣṇa and Rāma). Arguably, among spiritual masters of the world's religions, the incarnational status of Jesus the Christ has been subject to the most intense theological debate. Christians who call Jesus the Son of God base their understanding on numerous passages of their biblical New Testament; and theological inquiries about his status as both fully God and fully man worked out at the First Council of Nicaea (325 CE), the Council of Ephesus (431 CE), and the Council of Chalcedon (451 CE).

Revelation

Perhaps prophets stand as the prime examples of spiritual masters whose function is to mediate the divine. They are specially tasked with the difficult labor of flawlessly conveying messages that are revealed to them—often at the expense of their very lives. Prophets, who are said to convey God's words, gain moral authority in their role as mouthpieces of the divine. During moments when they are functioning directly as charismatic mediators, their authority is unsurpassed among humans. When not performing direct charismatic mediation, the authority of prophets can be likened to that of other authoritative masters of traditions. For example, Prophet Muḥammad is the spiritual master par excellence among Muslims. Words from his mouth said to be from Angel Gabriel are called the Qur'ān, Recitation. Words from his mouth that come from his own human insight are called *ḥadīth*s, traditions.

The Sikh *gurūs*, both human and scriptural, can be counted among those whose moral authority derives fundamentally from revelation. In the case of transmission of the *jot*, the charismatic authority is immune from routinization. In a profound esoteric sense, one should not speak of a spiritual lineage of the Sikh *gurūs*, because there is no hierarchy of the *jot*, and there is no temporality or historicity of the *jot*. Each Sikh *gurū* is a vessel of the selfsame divine light, which, itself, is eternal.

Spiritual Lineage

Religious traditions are established through the transmission of charisma in the context of a spiritual lineage. Frequently, the spiritual lineage emerges in the event of a hierophany, wherein a sacred initiator breaks into the profane world to start a charismatic chain of command. A spiritual lineage might be initiated by one believed to be an incarnation of God, by one to whom a revelation was bestowed through an angel, or by one who had a contemplative breakthrough. For examples: Jesus initiated a spiritual lineage through Peter, who became the first pope in a long line of Roman Catholic popes; Ṣūfīs pass on the *barakah muḥammadīyah,* the grace of Muḥammad, through a spiritual lineage initiated by the Prophet of Islam; and Zen Buddhist masters trace their lineage back to Gautama Buddha, who gave the transmission Mahākāśyapa during his Flower Sermon.

Normally, spiritual lineage transmission occurs in the context of a ritual that is symbolically designed to recapitulate an original hierophany involving the lineage founder. Lineage holders do not have the same degree of charismatic authority as the founder. Thus, the historical course of transfer of charismatic authority through a spiritual lineage might well undergo a Weberian process of routinization, with its characteristic loss of charismatic authority.

The Spiritual Master Personally Supports Religious Vitality

The third portion of our definition of *spiritual master* signals a *modus operandi* of the authoritative teacher and charismatic mediator: PERSONALLY SUPPORTING RELIGIOUS VITALITY. Authoritatively teaching traditions while charismatically mediating the sacred occurs in a *personal* context. *Supporting* indicates that the outcome of the interaction provides sustenance in both private and public arenas—moving from impact on an individual to society and culture, and visa verse. *Vitality* is life force, power, and energy supporting inner life and outer tradition. *Religious* indicates that the spiritual master works from the cultural context of religious traditions and institutions.

Weber noted that charismatic individuals "mold ethical ways of life, with the ultimate goal of influencing the crystallization of ethical regulations."[46] His observation suggests that a spiritual master personally supports religious vitality by serving as a role model for the ideal way of life. In the case of a holy scripture, such as Gurū Granth Sāhib, the personal support of religious vitality comes in the moral authority conveyed through the charisma of the object.

The Spiritual Master as a Role Model

A prime example of the power of a role model in promoting an ethical way of life is seen among the Ṣūfīs, who emulate Prophet Muḥammad. They carry on traditions of dress, greeting, prayer, and other traditional forms, seeking proximity to divine revelation. That is, they aspire to reach symbolically back to the original hierophany of the Prophet's revelation. Bakar, in his chapter on Muslim spiritual masters, emphasizes the critical role of Ṣūfī teachers in conserving their exoteric religious tradition by keeping alive its wellspring, which is experience based on esoteric teachings:

> We are speaking here primarily of forms connected to spiritual life, including: the traditional clothes the Ṣūfīs wear (at least during spiritual gatherings, if not in public), their manner of greeting each other, the way they conduct prayers and other spiritual exercises, the kind of music to which they listen, and art objects that make up their cultural ambience.
>
> Beyond their immersion in the spiritual forms of traditional culture, Ṣūfīs are also traditional in their actions as they strive to emulate the Prophet's ethical behavior in everyday life. From the Ṣūfī point of view, it is important to be as traditional as possible in one's life, because authentic tradition implies proximity to the origin of divine revelation—and, therefore, to the life of the Prophet. Attachment to traditional forms, including leading a life guided by the Prophet's spiritual ethics, is an essential way of remaining close to the origin and essence of religion, no matter how far distant in time one lives from that origin. (93–94)

The obligation of obedience garnered by a charismatic role model yields the legitimate authority to mold normative ethical ways of life for outer tradition based on the safeguarding of the tradition in the inner life of its religious specialists. The case of Gautama Buddha who "woke up" under the Indian Bodhi Tree shows this. His enlightenment set the standard for spiritual mastery, and ethical ways of life in the tradition known as *buddha-dharma*. Over time, specialized communities of nuns and monks who mastered the teachings through study, contemplation, and personal relationships based in altruism devised culturally diverse methods of "waking up" that would impact individuals and social institutions across broad geographic zones.
A spiritual master is already presumed to be a charismatic individual and an authoritative teacher of traditions. Both of these qualifications contribute to the support of religious vitality. This support becomes very personal as the spiritual master becomes a role model. In a role model, the symbolic body and symbolic conduct, which mark the spiritual master as a charismatic mediator, are enhanced by the cultural

appurtenances they adopt. The symbolic character of the physical person is magnified by symbolic garb, and the teaching is deepened by the sense of responsibility of a spiritual master towards disciples.

The Symbolic Garb of a Role Model

Spiritual masters often adopt a distinctive mode of dress, hairstyle, or ornamentation (e.g., rosary, body tattoo) that carries symbolic meaning. Instructive are three examples from India that show how single cultural theme of world renunciation can be variously interpreted. Here, we will see how the clothing derives from a cultural repository, a religious tradition, and personal idiosyncrasy: (1) The Benedictine monk, Bede Griffiths (1906–1993) was deeply influenced by a lengthy residence in India, and drew from its cultural repository. He integrated aspects of Hindu worship into Christian rituals, and his garb often resembled that of a *sādhu* (Hindu holy man) including a bead rosary and clothing of the saffron color. In spite of all this, Father Bede sustained deep Christian convictions. The case of Bede Griffiths indicates that clothes can reflect a host culture, without reflecting a religious identity. (2) Buddhist monks wear robes whose color and style is based on the garb adopted by Gautama in sixth century BCE India. The basic template of Buddhist robes hearkens back to its founder; and while they were modified in various parts of Asia, the wearing of such robes developed into a long standing tradition that continues to this day. The case of Buddhist monks indicates that clothes can reflect a religious identity without reflecting a current culture. (3) Traditional Digambhara (sky-clad) Jain monks wear no clothes. They imitate Pārśva (fl. 800 BCE) whose robe got snagged on thorns and came off. Being nonattached to material goods, Pārśva never replaced it. To this day, sky-clad monks follow the long-standing tradition based on the personal idiosyncrasy of Pārśva.

The Personal Touch of a Role Model

Clothing and other aspects of material culture are displayed by a spiritual master in the context of outer tradition. But the impact reaches to the inner life of disciples. The traditional cultural forms of clothing and hairstyle—along with various elements of discourse, such as greetings and prayers—function symbolically to provide a rich fount of existential meaning. The existential meaning is nourished not only through rituals, teachings, and symbols of outer tradition, but also through the private communication whose effect depends on the religious perception of a ready disciple. This esoteric communication can occur in radical ways. Sharma presents a traditional Hindu understanding of the intimate master-disciple relationship in which esoteric communication occurs by means of thinking, looking, or touching:

> "The guru can bestow his grace [give *dīkshā*] either by thought, as the turtle hatches its eggs by merely thinking about them, or by look as the fish hatches its eggs by looking at them, or by touch as the hen hatches its eggs by sitting on them." But *dīkshā* by thought is said to be the best. (122)[47]

A spiritual master need not be physically present to attend to the spiritual needs of disciples by giving a personal touch. In the Christian chapter, Wiseman reports that Jesus taught Thérèse of Lisieux despite a time gap of eighteen hundred years. She wrote in *Story of a Soul*:

> Jesus has no need of books or teachers to instruct souls; he teaches without the noise of words. Never have I heard Him speak, but I feel that He is within me at each moment; He is guiding and inspiring me with what I must say and do. I find just when I need them certain lights that I had not seen until then. (78)[48]

Cultural traditions have an exoteric dimension that is visibly represented to the public—a community of individuals—in conventional forms, and an esoteric dimension that becomes evident to individuals in the private arena according to their categories of religious perception. Personal connection with a spiritual master on the esoteric level, as seen in the case of Thérèse of Lisieux, supports a religious tradition on the revealed, exoteric level. Bakar reminds of this cultural dynamic in connection with Muslim spiritual masters, saying, "Without its inner dimension of the *ṭarīqah,* or esoteric Ṣūfī Path, Islam would be a religion with a body, but without a soul" (95). The reverse is also true, as the exoteric activities of a spiritual master provide a cultural framework for both esoteric and exoteric religious experience.

The spiritual master who makes the connection between outer tradition and inner life by means of personal communication becomes an effective role model, because disciples take the relationship to heart. A spiritual master personally supports religious vitality by taking responsibility for the welfare of disciples. Their welfare is typically entwined in an ethical way of life in order to produce valued results for either this life or the future. The personal touch gives special efficacy to the spiritual master as a role model. This efficacy, which brings what Weber called a "crystallization of ethical regulations," is derived from the moral authority garnered by a charismatic individual. But, suppose that the spiritual master does not have the best interests of disciples at heart, and has lost moral authority?

Moral Exhaustion

Bruce Lincoln identifies the phenomenon of "moral exhaustion," whereby dehumanizing activities are performed after overriding the "moral hesitation" characteristic of normal human behavior. Speaking of the Old Persian Empire, and foreshadowing the moral depravity seen in many countries around the world, including the United States of America, he notes:

> Having overcome the problem of moral hesitation by wrapping even its most distasteful actions in an ennobling, sanctifying discourse, the empire now faces the possibility of moral exhaustion, in which its animating discourse loses all credibility, by virtue of its complicit relation to those same repugnant actions [that had previously been restrained by moral hesitation].[49]

We can bring this concept of moral exhaustion to bear on the conduct of individual religious leaders whose authority grows to ungodly proportions. In doing so, we are thrown back to Max Weber's timely inquiry—at the start of the twentieth century—into the acquisition of religious authority. These were the years that ominously opened the way for Nazi political domination of Europe.

Instances of the abuse of power among religious leaders nag at us, even now, as we are immersed in the day's news. This is a point to which Sharma draws our attention, in quoting Huston Smith:

> The shadow side [of the spiritual master], of course, is that like every good it can be perverted. And, as the Latin warns us, *corruptio optimi pessima*—the corruption of the best produces the worst. (123)[50]

Weber's genius was to recognize that religious leaders garner authority on the basis of an obligation of obedience. His work helps us to understand that an obligation of obedience might derive from any number of sources, be they psychological, political, religious, sociological, or whatnot. Commanding leaders have powerful ways to garner authority, aside from being democratically elected and based on unanimity of views grounded in a uniform definition of greatness. Bystanders who fail to think deeply about what does and what does not make a true spiritual master, might unwittingly tolerate the override of moral hesitation in religious leaders.

Tracking abuse of authority from a reductionist perspective balances with social realism a religionist view of spiritual masters as having privileged access to a purported sacred reality. A reductionist inquiry introduces a healthy critique of spiritual masters who present themselves as authoritative sacred mediators, or who fill an office expediently claiming sacred mediation for psychologically disturbed or power hungry reasons. Beyond that, both reductionist and religionist critiques help the bystander to identify situations that do not promote religious vitality for individuals in their charge, thence not for society.

Does it not happen that the eyes of many beholders find attractive religious leaders whose authoritative teaching of traditions enhance discord and threaten life? Some religious leaders might resemble spiritual masters in terms of how they dress, how they act, what they teach, and so forth. And while these religious leaders might not exhibit an aura of loving-kindness to the eyes of some, they might attract followers through a *mysterium fascinans* or *mysterium tremendum* that evoke an obligation of obedience. What, then, might be some criteria for evaluating whether or not *supporting religious vitality* was an outcome of the activities of a spiritual master? This question should be asked by readers who become engaged in the discussions of the eight religious traditions offered in the chapters to come.

Testing the Definition of *Spiritual Master*

Osama bin Laden, Abraham Heschel, Tenzin Gyatso, Jim Jones, Karol Jósef Wojtyla, Jerry Falwell, Dorothy Day—who among these people of our times is a spiritual master? Kṛṣṇa, Gautama, Devadatta, Confucius, Jesus, Muḥammad, Shabbatai Tsevi, Bahá'u'lláh—who among these historical figures is a spiritual master? With a handful of cases, let us test our definition of spiritual master as A CHARISMATIC MEDIATOR WHO AUTHORITATIVELY TEACHES TRADITIONS, PERSONALLY SUPPORTING RELIGIOUS VITALITY. We invite readers to begin forming their own views about these, as well as other figures presented in this book.

James Warren Jones (aka Jim Jones) presided over the mass "revolutionary suicide" achieved by communal drinking of cyanide-laced Flavor Aid at his Peoples Temple in Guyana, South America, on

November 18, 1978. Some say that Jim Jones did not "brainwash" his followers, some nine hundred of whom died on that fateful day. Rather, he merely "socialized" them in a totalistic environment that was freely entered.[52] Michael Prokes, a public relations man for the Peoples Temple, explains the benefit some members found in his teaching:

> Jones was a hell of an eye-opening experience. It wasn't brainwashing that Jones was engaged in—it was more like deprogramming. Jones was educating and the effect was therapeutic for thousands who heard him and whose lives were in a state of confusion from feeling imprisoned in a society they were told was free. He liberated many minds out of their confused states by demonstrating why there are huge ghettoes in every city of America and why those ghettoes are populated mostly by blacks. He laid the blame squarely at the feet of white racism and a socio-economic system that clearly puts profit motives above human values.[53]

Would Jim Jones qualify as a spiritual master? Was he a charismatic mediator? Did he authoritatively teach traditions? Did his teaching have a deeply personal impact? Did he support religious vitality? If all of these questions produce an affirmative answer, Jim Jones would qualify.

Osama bin Laden (d.2011), the late leader of al-Qaeda who is credited with masterminding the attack on New York's Twin Towers and the U.S. Pentagon on 9/11/2001 is a hero to many. Richard Holbrooke, ambassador to the United States under President Bill Clinton wrote these words about him:

> He remains a folk hero to millions of Muslims; youths wear T-shirts of him and children are named after him throughout the Muslim world. . . . *He is a false prophet who incites mass murder, but he is clearly eloquent and charismatic. His ideas, no matter how insane they seem to us, appeal to many people. (Hitler had those qualities, too.)*[54]

Would Osama bin Laden qualify as a spiritual master? Was he a charismatic mediator? Did he authoritatively teach traditions? Did his teaching have a deeply personal impact? Did he support religious vitality? If all of these questions produce an affirmative answer, Osama bin Laden would qualify.

The Polish archbishop Karol Jósef Wojtyla (d. 2005) became Pope John Paul II in 1978. As leader of the Roman Catholic Church, could he—by virtue of being pope—automatically be called a spiritual master? Would Pope Urban II who launched the First Crusade in 1095 to militarily reestablish the Holy Land under Christian rule be counted as a spiritual master? Does advocacy of killing automatically disqualify one as a spiritual master? If so, would Lord Kṛṣṇa be disqualified? According to the Hindu *Bhagavadgītā,* this singular personality mentally prepared the warrior Arjuna for battle against his kinsmen. Might advocates of such a spiritual master appeal to a Just War theory that allows killing in the interest of the greater good as a means of supporting religious vitality?

Religiously impacting the lives of others through political force or brainwashing does not satisfy the final clause of our core definition, which speaks of SUPPORTING RELIGIOUS VITALITY. Compulsion or devious means of transforming a person's beliefs, attitude, and practices are not life-enhancing elements that support religious vitality. Arguably, religious dogma and rituals exerted through political mandates and psychological manipulation tend to deplete the life force of individuals. Thus, masterful authorities who exert such "religious" pressures do not count as spiritual masters. Spiritual masters are role models with moral authority who transmit religious traditions that effectively enhance life by encouraging such things as health and religious insight in the private arena, and such things as social harmony and life-giving activities in the public arena.

The Question of Value Judgments

Weber and Gold both worked as scientists, and did not center their analyses on value judgments about abuses of power. However, they both observed the processes by which obedience to authority is garnered and lost. In the academic disciplines of sociology and the history of religions, value judgments are avoided on principle. They are to be checked by scholars through overt self-reflection on their biases. Yet, the ideally value-free scholarship done in these fields should render the general public better equipped to deal with the problem of spiritual masters—in theory, and in their lives. Accordingly, research on the nature and function of a spiritual master should provide intellectual leverage to help interested persons determine the extent to which they are willing to grant an obligation of obedience to a religious leader.

Scholarship in the social and human sciences is not completely without its practical application. Once a value judgment has been made and socially accepted as legitimate, scholars might be of help in resolving what are taken to be social problems. Yet, it is left to the individual members of society to think through the issues that beset them, and make their voices heard. Steve Hoenisch, developer of the online blog, Criticism.Com, wrote a cogent essay on Max Weber's value-free sociological method; and much of what he says here applies to method in the history of religions as well.

> Weber maintained a two-tiered approach to value-free social science. On the one hand, he believed that ultimate values could not be justified "scientifically," that is, through value-free analysis. Thus, in comparing different religious, political or social systems, one system could not be chosen over another without taking a value or end into consideration; the choice would necessarily be dictated by the analyst's values. On the other hand, Weber believed that once a value, end, purpose, or perspective had been established, then a social scientist could conduct a value-free investigation into the most effective means within a system of bringing about the established end. Similarly, Weber believed that objective comparisons among systems could also be made once a particular end had been established, acknowledged, and agreed upon, a position that allowed Weber to make what he considered objective comparisons among such economic systems as capitalism and socialism. Thus, even though Weber maintained that ultimate values could not be evaluated objectively, this belief did not keep him from believing that social problems could be scientifically resolved—once a particular value or end had been established.[51]

After a standard has been articulated, then legitimated outside of the value-free zone of scholarship, tools of the scholar can again become useful to assess whether or not a religious leader qualifies as spiritual master. In line with their professions, contributors to this book discuss value judgments intrinsic to the religious traditions at hand, without offering their own—except in the perhaps inevitable sense that their *choice* of exemplars already stems from bias.

Resisting the Obligation of Obedience

In general, we can say that our working definition of *spiritual master* provides rational leverage for understanding the machinations of religious leaders. Having little conceptual grasp on the nature of religious leadership, a bystander can easily succumb to an obligation of obedience. Religious leaders garnering authority based on such obligations of obedience may or may not abuse that authority—but the stakes are high. In the end, we must recognize that religious leaders hold a powerful connection with people's sense of themselves. Perhaps religious leaders have great potential to become dangerous in private and public arenas because they have a complex relationship to what Sharma calls "interiority." But according to our definition, spiritual masters who abuse their authority forego the qualification of *spiritual*. *Spirare* connects to staying alive, and purported spiritual masters who do not support religious vitality do not live up to the name.

Regardless of how spiritual masters appear—as human or not human—the personal effect of supporting religious vitality depends ultimately on the disciple. Some traditions suggest that faith is the key element that determines how a spiritual master appears to disciples, while others point to such things as level of spiritual development. Geshe Rabten, a contemporary Tibetan Buddhist monk, claims that

> gurus act as a mirror of your mind. When you see them as having faults, these flaws are projections of cloudy delusions obscuring the pure nature of your own mind and mirror back to you what you must work on and learn about in order to gain liberation.[55]

Ultimately, the obligation of obedience granted to a spiritual master relies on categories of religious perception. Both cultural constructs and the vagaries of personal experience shape these categories, such that they might accommodate existentially meaningful inanimate objects.

Disciples bear immense responsibility in the relationship with a spiritual master. A key quality for disciples noted in some traditions is the ability to surrender to the spiritual master. Ramana Maharshi says:

> The disciple surrenders himself to the master. That means there is no vestige of individuality retained by the disciple. If the surrender is complete all sense of individuality is lost and there is thus no cause for misery. The eternal being is only happiness. This is revealed. (124)[56]

This aspect of surrender is noted by Bakar, speaking of the Ṣūfī master-disciple relationship:

> Shaykhs know their disciples, and indeed know them only too well—better in fact than the disciples know themselves. They know the psychological state and the spiritual needs of disciples. In a sense, the shaykhs have conquered their disciples, since the disciples have surrendered themselves to their spiritual masters for the purpose of spiritual rebirth and transformation. As experienced spiritual psychologists, shaykhs know the elements and tendencies that can distract and derail disciples from the Path. They also know the elements and inclinations that need to be guided and developed to perfection. (104)

It must be said that surrender is a feature of the relationship between a *highly qualified* spiritual master and a *highly qualified* disciple. The master assumes personal responsibility for the disciple, and thus the disciple should be safe in the hands of the teacher. The absolute surrender of a student to a teacher who lacks compassion is playing with fire. Milarepa, the yogi who submitted himself thoroughly to his lama Marpa warns:

> To serve a lama without compassion
> Is like worshipping a one-eyed demon;
> He and patron alike will misfortune meet. (164)[5]

Gautama Buddha said that one must be convinced of the true value of the teacher—and urged his disciples not to follow his words simply because he was a buddha. Kennick notes that Gautama used the metaphor of a goldsmith who tests metal to see whether or not it is real gold by biting, scraping, and burning it. Like the smith who probes metal to determine its value, so a buddha's disciples should investigate *buddha-dharma* to determine whether or not the teachings are truthful and worthwhile.

Conclusion

Religious leaders are not necessarily spiritual masters, and there seems to be a growing sense in the world today that people have a responsibility to scrutinize those who ask for their surrender in the name of religion. Such surrender results in what Weber identified as an obligation of obedience that grants authority to the religious leader; and we must keep in mind that exercise of authority often leads to abuse of authority. Sharma notes a healthy modern wariness toward "masters" with regard to their intrusive nature.

> It may be helpful to try to identify the real cause of discomfort such a need for a "master" generates in us, and the situation may be explained as follows. Almost all spiritual paths require that we reconfigure our sense of the self—of who we are—significantly. In fact, this sense of self, or "ego," is said to be the main obstacle we need to overcome to progress on the spiritual path. It becomes the duty of the master to dilute our ego, if we then approach a master on the spiritual path instead of going our own way. This is highly problematical. (247–48)

In this day of the Arab Spring and its subsequent seasons, the legitimacy of long-established authoritarian political leaders is being questioned, challenged, and cancelled. With the same enterprising spirit, adherents of the world's religious traditions may become disenchanted with religious leaders, no matter how charismatic they appear. Perhaps the meaning of *surrender to authority* will change dramatically in the coming years, if the obligation of obedience emerges with the profound exercise of critical intelligence and judgment. If this occurs, we can expect a more vital manifestation of arguably the most profound of all human relationships—that between spiritual master and disciple.

In the Hindu context, Sharma notes that "ultimately there are no teachers, only disciples. That is to say, it is the faith of the disciple in the master that bears fruit—be it secular or sacred" (117). If we accept as a premise that spiritual masters ultimately depend on others for their authority, it is imperative that beholders be more than bystanders in order to prevent abuse of that authority. The intellectual leverage provided by a working definition of *spiritual master* helps beholders to assess the quality of religious leaders and to refrain from unwarranted obligations of obedience.

Notes

In this volume, words and names are provided with diacritical marks that follow, for the most part, the conventions adopted in Lindsay Jones, ed. in chief, *The Encyclopedia of Religion,* 2nd ed. (Detroit: Macmillan, 2005). In this chapter, Biblical quotations are English translations found in the New International Version (NIV).

1. Procrustes is a character of Greek myths. He was a strange host indeed. Living near Eleusis on the coast of Attica, he invited guests to spend the night with the prospect of sleeping on a marvelous bed. After they died on the procrustean bed, he stole their goods. Finally, the heroic Theseus put Procrustes to death upon this bed.

2. The terms for spiritual master mentioned by contributors include: *murshid* and *shaykh* (Arabic), *sheng* (Chinese), *didaskalē, epistata,* and *kyriē* (Greek), *gadol ḥador, ga'on, ḥakham, ḥasid, talmid ḥakham,* and *tzaddik* (Hebrew), *tuan gurū* (Malay), *pīr* (Persian), *ācārya, arhat, bodhisattva, buddha, gurū, samyaksambuddha,* and *upādhyāya* (Sanskrit), and *bla-ma* (Tibetan).

3. Our notion of charisma builds on Max Weber's groundbreaking analysis of *Herrschaft* ("rule," "domination" in German), which he classified into three types of authority: legal, traditional, and charismatic. Of *charisma,* Weber says, "The concept of 'charisma' (the 'gift of grace') is taken from the vocabulary of early Christianity. . . . It is nothing new." *Theory of Social and Economic Organization,* trans. A. R. Anderson and Talcott Parsons (1922; repr. New York: Oxford University Press, 1947), 328.

4. For a pertinent comment on the related adjectives *spiritualis* and *vitalis,* and the observation that "the adjective 'spiritualis' relates to the noun *spiritus* in its meaning as 'breath' and has no theological or mystical connotations," see Charles Burnett, "The Chapter on the Spirits in the *Pantegni* of Constantine the African," in *Constantine the African and ʿAlī ibn al-ʿAbbās al-Maǧūsī: The* Pantegni *and Related Texts,* ed. Charles Burnett and Danielle Jacquart (Leiden: E. J. Brill, 1994), 103, n.10.

5. Mircea Eliade, *Shamanism: Archaic Techniques of Ecstasy,* trans. from French by Willard R. Trask (New York: Bollingen Foundation, 1964); preface, xv. Eliade wrote this with the mentality of an early historian of religions who was carving out the academic discipline in contrast to both theology, and the social sciences. Some historians of religions adopt reductionism to correct a religionist tendency to erode the boundary between history of religions and theology. They risk eroding the boundary between history of religions and the social sciences. See Russell T. McCutcheon, *Critics Not Caretakers* (Albany: State University of New York Press, 2001), and Bruce Lincoln, ed., *Religion, Rebellion, and Revolution* (New York: St. Martin's Press, 1985).

6. Ibid., preface, xv.

7. Ewert Cousins, preface to the series, World Spirituality: An Encyclopedic History of the Religious Quest, 25 vols., Islamic Spirituality: Foundations, gen. ed. Ewert Cousins, 19: xiv.

8. Bruce Lincoln, "Culture," in *Guide to the Study of Religion,* ed. Willi Braun and Russell T. McCutcheon (London, New York: Cassell, 2000), 416.

9. As Weber introduced "the three pure types of legitimate authority," he cautioned readers about the limits of ideal types; he also defended the use of typologies:

> The fact that none of these three ideal types [of legitimate authority] . . . is usually to be found in historical cases in "pure" form, is naturally not a valid objection to attempting their conceptual formulation in the

sharpest possible form. In this respect the present case is no different from many others. . . . But even so it may be said of every empirically historical phenomenon of authority that it is not likely to be "as an open book." Analysis in terms of sociological types has, after all, as compared with purely empirical historical investigation, certain advantages which should not be minimized. That is, it can in the particular case of a concrete form of authority determine what conforms to or approximates such types as "charisma," "hereditary charisma," . . . and in so doing it can work with relatively unambiguous concepts. But the idea that the whole of concrete historical reality can be exhausted in the conceptual scheme about to be developed is as far from the author's thoughts as anything could be. *Theory*, 329.

10. Ibid., 328.

11. Ibid.

12. Max Weber, *The Sociology of Religion* (1922; repr., Boston: Beacon Press, 1993), 25. Each of Weber's types of charismatic individual is, more or less, connected to a specific cultural context, and the term spiritual master might offer a more culturally neutral option that is suited to a nontheistic religious environment, for example. We say "provisionally" spiritual master should be counted as a fourth type of charismatic individual, not because we have anything structurally significant to propose, but simply to set our subject matter into the fruitful context of Weber's insightful theory of the legitimation of authority.

13. Weber, *Theory*, 358–59.

14. Weber, *Sociology*, 47.

15. Weber, *Theory*, 361–62.

16. Ibid.

17. Ibid., 363–64.

18. Ibid., 364.

19. Ibid.

20. Ibid.

21. See note 3 above. Weber reformulated the term *charisma* that was "taken from the vocabulary of early Christianity," where it denoted a gift of grace. Ibid., 328. Weber transposed the concept from theology to sociology. Further, Dan Gold transposed the notion, which he identifies as divine grace, to the history of religions by making an epistemological turn. In a cultural or scientific paradigm shift, a new paradigm does not necessarily render the old one useless. Each may have its due strength in the proper context.

22. Daniel Gold, *Comprehending the Guru: Toward a Grammar of Religious Perception* (Atlanta: Scholars Press, 1988), 6–7.

23. Ibid., 6.

24. Ibid., 17. Although Gold does not use the term "charisma," Weber's notion is certainly reflected in what he calls here "divine grace, knowledge, and power [that] are mediated to humankind." Moreover, Weber's typology of *Herrschaft* appears transformed in the morphological frame of the immanent foci. From Gold's descriptions, we can see that traditional authority is specified in the eternal heritage, legal (rational) authority is specified in the

singular personality, and charismatic authority is specified in the holy man. Doing this, Gold generalizes the function of the charismatic personality into the other two contexts of *Herrschaft*, as each type of Weberian authority can be exercised by a *gurū*.

25. Ibid.

26. Ibid., 21. In our discussion of spiritual master, we avoid the terms *divine* and *immanent*, although their juxtaposition in Gold's model neatly establishes the function of meditation of the *gurū*. For our purposes, connotations of *divine* as opposed to *immanent* are more trouble than help—partly for the theistic language of the former, and the structural implications of the latter. We set Gold's immanent foci of the divine on a horizontal axis to avoid implying that only what is transcendent is mediated; and to emphasize the nonhierarchical character of the morphological frame, we think of his categories of esoteric and exoteric along a vertical axis, as two levels of religious perception, with no ontological implications.

27. Ibid., 89.

28. Ibid., 74.

29. Ibid., 20–21.

30. Ibid., 82–83.

31. Daniel Gold, *The Lord as Guru: Hindi Saints in North Indian Tradition* (New York: Oxford University Press, 1987), 7–8. Specifically: (1) the holy man offers "spiritual aid" as the basis of personal salvation, which is "the master's discourse and example" on the revealed level, and "esoteric help" on the hidden level. Further, the holy man offers "personal authority" as the basis of religious community, which is "the master's orders" on the revealed level, and "the master's mission" on the hidden level. (2) The singular personality offers "saving communication from the divine" as the basis of personal salvation, which is the "holy book" on the revealed level, and "saving power" on the hidden level. Further, the singular personality offers "sacred institution" as the basis of religious community, which is "sacramental tradition" on the revealed level, and "the elect, the true church" on the hidden level. (3) The eternal heritage offers "ancient knowledge" as the basis of personal salvation, which is "received myth and ritual" on the revealed level, and "esoteric wisdom" on the hidden level. Further, the eternal heritage offers "ancient ways" as the basis of religious community, which is "developed customary law" on the revealed level, and "an organic order of the divine" on the hidden level. (4) The unifying truth offers "the one divine truth" as the basis of personal salvation, which is "all scriptures" on the revealed level, and "their correct interpretation" on the hidden level. Further, unifying truth offers "the brotherhood of all men" as the basis of religious community, which is "all traditions" on the revealed level, and "the secret brotherhood of the wise," on the hidden level. Gold, *Comprehending*, 22.

32. Gold utilizes insightful terms with reference to "comprehending the guru," beginning with *grammar* in his subtitle, which describes the set of structural rules that govern the categories of religious perception. Methodologically, he made use of "types," such as holy man, and singular

personality; "definitions," of Hinduism, and so forth; and "broadly conceived processes," such as the Weberian routinization—admitting that these were "simpler than the connected concepts emerging from Eliade's eminently articulate world-vision" (Ibid., 6). Gold's suggestive terms include, "complex landscapes," "circle of meanings," "morphology of religious life," and "continuous fields of religious phenomena" (Ibid., 105, 34, 35, 105).

33. Ibid., 33.

34. Ibid., 25.

35. Ibid., 56-57.

36. Ibid., 22–23.

37. Ibid., 19.

38. Ibid., 88.

39. Ibid., 24.

40. Ibid., 14.

41. It would be foolish to discard work that is relevant and well done. Accordingly, we invite readers to more extensively study Weber's typology of *Herrschaft* and Gold's grammar of religious perception. Their disciplines of sociology and history of religions provide a suitable mix of reductionist and religionist questions, issues, and terms for a fruitful inquiry. Here, the distinctions made in unpacking the definition should not be taken as types or new categories of religious perception. Nor are they as a mere list of descriptive characteristics. Rather, they are basic structural classifications deduced from a body of material pertaining to religious teachers found in the history of the world's religions. The definition delimits an object of study that can be applied in those models; but the object of study—spiritual masters, according to the definition—is free to be applied in other contexts as well, not bound by those models. Words of the definition are meant to be enhanced by connotations that stem from preexisting models.

The Weberian connotations of *charisma, mediator,* and *authority* are welcome to thicken the description of *spiritual master*. Also welcome is Gold's understanding that the immanent foci of the divine mediate by allowing "spiritual power" to find "a center on earth" (17). *Personally* plays off the argument that the spiritual master, whether animate or not, is a *person* in the expanded sense disallowed by Weberian categories, but integral to Gold's *gurū,* who has an intimate relationship with disciples through the four foci. Beyond that, *teaches* indicates that spiritual masters have students who learn from them some body of traditions; *traditions* further establishes the spiritual master in a cultural context; and *supporting religious vitality* invites a critique of spiritual masters whereby they are distinguished from religious leaders, per se.

42. Weber, *Theory,* 358. See note 3 above. True to the brilliant and careful application of his social science method, Weber makes no judgment here as to whether or not the charismatic individual actually is endowed with charisma in the *theological* sense of "gift of grace." Similarly, in what follows, we do not intend to posit truth claims.

43. L. Ouspensky, *Theology of the Icon* (Crestwood, NY: St. Vladimir's Seminary Press, 1978), 208.

44. Rudolf Otto, *The Idea of the Holy: An Inquiry into the Non-rational Factor in the Idea of the Divine and Its Relation to the Rational,* trans. John W. Harvey (London: Oxford University Press, 1923), 31. For a classic discussion of the *mysterium tremendum* and *mysterium fascinans* as the two forms taken by the numinous content of the divine in the experience of human beings, see Ibid., 12-24, 31-41.

45. See Lincoln, *Religion, Rebellion, and Revolution,* 268–81.

46. Weber, *Sociology,* 52. Being a charismatic mediator, and authoritatively teaching traditions contributes to the spiritual master's personal support of religious vitality. But, more specific to the function of spiritual masters, per se, is activity that personally inspires disciples to live a life according to their example. Just as not every charismatic individual is an authoritative teacher of traditions, so not every charismatic mediator who authoritatively teaches traditions is one whose activities personally support religious vitality. Recall here our model of the Venn diagram, wherein *spiritual master* is a particular subset of those who are: (1) charismatic mediators, and (2) authoritative teachers of traditions, and (3) personally supporting religious vitality. Accordingly, while discussing the third portion of the definition, the focus is on the spiritual master as role model.

47. A. Devaraja Mudaliar, *My Recollections of Bhagavan Sri Ramana* (1960; repr., Tiruvannamalai: Sri Ramanasramam, 1992), 109, 110.

48. Thérèse of Lisieux, *Story of a Soul,* 3rd ed., trans. John Clarke (Washington, DC: ICS Publications, 1996), 179.

49. Bruce Lincoln, *Religion, Empire, and Torture: The Case of Achaemenian Persia With a Postscript on Abu Ghraib* (Chicago and London: University of Chicago Press, 2007), 96.

50. Phil Cousineau, ed., *The Way Things Are: Conversations with Huston Smith on the Spiritual Life* (Berkeley: University of California Press, 2003), 75.

51. Steve Hoenisch, "Max Weber's View of Objectivity in Social Science," Criticism.com, May 8, 2006.

52. Judith Mary Weightman, *Making Sense of the Jonestown Suicides: A Sociological History of Peoples Temple* (New York and Toronto: Edwin Mellen Press, 1983), 156.

53. Mark Lane, *The Strongest Poison* (New York: Hawthorn Books, 1980), 223–24, quoted in Weightman, *Jonestown Suicides,* 159.

54. Richard C. Holbrooke, "Elite reaction to Bin Laden," *Kharblog,* September 10, 2005, http://kwharbaugh.blogspot.com/2005/09/osama-bin-laden.html#holbrooke.

55. Geshe Rabten and Geshe Ngawang Dhargyay, *Advice from the Spiritual Friend: Tibetan Teachings on Buddhist Thought and Transformation* (New Delhi: Publications for Wisdom Culture, 1977), xvi.

56. Ramana Maharshi, *Talks with Sri Ramana Maharshi,* recorded by Swami Ramananda Saraswati (Tiruvannamalai: Sri Ramanasramam, 1984), 318.

57. Garma C. C. Chang, trans., *The Hundred Thousand Songs of Milarepa* (Seacaucus, NJ: University Books, 1962), 2:559.

1

Jewish Spiritual Masters

Harold Kasimow

And ye shall be unto Me a kingdom of priests, and a holy nation.

—Exodus 19:6

Ye shall be holy; for I the Lord Your God am holy.

—Leviticus 19:2

Introduction

When I recently told a rabbi that I was writing an essay on Jewish saints, he was somewhat puzzled. I am not surprised. When Jews think about saints, they usually think of Christianity. They think of the Catholic process of beatification and canonization by which the Church declares a person to be a saint. In Judaism there is no official religious body that can recognize someone as a saint. But there are saints in the Jewish tradition. When a person lives a holy, pious life, the Jewish community may come to recognize that human being as a saint. In the Jewish tradition a saint, or a spiritual master, may be called a *talmid ḥakham* (disciple of the wise), *tzaddik* (righteous person), or *ḥasid* (pious person). There are also other terms for the spiritually elite in the Jewish tradition, such as *ga'on* (genius) and *gadol ḥador* (Torah leader of the generation).

But how does Judaism define a saint? I would define a saint as a person who views *Imitatio Dei* as the ultimate purpose of life,[1] and who is totally committed to the following two commandments from the Torah: "You must love the Lord your God with all your heart and with all your soul and with all your might" (Dt 6:4) and "Love your neighbor as yourself" (Lv 19:17).[2] The test of a holy life is the willingness to give up one's life for the sake of the commandments. Saints are always ready to die for God.

Because the Jewish tradition places such a strong emphasis on study, on the mind, the Jewish saint will most likely come from the ranks of the *talmid ḥakhamim,* a sage who has mastered the Torah in an astonishing way and attained great stature in the community.[3] Classical Judaism sees such a person as the ideal because the Torah is believed to be the word of God and study of the Torah is seen as "holiness in words." Study, it is said, not only leads to paradise; it itself is paradise. By studying the Torah we can discern the will of God and fulfill all the *mitzvot* (commandments).[4] The person who submits to God's will and fulfills both the ritual *mitzvot* and the ethical *mitzvot* becomes holy.

The Jewish tradition sees Rabbi Elijah ben Solomon of Vilna (1720–1797), who is known as the Vilna Gaon and who studied Torah eighteen hours a day, as the ideal spiritual master in the Jewish tradition. He was known as *ha-Ga'on he-Ḥasid.*[5]

However, some Jews who are not great scholars may also be considered saints. They may be recognized as saints because of their intense love of God or their humility or because they may be blessed with divine inspiration, which gives them special power to influence God. The greatest challenge to the classical conception of a Jewish saint was the Baal Shem Tov (1700–1760), the founder of the Ḥasidic movement, who did not come from the ranks of the *talmid ḥakhamim* and was not known for his extraordinary knowledge of the Torah. The Baal Shem Tov gave greater emphasis to the heart than to the mind. He himself was a teacher of small children and a laborer who spent a great deal of time meditating in the forest rather than in the study hall. For the Baal Shem Tov, prayer with concentration, with joy, with ecstasy was a better way to cleave to God than study of the Torah.

The Baal Shem Tov was viewed by his followers as the ideal saint, the ideal master, the great *tzaddik.* His followers began to emphasize the doctrine of the *tzaddik,* whom they saw as an intermediary between themselves and God. According to the doctrine of the *tzaddik,* if we want to become attached to God we must attach ourselves to the *tzaddik,* whose thoughts are entirely God-centered. According to Louis Jacobs, the Ḥasidic master Elimelech of Lizensk (1717–1787) claimed that the *tzaddik* "brings man near to God and he brings down God's grace from heaven to earth."[6] We should not be surprised, therefore, that the Gaon of Vilna banned the Ḥasidic movement.

Moses Maimonides (1135–1204), the great Jewish philosopher, of whom it is said, "From Moses to Moses there was none like Moses," distinguishes between two types of ideal people: the *ḥakham,* that is, the sage, and the *ḥasid,* that is, the saint. Rabbi Jonathan Sacks claims that Maimonides favors the sage over the saint because "*the sage is concerned with the perfection of society. The saint is concerned with the perfection of self.*"[7] This is a useful distinction, but it does not always work so neatly in reality. The greatest Jewish sage, the Vilna Gaon, is also seen as a great saint. The sage from Vilna devoted so much time to the study of the Torah that it left him very little time to become involved in the affairs of his community. He never accepted a rabbinic position.

> The Gaon's way of life, as portrayed by his sons and his students, was characterized by the maximum channeling of the powers of body and soul to one exclusive goal: the study of the Torah. In practice, the Gaon understood absolute devotion to Torah study as one side of the coin; the other side was the value of asceticism and withdrawal from society as a guiding principle and way of life. . . . The Gaon saw the main significance of asceticism in its channeling of the majority of an individual's physical and spiritual resources toward the purpose of Torah study. He therefore particularly stressed the value of separation from the society of other people, as social contact brings in its wake the loss of time from Torah study, while isolation from society assists in constancy of study.[8]

In his last book, *A Passion for Truth,* Abraham Joshua Heschel points out the affinity that the major Ḥasidic leader Rabbi Mendel of Kotzk, known as the Kotzker, had for the Gaon of Vilna by citing the following passage about the Gaon:

> The Gaon would not receive people in order to save all his time for his studies. When his sister came to see him after an absence of twelve years, he said to his attendant, "Tell her we'll see each other in the next world. I have no time for such meetings here."[9]

Heschel claims that the Kotzker had a somewhat similar view: "Both lived in solitude, cut off from the world."[10] In his excellent article "Ascetical Aspects of Ancient Judaism," Steven D. Fraade, professor at Yale University, states: "If the central religious obligation is that of the study of Torah (and attachment to God through it), then worldly preoccupations such as family are bound to be distracting for reasons of time, energy, and purity."[11] Here we can see the strong ascetic strain in the Jewish tradition, which we will find in Moses Hayyim Luzzatto's path to holiness.

In contrast, the Baal Shem Tov, who revealed himself as a spiritual master when he was thirty-six years old, did not believe that to live a spiritual life it is necessary to divorce oneself from this world. He stressed a passage from the prophet Isaiah that "the whole world is full of His presence" (Is 6:1). Even more central to his teaching is his interpretation of the phrase from Proverbs, "In all your ways know God" (Prv 3:6). For the Baal Shem Tov, people have different paths to God. Study may not be the path for everyone; each person needs to find the right path for himself. The Baal Shem Tov felt that the highest peak of spiritual living is attained through immersion in everyday life. Heschel's statement on the Baal Shem Tov helps us see the contrast between the Baal Shem Tov and the Gaon of Vilna:

> Before the Baal Shem's time, pious Jews felt that to be close to God, the body must be chastised, one must fast and scourge oneself. Bodily enjoyment was considered despicable; sexual pleasures filled them with revulsion. But the Baal Shem and his followers held that all delights come from Eden. "A longing for things material is an instrument by which one may approach the love of God; even through coarse desires one may come to love the Creator." Lust, desire, evil inclination, all should be elevated, not uprooted.[12]

"For the Baal Shem Tov," says Heschel, "saintliness and worldliness are not mutually exclusive."[13]

For the Mithnagdim, the traditional Jews who opposed the Ḥasidim, Ḥasidic beliefs seem to blur the distinction between the sacred and profane. Especially troubling to them and their leader, the Gaon of Vilna, was the Ḥasidic sanctification of food and drink. The Gaon of Vilna discouraged excessive eating even on the Sabbath. One of his students recounts the following conversation:

> When I spoke of this matter before my teacher, the Gaon, of blessed memory, he told me that he had a general principle that even though it is a *mitzvah* to eat and drink on the Sabbath, it is also a *mitzvah* to study Torah on the Sabbath. It is then much better to increase one's study than to increase one's eating and drinking. For increasing study will help develop study habits, and study is a *mitzvah* at all other times as well. On the other hand, eating on the Sabbath will lead to a greater appetite on weekdays as well.[14]

It may seem that the Mithnagdic and the Ḥasidic conceptions of the saint cannot be reconciled. But as I will demonstrate in the final section, there is a modern-day saint who combines the virtues of both models of the saint.

The Path to Holiness in Jewish Thought

We have some sense of what a Jewish saint is. But how does one become a saint? The best description of a path to holiness in the classical Jewish tradition comes from the great Jewish mystic and ethical writer from Italy, Moses Hayyim Luzzatto (1707–1746), and his *Mesillat Yesharim* (*The Path of the Upright*). Perhaps the most influential Jewish book on ethics, *Mesillat Yesharim* presents a systematic, step-by-step path on how to attain holiness: "Holiness is of a twofold nature; it begins as a quality of the service rendered to God, but it ends as a reward for such service. It is at first a type of spiritual effort, and then a kind of spiritual gift. A man must first strive to be holy, and then he is endowed with holiness."[15]

Luzzatto's work is actually an investigation into a single teaching from the second century rabbi Phinehas ben Yair, who stated: "The knowledge of Torah leads to watchfulness, watchfulness to zeal, zeal to cleanness, cleanness to abstinence, abstinence to purity, purity to saintliness, saintliness to humility, humility to fear of sin, and fear of sin to holiness."[16] Luzzatto transformed his hierarchy of qualities into a detailed guide to how man could perfect himself.

Luzzatto based his arguments on the belief that human beings, because they are imbued with a divine soul, cannot be satisfied with anything that can be found in this world. Rather, human beings were created to enjoy the world to come. Luzzatto writes: "Likewise, if thou were to offer the soul all the pleasures of the world, she would remain indifferent to them, because she belongs to a higher order of existence" (Koheleth R. to 6.7).[17] Therefore, this world should be viewed only as a path to fulfillment in the world to come.

Luzzatto says, "All of man's strivings should be directed toward the Creator, blessed be He. A man should have no other purpose in whatever he does, be it great or small, than to draw nigh to God and to break down all separating walls, that is, all things of a material nature, between himself and his Master, so that he may be drawn to God as iron to a magnet."[18]

Watchfulness

Following Rabbi Phinehas ben Yair's model, the first step to holiness begins with watchfulness. By watchfulness, Luzzatto means great care to avoid the evil inclination inside oneself. Only by studying the Torah and taking time to consider its ethical lessons can one avoid the evil inclination: "In fine, a man should at all times consider carefully what course to pursue so as to conform with the laws of the Torah. He should also set aside stated periods when he may contemplate in solitude."[19] But watchfulness is endangered by three factors: "The first is preoccupation with worldly affairs; the second is frivolity and levity; the third is the society of evil companions."[20]

All three factors that endanger watchfulness might compromise one's intent to live by the code of the Torah. Of these three, Luzzatto is most concerned about the danger of involvement in worldly affairs. He feels that this is the most common enemy and also the one factor that is easiest to overcome. At the same time, Luzzatto is opposed to severe asceticism. He realized that a human being must devote a certain amount of time to making a livelihood. But he was certain that devoting one's life to materialism would not deliver lasting bliss or salvation.

Zeal

The next step is zeal. Luzzatto explains that watchfulness pertains to the negative commandments while zeal pertains to the positive ones. He who is watchful merely avoids sin; he who is zealous also does good. Zeal means a commitment to do the *mitzvot* whenever possible. To acquire this commitment is no simple task; it requires great strength. Luzzatto writes: "It should be borne in mind that it is the nature of man to be inert, and that the earthiness of the physical element in him acts as a weight upon him. Man, therefore, seeks to avoid all toil and effort. Accordingly, a man who desires the privilege of worshiping the Creator, blessed be He, must be able to prevail over his own nature, and act with strength and energy."[21]

Cleanness

Luzzatto proceeds to the higher stage of cleanness. He tells us that "The quality of cleanness consists in being free from the evil traits as well as from sin."[22] Cleanness of soul is higher than watchfulness and zeal because the person who acquires the stages of watchfulness and zeal only succeeds in keeping his evil inclination in check, but he does not eradicate it. The person who has attained the higher stage of cleanness is beyond the evil inclination—beyond lust, beyond temptation. As a person becomes clean, the fire of lust will die out in his heart and its cessation will bring about a longing for the divine: "The true way to acquire the trait of spiritual cleanness is to read assiduously the words of our Sages, both their legal enactments and their ethical exhortations."[23] According to Luzzatto most people are only capable of reaching the stage of cleanness. Only a few can become saints.

Abstinence

With the next step we begin to approach the stages that lead to sainthood. The stage of abstinence marks the way to saintliness. The great enemy of abstinence is the craving and attachment to the pleasures of the world. The senses are indeed powerful antagonists to the greatest of men and women. The eyes of human beings are captivated by things that are outwardly beautiful and charming. It was these perceptions that "lead to man's original sin, as scripture testifies."[24] The way to attain abstinence is by realizing the true nature of pleasures. Luzzatto finds pleasures to be useless, worthless, and transient. Once a human being has attained abstinence he will no longer be allured by physical pleasures, "for he will know that he may enjoy in this world only those things without which he can't live."[25]

Purity

Purity follows abstinence. The essence of purity is the perfecting of one's heart and one's thought. Above all, to be pure is to attain perfect worship: "It can be called perfect only when it is pure and is rendered for no reason except that of serving God."[26] Before one reaches this stage one must realize that human glory is vanity, and one must view ambition as merely striving after the wind. Purity is zeal stripped of ego. It is higher than cleanness because cleanness involves only eradicating the evil inclination, while purity involves the actual performance of *mitzvot.* By meditating for many hours one prepares oneself for the performance of a mitzvah and in so doing becomes one with it. Only at this point "will he perform his religious duties with no thought of the praise he might win; his mind will then be directed wholly toward his Master. He alone is our glory, our good, and our perfection."[27]

Saintliness

Purity leads to saintliness, which is different in Luzzatto's view from holiness. Man alone can achieve saintliness; holiness requires the intervention of God. Luzzatto compares the saint to a lover who is always ready to do more than what is required. As a lover of God the aim is always to give happiness to one's Creator. Luzzatto devotes four chapters to saintliness, placing great stress on wisdom and the centrality of the study of the Torah. He states: "Saintliness should be reared upon great wisdom and upon the adjustment of conduct to the aims worthy of the truly wise. Only the wise can truly grasp the nature of saintliness; as our Sages said, 'The ignorant man cannot be saintly.'"[28] The need to attain wisdom by studying Torah day and night may be a major reason why Luzzatto, who clearly favors the world to come over this world, is opposed to prolonged fasting and other ascetic practices. Luzzatto was surely familiar with the rabbinic view that "a Torah scholar may not fast because he is detracting from the work of heaven."[29]

Humility

Also essential for the saint is the practice of loving-kindness, which forbids the infliction of pain upon any living creature. The saint's heart must be full of compassion and benevolence. We are faced here with a Jewish version of *ahiṃsā,* the Hindu belief of nonviolence. Withdrawing to solitude and concentrating upon the truth of the perfect and exalted nature of God will lead the saint to a state in which he ceases to regard himself with self-esteem. At the point at which the saint does not think of himself at all, since his whole being is concerned with the glory of God, he has reached the stage of humility—the all-consuming submission of one to God's will. Constant humility can only be achieved through reflection and training. This means habituating oneself in humbleness until humility is an implicit part of being.

Fear of Sin

The stage of humility is followed by the stage of the fear of sin. By the fear of sin Luzzatto does not mean only the fear of punishment but also a sense of awe for the glory of God. We can see how this sense of awe would be an inevitable result of submitting one's entire self to the will of God. Since Luzzatto believed that the fate of the world depends on our conduct, fearing sin is equivalent to fearing the destruction of the world.

Holiness

While great commitment can allow man to ascend through the earlier stages, the final stage of Luzzatto's path—holiness—is beyond the effort of human beings alone. He writes:

> But since it is impossible for a man to attain this status through his own efforts—for he is, after all, only a physical being, mere flesh and blood—holiness has to be finally granted to him as a gift. . . . It is the Holy One, blessed be He, who leads man in the path he has chosen, and who imparts to him some of His own holiness, thereby rendering him holy. The man who is holy, he who is always in communion with his God . . . is accounted as though he beheld the presence of the Lord, notwithstanding that he is still in this world.[30]

Judaism as well as Christianity and Islam are sometimes characterized as religions of faith, in contrast to Asian religions, which are said to be religions of experience. It is claimed that the Jew is required only to have faith in God and God's revelation. A reading of Luzzatto reveals that the saint not only has faith but that he has real experiences of God in this life. Luzzatto claims that faith in God combined with the will to holiness can lead one step by step "until there is poured upon him a spirit from on high and the name of the Creator, blessed be He, will abide within him as it does within all holy things."[31]

Like the Buddhist eightfold path, Luzzatto's path begins with watchfulness and, as one continues to struggle on this path, one may reach the stage of fear of sin. When one reaches that stage, the Holy Spirit may then descend and one attains holiness. Once one is granted holiness by God, claims Luzzatto, one has the power to resurrect the dead.

Mesillat Yesharim became an important ethical text for both the Mithnagdim and the Ḥasidim. The Ḥasidim, who elevated prayer over Torah study and made *devekut* (communion with God) their central goal, felt a strong affinity for Luzzatto's holy path, because they felt it leads to *devekut*. At the same time, the Gaon of Vilna is said to have stated that he could not find a superfluous word in the first seven chapters of *Mesillat Yesharim*—and were Luzzatto still alive, he would walk across Europe to study with him.

But Luzzatto's greatest influence was among the devotees of the Musar movement, an ethical self-perfection movement founded in Vilnius by Rabbi Israel Salanter (1810–1883). Salanter, one of the most influential Orthodox thinkers of the nineteenth century, felt a strong affinity for Luzzatto, stressing that the primary goal of a human being is to strive for ethical perfection. Rabbi Dov Katz, a third-generation disciple of Salanter, wrote: "His avowed aim in life was the attainment of spiritual perfection. He regarded ethical perfection as the entire purpose for being on earth."[32] Salanter believed that "it was more difficult to change a single character trait than to cover the entire Talmud."[33] Yet for him this was a task that must be undertaken and that would ultimately lead to the transformation of the individual:

> Yet let no one say: What God has made cannot be changed. He, may He be blessed, has infused an evil drive in me; how can I ever hope to eradicate it? It is not so. Man's drives can be subdued and even changed. . . . It is within his power to conquer his evil nature and prevent its functioning, and also to change his nature to good by study and training.[34]

In the preface to his book *Mesillat Yesharim* Luzzatto complains that people are devoting too much time to the study of Jewish law and are not paying sufficient attention to the study of Musar: "There are but few who study the nature of the love and the fear of God, of communion, or any other phase of saintliness."[35] This captures precisely the view of Salanter, who made the study of Musar texts central to achieving a holy life and who helped Luzzatto's *Mesillat Yesharim* become the most widely used basic text among the *Yeshivot* of Lithuania.[36]

At the beginning of the twenty-first century, there are only a few *yeshivot* in the United States and Israel that emphasize Musar in their curriculum. Although there are four English translations of *Mesillat Yesharim,* the Jewish world as a whole is not familiar with the Musar movement and its preeminent ethical text.[37]

A Jewish Saint of the Twentieth Century

Today there is a new, beautiful ethical text that is capturing the minds and hearts of Jews and members of other faiths throughout the world, especially in America. This work, *God in Search of Man: A Philosophy of Judaism,* was first published in 1955 by Rabbi Abraham Joshua Heschel (1907–1972). I—along with many other Jews and Christians—consider Heschel to be the Jewish saint of the twentieth century. His first student in America, Rabbi Samuel Dresner, claimed that Heschel was "*zaddik hador,*" the saint of our generation.[38] For Heschel's disciple Byron Sherwin, "Abraham Joshua Heschel was a jewel from God's treasure chest."[39] Christians speak of Heschel as the most significant spiritual writer of our time and often call him a prophet.[40] I view Heschel's *God in Search of Man* as a modern equivalent of Luzzatto's Jewish path to holiness. Heschel's book can be seen as "a way of developing sensitivity to God and attachment to His presence."[41]

God in Search of Man is devoted to three interrelated aspects of a Jewish path through which contemporary Jews can open themselves to God or, more precisely, through which we can respond to God, who according to Heschel, needs human beings. In Heschel's words, "There are three starting points of contemplation about God; three trails that lead to Him. The first is the way of sensing the presence of God in the world, in things; the second is the way of sensing His presence in the Bible; the third is the way of sensing His presence in sacred deeds."[42]

Heschel has been called the philosopher of wonder because he believed that awareness of the divine begins with wonder. For Heschel, radical amazement can help us to experience the realm of the ineffable. Heschel takes as his task in the first path to tell us how to sense wonder and awe, how to see the holy in the everyday, to see that all of life is sacred.

The second of Heschel's paths to God is encountering God through the words of the Bible. Heschel asserts that the Bible is the ideal path through which Jews can encounter God. However, mere biblical study will not disclose the presence of God. We must approach the Bible with our whole being. We must also cultivate certain virtues, such as humility and truthfulness, and attempt to rid ourselves of pride, pettiness, and falsehood.

In Heschel's third path, the way of sensing God's presence in sacred deeds, he claims that modern human beings who have difficulty with the first two paths, who still cannot open their eyes, have a final alternative. Heschel presents a most challenging and provocative claim. He contends that performing the *mitzvot,* the commandments, is not merely our response to the demands of God. They may also serve as a path *to* God. The fact that contemporary human beings are callous to the mystery of existence and detached from the biblical tradition leads Heschel to say that the way through deeds may be our last hope. The significance that Heschel attaches to sacred deeds becomes apparent when he states, "A Jew is asked to take a leap of action rather than a leap of thought. He is asked to surpass his needs, to do more than he understands in order to understand more than he does. In carrying out the words of the Torah he is ushered into the presence of spiritual meaning. Through the ecstasy of deeds, he learns to be certain of the hereness of God. Right living is a way of right thinking."[43] Farther along, Heschel explains more fully why the Jew is asked to take a leap of action:

> The mitzvah is a supreme source of religious insight and experience. The way to God is a way of God, and the mitzvah is a way of God, a way where the self-evidence of the holy is disclosed. . . . A mitzvah is where God and man meet. . . . To meet Him means to come upon an inner certainty of His realness, upon an awareness of His will. Such a meaning, such presence we experience in deeds.[44]

Conclusion

There are clearly major affinities as well as differences between the works of Luzzatto and Heschel. Luzzatto was writing during a time when, for most Jews, God was a reality. His aim was to lead ordinary Jews to saintliness. Heschel, on the other hand, wrote during a time when the belief in a supernatural concept of God was no longer a reality for many Jews. His aim was to convince Jews that awareness of God's reality would help lead them to a more spiritual, holy life.

Luzzatto's path is more otherworldly than Heschel's path, with a strong stress on personal transformation. Because of the intense effort that is necessary to attain saintliness, there is little time in Luzzatto's path for one to be involved in the community. Heschel, on the other hand, is deeply concerned with the everyday. He became involved in a number of compelling social and political issues of his day. He devoted a great deal of time to the civil rights movement, led by Martin Luther King Jr., and to opposing the war in Viet Nam. He also addressed himself to the plight of Jews in the Soviet Union.

Judaism commands love of both God and neighbor. The question that has often been asked is: Does love of God take priority over love of neighbor? I would argue that that is the case for Luzzatto. For Heschel, who always attempted to create a balance between the polarities in Judaism, human beings come first. Heschel observed, "Every human being is made in the image of God. Therefore, if we are serving our fellow human beings, in a very real sense we are serving God as well."[45] This is how Heschel characterized a saint: "A saint was he who did not know how it is possible not to love, not to help, not to be sensitive to the anxiety of others."[46]

With his attention to the world and the divine, Heschel combined the hallowing of the everyday of the Baal Shem Tov with the brilliant scholarship of the Gaon of Vilna and the ethical fervor of Israel Salanter. Heschel described—and lived—a modern path to sainthood.

Notes

1. Solomon Schechter (1847–1915) in his classic book, *Aspects of Rabbinic Theology: Major Concepts of the Talmud* (1909; repr. New York: Schocken Books, 1961), presents a very helpful analysis of holiness in rabbinic literature. He discerns a distinction between holiness and saintliness, which is not always made clear by the rabbis. In his discussion of holiness and saintliness, he states that "the former moves more within the limits of the Law, though occasionally exceeding it, while the latter, aspiring to a superior kind of holiness, not only supplements the Law, but also proves a certain corrective to it" (201). His later comment on rabbinic Judaism is very helpful in showing the affinity between Judaism and Christianity: "Impure thinking was, in the Rabbinic view, the antecedent to impure doing, and the ideal saint was as pure of heart as of hand, acting no impurity and thinking none" (210–11).

2. Jesus was reflecting Jewish thinking when he cited these two commandments as the most important verses of the Torah; see Mk 12:28–34. In this chapter, scriptural passages from the Hebrew Bible are from the 1955 and 1962 translations of *The Holy Scriptures* by the Jewish Publication Society of America.

3. The ethical classic *Pirke Avot* is the best-known rabbinic text; see *Pirke Avot: A Modern Commentary on Jewish Ethics*, ed. and trans. Leonard

Kravitz and Kerry M. Olitzky (New York: UAHC Press, 1993). This text teaches that "the ignoramus will not be saintly (Avot 2:5)." Ibid., 21. *Pirke Avot* is the only part of the Talmud that was incorporated into the Jewish prayer book. The rabbis stated: "Whoever aspires to saintliness, let him fulfill the teaching of avot" (Baba Kamma, 30a).

4. Jewish mystics go even farther. For them, the words of the Torah are a rendezvous point where humans meet God, who is "in the letters of the Torah." So, study is a way toward *devekut,* and not only a way of discerning God's will.

5. In his chapter, "The Gaon, Rabbi Elijah Wilna," written in 1928, Louis Ginzberg writes: "The earliest documents in which the Gaon is mentioned, one dating from the time he was thirty, the other from a time when he was thirty-five, call him Rabbi Elijah the Saint, and to this day his synagogue in Wilna is known as the synagogue of the saint." *Students, Scholars and Saints* (1928; repr. New York: Meridian Books, 1960), 141.

6. Louis Jacobs, "The Doctrine of the Zaddik in the Thought of Elimelech of Lizensk," The Rabbi Louis Feinberg Memorial Lecture in Judaic Studies, University of Cincinnati, February 9, 1978, 3. Jacobs claims that according to Elimelech of Lizensk, "the Zaddik has power over life and death." This power is given by God to the *tzaddik* because "God so desires the prayers of the righteous" ("Doctrine of the Zaddik," 6). To this day, many Ḥasidim visit the graves of their Ḥasidic masters because they believe that their masters still retain their miracle-making powers and may intervene on their behalf. In a recent pioneering work entitled *Workers of Wonders,* Byron Sherwin argues that the most influential Jewish leaders throughout history were also miracle workers. The veneration of saints who are believed to be miracle workers was an especially widely practiced phenomenon among North African Jews, who continue this practice today in Israel; see Alex Weingrod, *The Saint of Beersheba* (Albany: State University of New York Press, 1990), and Byron L. Sherwin, *Workers of Wonders: A Model for Effective Religious Leadership from Scripture to Today* (Lanham, MD: Rowman and Littlefield, 2004); for a more in-depth discussion of the idea of drawing down divine grace, see Byron L. Sherwin, *Kabbalah: An Introduction to Jewish Mysticism* (New York: Rowman and Littlefield, 2006), esp. chap. 7. I am deeply grateful to Byron Sherwin for his careful reading of this essay and for his helpful comments.

7. Jonathan Sacks, *To Heal A Fractured World: The Ethics of Responsibility* (New York: Schocken Books, 2005), 245; emphasis in the original.

8. Immanuel Etkes, *Rabbi Israel Salanter and the Mussar Movement: Seeking the Torah of Truth* (Philadelphia: The Jewish Publication Society, 1993), 18.

9. Abraham Joshua Heschel, *A Passion for Truth* (New York: Farrar, Straus, and Giroux, 1973), 82.

10. Ibid.

11. Steven D. Fraade, "Ascetical Aspects of Ancient Judaism," in *Jewish Spirituality: From the Bible through the Middle Ages,* ed. Arthur Green (New York: Crossroad Publishing, 1986), 274–75.

12. Heschel, *A Passion,* 25.

13. Ibid., 24.

14. Qtd. in Allan Nadler, *The Faith of the Mithnagdim: Rabbinic Responses to Hasidic Rapture* (Baltimore: Johns Hopkins University Press, 1997), 86.

15. Moses Hayyim Luzzatto, *Mesillat Yesharim: The Path of the Upright*, trans. Mordecai M. Kaplan (Philadelphia: The Jewish Publication Society of America, 1966), 442. I find it somewhat paradoxical that Kaplan (1881–1983), founder of the Reconstructionist Movement in Judaism, whose reinterpretation of the Jewish tradition rejects the concept of a supernatural God, devoted so much time to translating a text written by one of the greatest mystics that Judaism has produced. In the introduction Kaplan explains why he did so: "*Mesillat Yesharim* will ever serve as a true mirror reflecting the inwardness and spirituality which Judaism demanded of those who lived in conformity with its laws" (xxxvi).

16. Qtd. in Luzzatto, *Mesillat Yesharim*, 18.

17. Luzzatto, *Mesillat Yesharim*, 32.

18. Ibid., 36.

19. Ibid., 56.

20. Ibid., 80.

21. Ibid., 98.

22. Ibid., 134.

23. Ibid., 234.

24. Ibid., 262. The English translation of *Mesillat Yesharim* by Shiraga Silverstein translates this Hebrew passage as "first sin" rather than "original sin." I believe this is more in accord with Luzzatto's meaning and the Jewish tradition, which rejects the idea of original sin (New York and Jerusalem: Feldheim Publishers, 1966), 197.

25. Ibid., 266. With the focus on abstinence Luzzatto comes dangerously close to creating a monastic movement within Judaism. Following this idea to its logical conclusion, one should not marry. Any man who reached this stage would be faced with a real conflict, since he must fulfill the commandment to "be fruitful and multiply." Luzzatto himself was married and had children, for he could not go against the Torah.

It may be asked whether Luzzatto's emphasis on otherworldliness is consistent with what may be called normative Judaism. Dr. Guttmann's statement concerning the very influential medieval Jewish ethical writer Bahya ibn Pakuda helps us understand this point: "Bahya goes far beyond the clues provided by the Talmud; for though the Talmud places man's ultimate aim in the world to come, it does not view the moral and religious task of his life exclusively from the viewpoint of the hereafter." Julius Guttmann, *Philosophies of Judaism: The History of Jewish Philosophy from Biblical Times to Franz Rosenzweig* (New York: Anchor Books, 1966), 123. Seeing the world from the point of view of the world to come is precisely what Luzzatto does throughout his book.

26. Ibid., 276.

27. Ibid., 284.

28. Ibid., 290.

29. Eliezer Diamond, *Holy Men and Hunger Artists: Fasting and Asceticism in Rabbinic Culture* (New York: Oxford University Press, 2004), 117.

30. Ibid., 444–46.

31. Ibid., 452.

32. Dov Katz, *The Musar Movement,* trans. Leonard Oschry (Tel-Aviv: "Orly" Press, 1977), vol. 1, pt. 2, 138.

33. Ibid., 120.

34. Qtd. by Dov Katz in *Musar Movement,* 65. It is beyond the scope of the present essay to compare and contrast the holy person in Judaism and Buddhism. However, I do want to point out that a study of the methods of training advocated by the Buddha and Israel Salanter reveals some striking similarities. For example, both advocate meditation on death. I also find it quite striking that Salanter, like the Buddha, believes in the possibility of a radical transformation of the human being. Salanter's closest disciple, Rabbi Simcha Zissel Ziv of Kelm, Lithuania, taught "Take time, be exact, unclutter the mind." He also said, "The worst thing that can happen to a person is to remain asleep and untamed." I see these statements as central teachings of the Buddha.

35. Luzzatto, *Mesillat Yesharim,* 4.

36. Rabbi Norman Lamm, the former president of Yeshiva University in New York City, reminds us of the great popularity of *Mesillat Yesharim.* He writes: "Its wide popularity can be gauged by the fact that it was reprinted no less than sixty-six times in a period of one hundred and fifty-five years." *Torah; Lishmah: Torah for Torah's Sake in the Works of Rabbi Hayim of Volozhin and His Contemporaries* (Hoboken, NJ: Ktav Publishing House, 1989), 338.

37. The Musar movement had its greatest strength in Lithuania, where 95 percent of the Jews were killed during the Holocaust. Fortunately, a few students from the yeshiva in Slabodka, which was known as "the mother of yeshivas," and from the yeshiva of Volzhin, managed to survive. In *Climbing Jacob's Ladder: One Man's Rediscovery of a Jewish Spiritual Tradition,* Alan Morinis, a secular Jew and a Rhodes scholar who was a professor of Asian religions, tells the incredible story of his meeting with Rabbi Yechiel Yitzchok Perr, a great contemporary Musar teacher and how his life was transformed by this encounter (New York: Broadway Books, 2002).

38. Samuel H. Dresner, "Abraham Joshua Heschel: The Man," in *Prayer and Politics: The Twin Poles of Abraham Joshua Heschel,* ed. Joshua Stampfer (Portland, OR: Institute for Judaic Studies, 1985), 30.

39. Byron L. Sherwin, *Abraham Joshua Heschel* (Atlanta: John Knox Press, 1979), 1.

40. For example, Reinhold Niebuhr spoke of Heschel as "the most authentic prophet of religious life in our culture" (qtd. by Byron L. Sherwin, in "Abraham Joshua Heschel," *The Torch* [Spring 1969]: 7). Heschel's friend Martin Luther King Jr. often spoke of Heschel as a prophet. And at a recent conference in Switzerland, Professor Stanislaw Obirek from Warsaw, Poland, the land of Heschel's birth, called Heschel, "a real prophet." Heschel did not accept being praised as a prophet. He said that he hoped and prayed that

he was "worthy of being a descendent of the prophets." See "Carl Stern's Interview with Dr. Heschel," in *Moral Grandeur and Spiritual Audacity: Essays: Abraham Joshua Heschel,* ed. Susannah Heschel (New York: Farrar, Straus, and Giroux, 1996), 400.

41. Abraham Joshua Heschel, *God in Search of Man: A Philosophy of Judaism* (New York: Farrar, Straus, and Cudahy, 1955), 26.

42. Ibid., 31.

43. Ibid., 283.

44. Ibid., 312.

45. Qtd. in Bernard S. Raskas, *Jewish Spirituality and Ethics* (Hoboken, NJ: Ktav Publishing House, 1990), 9.

46. Abraham Joshua Heschel, *The Earth Is the Lord's* (New York: Farrar, Straus, and Giroux, 1978), 20–21.

2

Christian Spiritual Masters

James A. Wiseman

The Meaning of the Terms *Spiritual* and *Master*

A useful way to understand the basic meaning of words, even very common ones, is through their etymology. So I begin this chapter by looking at the derivation of the words *spiritual* and *master*. The latter comes from the Latin word *magister,* whose root *mag* also gives us the related adjective *magnus,* meaning "great" or "large." Accordingly, in ancient Rome the term *magister* was used of anyone who held a position of leadership. A dictator was often called the *magister populi* (leader of the people), while the captain of a ship was the *magister navis*. One of the very common places in any society for someone to assume a position of leadership is, of course, the classroom. So in Roman times the word *magister,* without any further specification, was often used of a teacher or educator. This usage has carried over into English with our word *schoolmaster*. We shall soon see how this magisterial teaching function is prominent in the notion of spiritual masters within the Christian tradition; but before turning to that point let us also examine the adjective *spiritual*.

The word *spiritual*, too, comes from a Latin word: *spiritualis*. It is derived from the verb *spirare*, whose root meaning is "to breathe." Since we need to breathe in order to stay alive, that verb also came to mean "to live, to be alive." The corresponding adjective *spiritualis* could, therefore, simply mean "belonging to breathing" or "to air." However, since breath and air cannot readily be seen, the adjective also came to mean "spiritual" as distinct from "tangible, or material." For this reason, and particularly within some circles of Christianity, the words *spiritual* and *spirituality* have often been regarded with considerable suspicion because they smacked of otherworldliness—suggesting disdain for the temporal, the bodily, the here-and-now. For many people the terms conjured up memories of the kind of objection that Karl Marx made against religion—religion was merely "the opium of the people," promising pie in the sky, and thereby distracting persons from the work of bringing about a more just society. More recently, the term *spiritual* has normally been used with much more positive connotations, as when a person says, "I'm not religious, but I'm spiritual." Here the word has connotations of open-mindedness, creativity, and freedom from the restraints of religious dogmas and laws.

As used in this chapter, *spiritual* does not imply any opposition to participating in a religious tradition, nor any lack of engagement in the pressing concerns of civil society. Within Christianity, the word ideally refers to being led, guided, or inspired by the one whom the Bible calls the Holy Spirit, which in mainline Christian thought has always referred to God's abiding, personal presence among us. As a preliminary definition of the spiritual master within Christian tradition, we could, therefore, say that the person is a Spirit-filled leader, one of whose main functions is to serve others through wise teaching.

Jesus Christ as the Preeminent Spiritual Master in Christianity

Even from our preliminary definition of a spiritual master—a Spirit-filled leader, one of whose main functions is to serve others through wise teaching—one could rightly conclude that the preeminent spiritual master within the Christian tradition is Christ Jesus himself. The two interrelated functions of leading and teaching are abundantly clear from a careful study of the titles given to Jesus in the Gospels. The word in the original Greek New Testament that most literally translates as "master" is *epistata,* often used of Jesus in the Gospel of Luke, as in his account of the stilling of a storm on the Sea of Galilee. For our purposes, it is instructive to see how Luke's account of the incident differs from those of two other evangelists, Mark and Matthew.

All three evangelists recount that on a particular occasion Jesus was asleep in a boat as he and his disciples were crossing the lake. When a storm struck and the boat was filling with water, the frightened disciples awakened Jesus, seeking his aid. In Luke's gospel, they address him with that term *epistata*: "Master, Master, we are perishing" (Lk 8:24 NRSV).[1] It is significant that in Mark's gospel, almost certainly written earlier than Luke's and known by Luke, the disciples address Jesus by a different title, "Teacher" (*didaskalē* in Greek): "Teacher, aren't you concerned that we are perishing?" (Mk 4:38). By contrast, in the corresponding passage of Matthew's gospel still another title is used, "Lord" (in Greek, *kyriē*): "Lord, save us, we are perishing" (Mt 8:25). All three evangelists clearly affirm the preeminence of Jesus, but the three different terms of address used in their accounts of the stilling of the storm tell us something important about mastership as it applies to Jesus in the Gospels: He is simultaneously *leader* and *teacher*. In addition, he is the *saving lord* to whom disciples can go in time of danger.

Not only that. We hear elsewhere in the Gospels that Jesus is to be considered the *only* master or teacher for those who would be his followers. In chapter 23 of Matthew's gospel, Jesus warns his disciples against those Pharisees who do things only to be seen by others: seeking places of honor at feasts, taking the best seats in the synagogues, and being called "Rabbi." Regarding this title *rabbi,* a common term of respect for leaders and teachers in the society of Jesus's day, he tells his followers: "You are not to be called rabbi, for you have one teacher, and all of you are brothers" (Mt 23:8). Thus, we see here, *one* teacher, *one* master. Whether or not most of Jesus's followers have explicitly reflected on this point across the centuries, there is no doubt that in the Christian tradition there is only one spiritual master par excellence, Jesus Christ. All others to whom the title can rightly be applied are masters only in a derived sense, and deserve the title only to the extent that they exemplify the qualities that marked Jesus's life and teaching. I will discuss five such qualities, and in each case show how one or more later Christians exercised their own spiritual mastery after the model they found in Jesus. I will then conclude with some thoughts on how one becomes a spiritual master and is (or is not) so recognized by others.

The Authoritative Nature of a Spiritual Master's Teaching

The first quality of spiritual mastery that I want to emphasize is the authoritative nature of Jesus's teaching. Several times in the Gospels we hear how the crowds were in awe of the words spoken by Jesus, so different were they from the words of others who spoke to them. Near the very beginning of Mark's gospel we read:

> [Jesus and his followers] came to Capernaum, and when the Sabbath came he entered the synagogue and taught. [The people] were astounded at his teaching, for he taught them as one having authority, and not as the scribes. (Mk 1:21–22)

One way of putting this is that Jesus was perceived by many to be filled with the power of God's Spirit. This point led Huston Smith, in the Christianity chapter of his best-selling book on the world's religions, to write: "That Jesus stood in the Jewish tradition of Spirit-filled mediators is the most important fact for understanding his historical career."[2]

Not everyone in Jesus's day acknowledged that Jesus was filled with God's Holy Spirit, however. The Gospels explain the opposition to Jesus by saying that there were people whose eyes and ears were closed to the salvific nature of his life and teaching. For those who did accept Jesus as their master—whether in first-century Palestine or in any century since—the attraction is to be found largely in the self-authenticating nature of what he did and said. This is true not only of simple believers who have discovered in Jesus the lodestone for their lives even if they have never studied a page of academic theology, but also of well-educated persons whose professional careers have been centered in that discipline. Thus, David Tracy, a highly regarded theologian of the University of Chicago Divinity School, writes in one of his books about what it means to find a gracious God in and through the one whom the New Testament calls "the beloved Son." In Tracy's words:

> [For Christians, Jesus] is *the* re-presentation, *the* Word, *the* Deed, *the* very Destiny of God himself. The God disclosed

> in the words, deeds, and destiny of Jesus the Christ is . . . a loving, righteous Father who promises the power of this new righteousness, this new possibility of self-sacrificing love to those who will hear and abide by The Word spoken in the words, deeds, and destiny of Jesus the Christ.[3]

There have been many other men and women in the past twenty centuries who have—to one degree or another—attracted hearers by what I have called the self-authenticating nature of their words. Of these teachers, the Roman Catholic Church has singled out a select group, numbering only thirty-three at the present time. It has named these individuals, "doctors of the Church." They are doctors in the sense of official teachers, as the word *doctor* derives from the Latin verb *docēre,* "to teach." Of these doctors, or master teachers, perhaps the most striking example is the one named most recently, St. Thérèse of Lisieux, who was accorded that rank by Pope John Paul II in 1998.

In many respects Thérèse's life was very different from Jesus's life. Having entered a strictly cloistered convent of Carmelite nuns in Normandy at the age of fifteen and having died of tuberculosis in 1897 at the age of twenty-four, she had no opportunity to be out among the people, speaking to crowds as Jesus once did. In fact, at the time of her death, when the sisters of her community were preparing the brief biographical notes that would appear on the death notice to be sent to other convents of the order, some of them wondered aloud what positive things could be said about Thérèse, so unobtrusive and apparently ordinary had her life been. Others in the convent, however, had already sensed the depth of her wisdom and had asked her to write several autobiographical manuscripts. When these were later pieced together and published in book form under the title *Story of a Soul,* the effect was monumental. The work has been translated into more than a dozen languages, has been read by millions, and led one pope to call her the greatest saint of the twentieth century.

I want to emphasize that there is nothing complicated about Thérèse's teaching. She herself would have said, rightly enough, that her writings are primarily a working out of some of the major themes of the Bible. Yet, she had a profound ability to go right to the heart of the matter in the way she understood such doctrines as the graciousness and mercy of God. This, together with straightforward accounts of ways in which she unobtrusively tried to live out the challenge of the Gospels that we love one another even as Christ has loved us, won for her a hearing that endures to this day. Thérèse became a genuine spiritual master because she drew her nourishment from what must always remain the wellspring of spiritual life for a Christian, namely, the Bible—and above all, the Gospels. At one point, she wrote that as she grew older most religious writing left her in a state of aridity, but such was never the case with the Gospels. In her words:

> It is especially the *Gospels* that sustain me during my hours of prayer, for in them I find what is necessary for my . . . soul. I am constantly discovering in them new lights, hidden and mysterious meanings. . . . Jesus has no need of books or teachers to instruct souls; he teaches without the noise of words. Never have I heard Him speak, but I feel that He is within me at each moment; He is guiding and inspiring me with what I must say and do. I find just when I need them certain lights that I had not seen until then.[4]

The Healing Function of a Spiritual Master

If persons such as Jesus and St. Thérèse were doctors in the sense of teachers, the more common English usage of *doctor* in the sense of healer or physician is also pertinent to our subject. One of the best-known passages in the Gospels is the account of one of Jesus's conflicts with the Pharisees, who objected that he was accustomed to eating with tax collectors and those known to be public sinners. When they asked his disciples how this could be justified, Jesus heard of their complaint and said, "Those who are well have no need of a physician, but those who are sick [have need of one]; I have come to call not the righteous but sinners" (Mk 2:17). Although his healing of those with physical ailments is reported frequently in the Gospels, what Jesus referred to in the passage just quoted was healing of another sort—spiritual healing.

Few passages in the Gospels are more moving than those in which someone long burdened with a sense of guilt is set free by his proclamation of forgiveness. Consider the episode where Jesus is dining at the house of a Pharisee named Simon. Luke writes that while Jesus was eating, a woman known in the city to be a sinner came in bearing an alabaster flask of ointment. She stood behind him, weeping; and then began to bathe his feet with her tears. She wiped his feet with her hair, kissed them, and anointed them with the ointment. His host was incensed at this scene, thinking that if Jesus knew what sort of woman this was, he would never have let her touch him. However, after telling Simon a brief parable about the different degrees of gratitude and love that will be felt by persons who have had different amounts of debt forgiven, Jesus went on to say:

> "Do you see this woman? I entered your house; you gave me no water for my feet, but she has bathed my feet with her tears and dried them with her hair. You gave me no kiss, but from the time I came in she has not stopped kissing my feet. You did not anoint my head with oil, but she has anointed my feet with ointment. Therefore, I tell you, her sins, which were many, have been forgiven; hence she has shown great love. But the one to whom little is forgiven, loves little." Then he said to her, "Your sins are forgiven." But those who were at the table with him began to say among themselves, "Who is this who even forgives sins?" And he said to the woman, "Your faith has saved you; go in peace." (Lk 7:44–50)

Here, as regularly in cases of spiritual healing, it was Jesus's relationship with a particular person rather than with a large crowd that was at issue. Christians who followed Jesus in this particular exercise of spiritual mastery have likewise regularly done so on a one-to-one basis. However, while Jesus is at times depicted in the Gospels as being able to read hearts and so know a person's spiritual state without having to ask probing questions, this is normally not the case with his followers. For this reason, one of the principal activities of a spiritual master and disciple is what is usually called "the revelation of thoughts"—something that is altogether basic to the work of many spiritual masters in Christian tradition.

Although the revelation or disclosure of thoughts may, at times, involve the confession of sins and the receiving of absolution from an ordained minister, the practice among Christian spiritual masters is actually much broader. In fact, the thoughts that are revealed will ideally not be sins at all; rather, they are likely to be subtle suggestions that could eventually lead to actual sin if not nipped in the bud. Among those who grasped the crucial importance of this practice were the spiritual fathers and mothers of the early monastic movement that began in Egypt, Palestine, and Syria in the late third century of the Common Era. Originally, much of their teaching only was given orally; but after several generations their wisdom came to be written down, lest it be lost to posterity. In one collection of these sayings, an anonymous elder had this to say to his disciple:

> When evil thoughts harass you, do not hide them but tell them at once to your spiritual father. The more one hides one's thoughts, the more they multiply and the stronger they become. As a serpent flees instantly as soon as it has left its hole, so an evil thought dissipates as soon as it begins to be disclosed. Like a worm in wood, so a hidden evil thought devastates the heart. The person who discloses his thoughts is soon healed. Whoever hides them makes himself sick through pride.[5]

It is not enough, of course, for a spiritual master simply to hear the disclosure of thoughts by the disciple. The response must be marked by the vitally important quality of compassionate discernment. Not everyone will receive exactly the same advice, since a genuine master will recognize the varying capacities of those who disclose their thoughts to accept and appropriate the counsel that is given. Above all, the advice must be characterized by charity and compassion, so that even a severe admonition will not lead to discouragement or despair. Another passage from that early monastic literature gives an account that illustrates both the wrong and the right ways to respond.

The story goes as follows: One day a young monk, among the most diligent, went to an elder hoping to make progress and be healed of his ills. He spoke of lustful temptations he had been experiencing, hoping that he would receive consolation and helpful advice. Instead, this elder rebuked him bitterly, saying that he was wretched and dishonorable for being agitated in this way. The young monk left, given over to despair and grief. Then he happened upon another elder named Apollos, who was one of the most trusted in that region. The monk Apollos guessed the trouble merely from the expression on his face and began to inquire more intently about the causes for such grief. The young man said he was on his way back to his village since, according to what he had been told, he was unworthy to remain in the community. At this, Apollos began to console him, saying that he too was daily troubled by such temptations, and that one should never be dismayed by the ferocity of such thoughts, which are to be overcome not so much by toil and exertion as by the Lord's grace and mercy. The young monk took his words to heart and persevered. The narrative goes on to recount how Apollos later prayed that the other elder, who had been so uncompassionate, should himself experience such temptations. This prayer having been answered, Apollos then confronted him with the following words:

> This has happened to you because of the young man. He came to you because he was being attacked by the common enemy of us all. You ought to have given him words of consolation to help him against the devil's attack, but instead you drove him to despair. . . . You did not remember our Savior's parable [where he says], "You should not break the bruised reed, nor quench the smoking flax."
>
> So saying, Apollos prayed again, and at once the old man was freed from his inner war. Abba Apollos urged him to ask God to give him the tongue of the wise, to know the time when it is best to speak.[6]

In the way he dealt with the young monk who felt weighed down by a burden of guilt, Abba Apollos was clearly acting after the example he had found in such Gospel accounts as the one we just considered, that of Jesus dining at the home of Simon the Pharisee.

A Spiritual Master as Servant of Others

Persons who have assumed leadership roles in any society or organization run the risk of becoming arrogant, seeking primarily their own welfare and aggrandizement. In this connection, one thinks of the robber barons of late-nineteenth-century American capitalism. Spiritual leadership or mastery at its best is of an entirely different nature, as exemplified by Jesus's words on a certain occasion when there was a dispute among his closest followers about who were most deserving of certain privileges. Mark's gospel has Jesus saying to them:

> You know that among the Gentiles those whom they recognize as their rulers lord it over them, and their great ones are tyrants over them. But it is not so among you; but whoever wishes to become great among you must be your servant, and whoever wishes to be first among you must be slave of all. For the Son of Man came not to be served but to serve, and to give his life as a ransom for many. (Mk 10:42–45)

Such dedication to the service of others marks the life of every spiritual master, but there may be no better example within the Christian tradition than the life of St. Augustine of Hippo (354–430)—a man of penetrating intellect, and one of the most influential theologians in the history of the Church.

After his conversion to Christianity, Augustine would instinctively have preferred to live a life of contemplative retirement among philosophically minded friends. He never sought ordination to the priesthood and the kind of service to others that it required, but it came to him anyway in a most unusual manner. He had traveled from his native town of Thagaste (in modern-day Algeria) to the harbor city of Hippo in order to give some spiritual advice to a government official who was undergoing some difficulties. On the Sunday of his visit, while he was part of a congregation that had crowded the large cathedral church, the aged bishop Valerius announced his intention of having a new priest chosen. Many in the crowd recognized Augustine, a former professor of rhetoric long noted for his eloquence and now also respected for his ascetic way of life. They literally seized him and firmly took him up to the bishop's chair, declaring that this was the man who should be chosen. Augustine gave in to their request and thereby began a career of outstanding service to the church that has had enormous influence down the centuries.

Augustine's life of service became even more demanding when he succeeded Valerius as bishop a few years later. The demands now placed on him, including issues that reached far beyond the borders of his diocese, were numerous and pressing. In a letter to the abbot of a secluded monastery on an island in the Mediterranean, Augustine confessed that he often envied him his quiet, adding that one could live more peacefully in the midst of the sea than in his episcopal audience chamber. That Augustine, despite this inclination, met in a heroic way the demands placed upon him shows in a convincing way that he was truly a saint—that is, a spiritual master and not merely an ecclesiastical potentate or a persuasive speaker or writer. He once said in a sermon:

> No one can long more than I to be free from troubles and cares, for nothing is better, nothing is more sweet, than to browse among the heavenly treasures, away from all distractions and noise. Yet it is the Gospel itself that makes me fear that way of life. I might well say, "Why should I feel responsible for others?" It is there that the Gospel holds me back.[7]

A Spiritual Master's Gift of Discernment

A fourth quality that marked the life of Jesus and the lives of other spiritual masters in the Christian tradition is that of discerning how to respond to others in particular situations. In other words, their teaching is not of the "one size fits all" variety. Jesus could be very harsh in speaking to those in whom he discerned hardness of heart, as when the Gospels show him castigating certain opponents as "blind fools" who are like "white-washed tombs, which on the outside look beautiful, but inside are full of the bones of the dead and of all kinds of filth. So you also on the outside look righteous to others, but inside you are full of hypocrisy and lawlessness" (Mt 23:17, 27–28). On the other hand, when Jesus sensed genuine sorrow in a person for his or her sinful ways, his response was one of gentleness and forgiveness. Perhaps the most striking example of such discernment concerns the account of a woman who had been caught in the act of adultery, and so was liable to death by stoning. On this occasion, after confronting her accusers with the challenge that the one who was himself without sin should cast the first stone and then seeing them slink away one by one, Jesus was left alone with the woman. He did not at all deny the wrongness of her behavior, but even while acknowledging that, he spoke a further word that held out the hope and even promise of conversion to a new way of life. The concluding dialogue goes as follows: "Woman, where are they? Has no one condemned you?" She replied: "No one, sir." Then Jesus said, "Neither do I condemn you. Go, and from now on do not sin any more" (Jn 8:10–11).[8]

One of the many Christian spiritual masters who showed a similar ability to make appropriate responses in given cases, without others being able to know for certain in advance just what that response would be, was St. Pachomius (ca. 290–347), generally recognized as founder of the communal or cenobitic form of monastic life, which is distinct from the more solitary lifestyle of hermits. In the course of his lifetime Pachomius founded eleven monasteries along the Nile, nine for men and two for women, with thousands of monks and nuns in residence. What drew so many to him was not only his gift of speaking convincingly about the Scriptures and living in accord with the words he preached, but also his ability to deal with persons of a character very different from his own, as exemplified by the following incident recounted in one of the early lives of this saint.

It happened that in a monastery Pachomius had founded, located near the one where he was then living, a young monk aspired to the position of steward. His local superior did not consider him qualified for the task, but the monk so pestered him with his request that the superior, in a ploy to put a stop to all this importunity, deceitfully told the monk that Pachomius himself had decided that he ought not be named steward. As one might guess, this only made matters worse, for now the young monk ran off to Pachomius's own monastery to confront him. He found the master doing some manual labor high up on the outer wall, called out to him in abusive language, and insisted that he come down. Pachomius, totally unaware of what this was all about, nevertheless came down, begged the young monk's forgiveness for any wrong he had done him. Once Pachomius had learned the truth of the situation, he went to the superior of the other monastery and asked that he allow the man to become steward after all, saying: "Grant him his request, that by this means we may snatch his soul from the enemy. For it happens that when good is done to a bad man, he may come to some perception of the good." The account concludes by saying that when the monk had obtained the position of steward, he returned immediately to Pachomius, greatly sobered, and embracing him said, "O man of God, you are much greater than we had heard. We have seen how you have conquered evil with good by sparing a foolish sinner like me. If you had not been truly patient and had said something against me, I would have rejected this monastic life and become estranged from God. Blessed are you, for thanks to you I live."[9]

The point of the story of the young monk who would be steward is not that one should always give in to the requests of others, no matter how unreasonable they might be. The point is simply that a genuine master will not always automatically try to defend himself or harshly rebuke another. In other circumstances, Pachomius himself may have refused a request of this sort. However, here we see that sometimes a more lenient and generous response will in the long run be more fruitful.

A Spiritual Master's Ability to Empathize with Others

The Gospel of John, which is marked by what theologians call a "high Christology" that emphasizes Jesus's divine traits, emphasizes his ability to know even what others are thinking. As John writes at one point, Jesus "needed no one to testify about anyone, for he himself knew what was in everyone" (Jn 2:25). Even the other three Gospels, however, remark on Jesus's ability to empathize with others and to speak in a way that regularly drew large crowds from all parts of Palestine. This same quality of understanding others and speaking the words they need to hear is clearly seen in some of the most remarkable Christian spiritual masters of recent times.

One such person was Henri Nouwen, who was born in the Netherlands in 1932 and died of a heart attack at a relatively young age while visiting his native land in 1996. During the many years he lived in the United States, Peru, and Canada, Nouwen attracted numerous people to hear him speak: in classrooms at Notre Dame, Yale, and Harvard; in churches and cathedrals; in conference halls and retreat centers; and through his numerous books that remain best-sellers to this day. When trying to fathom the "secret" of his popularity, one hears time and time again that people found in Nouwen someone who really understood their own problems. One of his earliest and best-known books is *The Wounded Healer,* a title that reflects a great deal of who Nouwen himself was. He was quite willing in his talks and writings to speak very openly of his own weaknesses and failings. Some of his publishers even felt they had to tone down parts of the manuscripts that he would submit to them; and one of them once said, "Henri liked the idea that what was most personal was most universal. We had to remind him that what was most personal was sometimes best kept private."[10]

A related point that contributed to Nouwen's appeal was his refusal to give pat answers to the deepest questions of human existence. One of his starkest avowals of the ineluctable suffering that, in one way or another, marks everyone's life is to be found in the above-named book, where he writes:

> We ignore what we already know with a deep-seated intuitive knowledge—that no love or friendship, no intimate embrace or tender kiss, no community, commune or collective, no man or woman, will ever be able to satisfy our desire to be released from our lonely condition. This truth is so disconcerting and painful that we are more prone to play games with our fantasies than to face the truth of our existence. . . . Such false hope leads us to make exhausting demands and prepares us for bitterness and dangerous hostility when we start discovering that nobody, and nothing, can live up to our absolutistic expectations.[11]

A contemporary of Nouwen's who is also considered by many to be among the greatest spiritual masters in the Christian tradition was Thomas Merton. He was born to artist parents in southwestern France in 1915; and, like Augustine, led a rather hedonistic life until his conversion in his early twenties. After embracing an austere monastic life at the Abbey of Gethsemani in Kentucky in 1941, Merton soon became a very popular author, perhaps the most widely read Christian monk of all time. Like Nouwen, he appealed to a huge readership in large part because of his willingness to write openly about his own weaknesses and spiritual false starts—especially in his early autobiography, *The Seven Storey Mountain*—as well as by his open admission that he did not have all the answers to the most profound questions of human life. One passage that captures this acknowledgment has been reproduced on countless prayer cards and reads in part:

> My Lord God, I have no idea where I am going. I do not see the road ahead of me. I cannot know for certain where it will end. Nor do I really know myself, and the fact that I think I am following your will does not mean that I am actually doing so. But I believe that the desire to please you does in fact please you. And I hope I have that desire in all that I am doing. . . . Therefore I will trust you always though I may seem to be lost and in the shadow of death. I will not fear, for you are ever with me, and you will never leave me to face my perils alone.[12]

Another aspect of Merton's thought that has led many to regard him as a great spiritual master was his ability, especially in the final decade of his life, to pass on to readers the riches that he found not only in his own Catholic tradition, but also in other Christian and non-Christian traditions. Merton himself admitted that in the years immediately following his baptism he was something of a Catholic bigot, at times writing disparagingly of other religious paths; but as he matured he came to see that the better course was to affirm and accept whatever good he found in them. One of the most explicit statements of this new-found openness was published in 1966, two years before his accidental death while on a long-awaited trip to Asia. Merton wrote:

> The more I am able to affirm others, to say "yes" to them in myself, by discovering them in myself and myself in them, the more real I am. I am more fully real if my own heart says *yes* to *everyone*.
>
> I will be a better Catholic, not if I can *refute* every shade of Protestantism, but if I can truly affirm the truth in it and still go further.
>
> So, too, with the Muslims, the Hindus, the Buddhists, etc. This does not mean syncretism, indifferentism, the vapid and careless friendliness that accepts everything by thinking of nothing. There is much that one cannot "affirm" and "accept," but first one must say "yes" where one really can.[13]

This affirmative attitude comes out especially in his various essays on Zen Buddhism, and in the posthumously published *Asian Journal*.[14] The many ways in which Merton expressed such a "yes" have led many to regard him as a spiritual master even though they themselves were not Christian.

On Becoming a Spiritual Master

Before concluding this chapter, I want to discuss the important question of how one comes to attain the position of spiritual master in the first place. Time and time again, Christian tradition emphasized that spiritual master is not a role to which one may blithely arrogate by oneself. What is needed first of all is self-mastery, so that one does not succumb to the tendencies that keep one from living as a genuine disciple of Christ—tendencies such as a craving for wealth or power or fame. That Jesus himself was confronted with such challenges is evident from the Gospel accounts of his temptations in the desert at the very beginning of his public ministry.

The time-honored means for equipping oneself to deal with temptations of any sort is asceticism, which is reminiscent of the training or discipline that athletes must undergo in order to succeed in their difficult endeavors. One finds such asceticism in the life of St. Antony of Egypt (ca. 251–356), who was often called the father of Christian monasticism. After Antony had resolved to follow the Gospels as carefully as he could, at around the age of twenty he set about visiting dedicated Christian ascetics living in the vicinity of his village. After learning all he could from them by observing their way of life and listening to their advice, he spent some years in almost complete solitude. Visited only by friends who would bring him food, Antony spent most of his time and energy on that difficult inner work of self-knowledge, without which a deep personal transformation is not possible. Only later did he yield to the importunate requests of others to abandon his solitary lifestyle and become their teacher—a pattern that one finds repeated over and over again in Christian tradition.

The Eastern Orthodox bishop Kallistos Ware once noted that because the demands placed on a spiritual master are so daunting—he or she must to some degree be simultaneously a teacher, healer, counselor, and intercessor—we may well be tempted to ask with St. Paul in his Second Letter to the Corinthians, "Who is sufficient for such things?" (2 Cor 2:16). The answer, in Bishop Ware's words, "must be that no one would dare to assume such a ministry, did he [or she] not feel compelled to it by love for others."[15] What is normally required in a spiritual master is a sense of having received a specific call from God, though not necessarily in the form of some inner inspiration; the call may just as likely be the repeated requests of others for help in their own spiritual journey.

Finally, we must also admit that becoming recognized as a Christian spiritual master is a process sometimes fraught with ambiguity. I have already discussed some of the common criteria: teaching in a way that many people find authoritative and self-authenticating, healing those who are troubled by offering words that encourage rather than drive to despair, leading a life characterized by willing and generous service to others, discerning how best to respond in given situations, and empathizing with persons in need. The two persons discussed in the previous section—Henri Nouwen and Thomas Merton—provide good examples of what I mean.

Although Nouwen was widely revered as a spiritual master in the United States, this was decidedly not the case in Europe, including his native land. Michael Ford notes that Nouwen was "often overlooked and criticized by his fellow Dutch priests, and at times experienced the indifference of his own family," although "toward the end of his life there was more of an appreciation of him in Holland, and his family are now reading his books with greater conviction. His brothers in Rotterdam say that since his death they have been challenged and changed by his words."[16] There have been similar differences of opinion about whether Thomas Merton should be called a spiritual master. For instance, there is a documentary film about his life produced by Paul Wilkes in which one of Merton's former novices, Abbot Flavian Burns, says that for him Merton was the most outstanding spiritual master he had ever encountered.[17] I myself have heard another Trappist monk say something similar. Nevertheless, this opinion is not universal. Dr. Jonathan Montaldo, a former president of the International Thomas Merton Society and the editor of one volume of Merton's journals, once gave a public lecture at my monastery during which he said in no uncertain terms that Merton, for all of his remarkable literary gifts, had too many faults and failings to be regarded as a spiritual master—an opinion voiced also by Dr. Alice von Hildebrand in her lecture, "The Tragedy of Thomas Merton."[18]

Such disagreement should come as no surprise. After all, some of St. Thérèse's fellow Carmelites saw nothing remarkable about her, while a number of writers today lay at the feet of St. Augustine the blame for much that they find wrong in Christian moral and political theory. There is no need for absolute unanimity about just who are the spiritual masters in the Christian or any other religious tradition. It is, however, surely helpful for each one of us to find at least some persons in our respective traditions who speak directly to our needs, redirecting us when we are at loose ends and lifting our spirits when we are prone to discouragement. These will be our own spiritual masters and they are the ones who count for us personally, regardless of what others may think of them.

Notes

1. In this chapter, all translations from the Bible are taken from the New Revised Standard Version (NRSV).

2. Huston Smith, *The World's Religions* (San Francisco: Harper, 1991), 320.

3. David Tracy, Blessed Rage for Order: The New Pluralism in Theology (New York: Seabury, 1975), 220.

4. Thérèse of Lisieux, *Story of a Soul,* 3rd ed., trans. John Clarke, OCD (Washington, DC: ICS Publications, 1996), 179.

5. Qtd. in Irénée Hausherr, *Spiritual Direction in the Early Christian East* (Kalamazoo, MI: Cistercian Publications, 1990), 157–58.

6. Owen Chadwick, trans. and ed., *The Sayings of the Fathers, in Western Asceticism* (Philadelphia: Westminster, 1958), 61–62.

7. Further details can be found in F. van der Meer, *Augustine the Bishop: The Life and Work of a Father of the Church,* trans. Brian Battershaw and G. R. Lamb (London: Sheed and Ward, 1961); see esp. ch. 1, "A Prisoner in the Lord."

8. Many ancient versions of the Gospels do not include this account; and it is found in the Gospel of Luke rather than in the Gospel of John. Even so, it regularly has been understood as revealing an important side of Jesus's character.

9. *The First Greek Life of Pachomius* 42, in *Pachomian Koinonia,* 3 vols., trans. Armand Veilleux (Kalamazoo, MI: Cistercian Publications, 1980), 1:327–28.

10. Qtd. in Michael Ford, *Wounded Prophet: A Portrait of Henri J. M. Nouwen* (New York: Doubleday, 1999), xv.

11. Henri Nouwen, *The Wounded Healer* (London: Darton, Longman, and Todd, 1994), 84–85.

12. Thomas Merton, *Thoughts in Solitude* (New York: Farrar, Straus, and Cudahy, 1956), 83.

13. Merton, *Conjectures of a Guilty Bystander* (Garden City, NY: Doubleday, 1966), 129.

14. See Merton, *Zen and the Birds of Appetite* (New York: New Directions, 1968), and *The Asian Journal of Thomas Merton,* ed. Naomi Burton Stone, et al. (New York: New Directions, 1973).

15. Kallistos Ware, "Foreword: The Spiritual Father in Saint John Climacus and Saint Symeon the New Theologian," in Hausherr, *Spiritual Direction*, xxvi.

16. Ford, *Wounded Prophet*, 214. See also a widely used anthology of Merton's writings, edited by Lawrence Cunningham of the University of Notre Dame, *Thomas Merton: Spiritual Master* (New York: Paulist Press, 1992).

17. Paul Wilkes and Audrey Glynn, *Merton: A Film Biography* (New York First Run Features, 1984), VHS recording; DVD released in 2004.

18. Alice von Hildebrand, "The Tragedy of Thomas Merton," (Online: Keep the Faith, Inc.), audio lecture 2361D, http://www.keepthefaith.org.

3

Muslim Spiritual Masters

Osman Bakar

Introduction

According to Islam, Prophet Muḥammad is the perfect role model for Muslims of all times and places. While most Muslims seek to emulate the Prophet in the exoteric aspects of his personal and public life, the Ṣūfīs have been exceptionally attracted to his esoteric spiritual substance and portrait. The living Ṣūfī tradition that has survived to the present day holds the deep-seated belief that through oral transmission, the core of spiritual knowledge and practice originating from the Prophet has been passed down from one generation of Ṣūfī masters to the next. Sufism is concerned essentially with the inner human quest for the divine. The ideal Ṣūfī master is someone who is extremely well versed in the mysteries of that quest, and therefore with the mysteries of the human soul and the God-man relationship. Ṣūfī masters become spiritual authorities by virtue of their expertise on the "science of the Path," the *ṭarīqah*. They know, inside and out, the intricacies of the spiritual Path to God, and what it takes for Path seekers to fully realize their spiritual journeys.

The main purpose of this chapter is to present the idea of the spiritual master as understood and realized within the Islamic mystical tradition, better known as Sufism or *taṣawwuf*.[1] It treats the traditional role of Ṣūfī masters by expounding Islamic spirituality in the context of their times. Our primary concern is with the spiritual duties of Ṣūfī masters rather than with their spiritual accomplishments. We focus on the traits of Ṣūfī masters as spiritual authorities, and on their fundamental role in guiding disciples to lead a spiritual life completely dedicated to God, in constant remembrance of Him. Reference is made also to the views and practices of a contemporary Ṣūfī master, as we examine the role of the spiritual master in expounding Islamic spirituality in a contemporary language easily understood by disciples.

The Spiritual Master as a "Traditional Man"

A Muslim mystic, who may either be a male or a female, is usually termed in the West as a Ṣūfī master; but among followers, he or she is known in Muslim languages as *shaykh, pīr, murshid, murād,* or *tuan gurū*.[2] Ṣūfī masters may have various social positions in public life from teacher to shopkeeper—or even warrior, such as the Algerian Amīr ʿAbd al-Qādir who led a strong resistance in 1840s against the French military occupation of his country. However, in terms of core features that pertain to spiritual and social roles, the portrait of a Ṣūfī master has changed little during all the passing centuries since Islam became an established religion in the first half of the seventh century of the Common Era.

A Ṣūfī master is "the traditional man" par excellence. In practice, there are degrees of accomplishment among Ṣūfī masters. The degree of accomplishment is related to the intensity of *barakah* (divine grace) believed to flow within the veins of spiritual masters—overflowing through them to others, including those who technically speaking do not belong to their Ṣūfī order (*turuq*). We often hear of Muslims not in the Path, claiming they have gone to see such and such a Ṣūfī *shaykh* just because they want to receive that spiritual master's *barakah*. More accomplished Ṣūfī masters are said to possess a "greater *barakah*" than the lesser ones.

Of all known interpretations of Islam's doctrines and teachings as contained in the Qurʾān and prophetic *ḥadīths*, Sufism is perhaps the most traditional in spirit and orientation.[3] Ṣūfīs have shown themselves to be far more persistent in attaching themselves to traditional ideas and forms than any other Muslim religious group. This traditionalism stems from the special emphasis Ṣūfīs have placed on the eternal truths that constitute the spiritual core of Islam. It is the deep immersion in these truths that inspired and sustained their love and respect for traditional forms—especially those originating from Islamic revelation and Prophet Muḥammad's spiritual life. For the Ṣūfīs, divinely revealed forms have a profound spiritual significance: they help humans to fulfill a perennial need, arising from the very nature of their existence as earthly creatures destined for the permanent spiritual world. In the words of a contemporary Ṣūfī teacher, Seyyed Hossein Nasr:[4]

> Unlike other forms, the religious and revealed forms open inwardly toward the Infinite, because it is from the supra-formal Center that they originate, the Center which contains all these forms and is yet above them. The reason for the persistence of traditional forms and symbols is none other than this fact that although outwardly they are forms subject to time and space, their inner content leads to the Infinite. Hence they reflect even in the transient world of time and space the permanence that belongs to the spiritual world. They thus fulfill that perennial need of man to transcend the finite, to go beyond the transient and seek the permanent.[5]

From the perspective of *taṣawwuf,* the Ṣūfī master is a representative on earth of the esoteric function of Prophet Muḥammad. The prophetic esoteric function—associated with *walāyah* or saintly initiation, and closely related to *wilāyah,* meaning "sanctity"[6]—is a permanent element in Islamic spirituality. It does not change with time and space. Its permanence is symbolized by forms rich in spiritual significance. By virtue of their spiritual association with the esoteric function of Prophet Muḥammad, Ṣūfī masters have jealously sought to preserve traditional forms. Following the spiritual master, disciples seek to do the same. We are speaking here primarily of forms connected to spiritual life, including: the traditional clothes the Ṣūfīs wear (at least during spiritual gatherings, if not in public), their manner of greeting each other, the way they conduct prayers and other spiritual exercises, the kind of music to which they listen, and art objects that make up their cultural ambience.

Beyond their immersion in the spiritual forms of traditional culture, Ṣūfīs are also traditional in their actions as they strive to emulate the Prophet's ethical behavior in everyday life. From the Ṣūfī point of view, it is important to be as traditional as possible in one's life, because authentic tradition implies proximity to the origin of divine revelation—and, therefore, to the life of the Prophet. Attachment to traditional forms, including leading a life guided by the Prophet's spiritual ethics, is an essential way of remaining close to the origin and essence of religion, no matter how far distant in time one lives from that origin.

Securing a Legitimate Place for Sufism in Islam

Earlier we alluded to the Ṣūfī commitment to the Qur'ānic revelation and the prophetic traditions (*ḥadīth*s), noting that the emphasis of spiritual masters is on the esoteric, inner dimension of these twin sources of Islam. Through their commitment to the revealed and prophetic traditions, Ṣūfīs have demonstrated their loyalty to "orthodoxy." But the fact is that many people question the Ṣūfī loyalty to religious orthodoxy.[7] Some Muslims and many non-Muslims hold a prevalent perception that Sufism is not rooted in Islam. They mistakenly think that Sufism is a later accretion to Islam from mystical traditions that came before it, such as those of Christians and Buddhists.

In Defense of Sufism

As this particular understanding goes, both Ṣūfī doctrines and practices are viewed as deviations from Islamic orthodoxy. Ṣūfīs are frequently accused by such people of loosely interpreting the Qur'ān, and using either weak or false *ḥadīth*s to support "unorthodox" theological beliefs and spiritual practices that are disapproved in the *sharīʿah* (Islamic law). Under these circumstances, the first general task of a Ṣūfī master is to defend Sufism from such charges, especially when they come from the exoteric *ʿulamā'*s (Islamic scholars of a literalist and legalist bent) who define orthodoxy narrowly. Such critics not only judge Sufism solely from the point of view of *sharīʿah*, but also interpret the *sharīʿah* in a narrow, legalistic sense.

For Ṣūfī masters living in a Muslim-majority society, the need to respond to the "accusation of unorthodoxy" becomes especially important. They must take the accusation seriously for both theological and practical reasons. Theologically speaking, a Ṣūfī master sees the challenge as nothing less than a battle for the soul of Islam. Without its inner dimension of the *ṭarīqah,* or esoteric Ṣūfī Path, Islam would be a religion with a body, but without a soul. The practical concern of Ṣūfī masters is with the adverse effect that religious enmity toward Sufism could have on their ability to play their full role as spiritual masters, thus enabling them to keep alive the Ṣūfī teachings for future generations. After all, the exoteric *ʿulamāʾ*s have much influence in contemporary Muslim societies—as they did in ages gone by. In parts of the Muslim world that are influenced by an excessive exoterism, opposition to Sufism goes beyond the intellectual level. It also manifests itself in the form of suppressive laws.

In several Muslim countries, religious authorities condemn Sufism as a deviation from "official Islam," and make its dissemination illegal. In some other Muslim countries, Ṣūfī masters and their respective orders are harassed and under close watch of the authorities. They are not even allowed to hold private gatherings where they could teach Ṣūfī doctrines to their disciples. Such a hostile religious climate has forced some Ṣūfī orders to go underground in certain countries. Still we do find in such environments Ṣūfī masters who, to a certain extent, have been able to function in their spiritual role with public visibility—thanks to their accomplished and respected position as scholars of Islamic law. By contrast, there are many Islamic societies in which Sufism is not fully suppressed. In fact, present-day Senegal in Africa may claim to be a "Ṣūfī-ruled" state inasmuch as political power in the country has been traditionally in the hands of members of a Ṣūfī order known as the Mourides.[8]

Regardless of whether Ṣūfī masters play their spiritual role openly or secretively in society, they have the immediate task of instilling confidence in their followers that Sufism is, indeed, an authentic and integral part of Islam. They also seek to spread the same message to the larger Muslim public, so that the Ṣūfī perspective is better understood. Through lectures and writings, some more intellectually oriented Ṣūfī teachers, such as Seyyed Hossein Nasr, have made it their duty to explain to the educated public the "correct" essential relationship between formal Islam and Sufism.[9]

Ṭarīqah as an Integral Dimension of Islam

Since Muslim opposition to Sufism is usually done in the name of the *sharīʿah,* Ṣūfī masters have sought to address the issue of the relation between the two major dimensions of Islam: the Ṣūfī *ṭarīqah* and the *sharīʿah.* In conformity with the Ṣūfī intellectual tradition, particularly its theological perspective, Nasr argues that as an integral dimension of Islam, the *ṭarīqah* is no less fundamental than the *sharīʿah*. The main difference between the two is that the Ṣūfī Path pertains to Islam's esoteric teachings, while the Islamic law is basically concerned with its exoteric teachings—particularly ethics and laws governing human actions at both individual and collective levels. From this point of view, the *ṭarīqah* is the soul of Islam, which is less visible to the general eye than the *sharīʿah*, the body of Islam. If the criterion of Islamic orthodoxy is conformity to the core teachings of the Qurʾān and prophetic *ḥadīths*, then the *ṭarīqah* is no less "orthodox" than the *sharīʿah*. All Ṣūfī doctrines are drawn from these two most authoritative sources of Islam. Similarly, Ṣūfī spiritual practices fall within the sphere of orthodoxy insofar as they are modeled after Prophet Muḥammad's spiritual and moral conduct, and are in conformity with the teachings of the *sharīʿah*. To be sure, there have been deviations here and there in both doctrinal understanding and spiritual practices committed in the name of Sufism; but misguided beliefs and practices are also to be found within other schools of interpreters of the Qurʾān and Islamic law.

Nasr's books and lectures emphasize the point that Ṣūfīs—like other Muslims—believe in the Qurʾān, the prophetic *ḥadīths*, and the necessity of the *sharīʿah*. They believe in the foundations of the religion as embodied in the six articles of faith (*arkan al-īmān*), and the five pillars of Islam (*arkan al-ʾislām*).[10] Their love for the Prophet and his family is proverbial. They have been the greatest defenders of Islam's spiritual teachings; and, in our day, when many modernized Muslims question the authenticity of some prophetic *ḥadīths* that have been traditionally accepted, the Ṣūfīs come to their articulate defense. In many instances, Ṣūfīs do interpret the Qurʾān and *ḥadīths* differently from—and even contrary to—other interpreters. But this is without denying exoteric interpretations on their own level. If Ṣūfīs are able to accept *ḥadīths* that others reject, it is because they see meanings that are in conformity with the Qurʾān and other *ḥadīths*. Being at odds with exoteric interpretations of the Qurʾān and *ḥadīths* that are posed by literalist *ʿulamāʾ*s and other groups of scholars is not a good enough reason to brand Sufism as deviationist or heretical. After all, Prophet Muḥammad taught respect for "differences of opinions among scholars and those endowed with knowledge."[11]

The Perpetual Tension between Sufism and the Sharīʿah

Over time, Ṣūfī views of sacred texts and the *sharīʿah* versus the corresponding views by exoteric *ʿulamāʾ*s have become "institutionalized" perspectives with rival tendencies. This resulted in a sort of perpetual tension between the two groups: Ṣūfī masters and their respective orders (*turuq*) represent the institutionalization of Sufism,[12] while a hierarchy of officers and courts constituting the official religious establishment represents the corresponding institutionalization of the *sharīʿah*. Yet, in Islamic religious history there has never been any clear line separating the two institutions. Many individual religious figures belonged to both institutions, thus serving as important bridges between them, demonstrating the inherent unity of Sufism and the *sharīʿah*.

In a sense, Nasr is such an individual. He has many writings on Sufism for which he is widely recognized as an authority. But his writings on the more popular Islamic sciences are also widely read in the Muslim world, and are recognized and consulted even by Muslims who do not share his views on Sufism. Insofar as he has gained acceptance both among sympathizers of Sufism and among scholars and students of the *sharīʿah,* Nasr has succeeded well in balancing his twin roles of defending these two major dimensions of Islam. That success has convinced many Muslims that Nasr is preaching an authentic Sufism.

The "perpetual tension" we have in mind between Sufism and the *sharīʿah* pertains, in part, to the uneasy relationship that exists politically between Sufism and the exoteric or literalist Islamic schools of thought. Politics is often an important factor influencing that relationship. In situations where the state sides with the latter group—usually out of political expediency—Ṣūfī masters find themselves restricted in their movements to lead their spiritual flocks. Above, we have given examples of such states. But there are also governments that are friendly to Sufism and the Ṣūfī orders.

Ṣūfī masters residing in the West are a growing phenomenon, and their respective orders are not subjected to "fluctuating fortunes" in their relations with the political rulers. Still, they must stay well informed about the attitudes toward Sufism of the governments of the day in various Muslim countries. They have a great interest in doing so. Many of them have disciples scattered all over the globe. It is the main responsibility of these spiritual masters to ensure that the security and spiritual welfare of their disciples, wherever they may be, are not in jeopardy. This is not a new phenomenon. Ever since the emergence of Ṣūfī orders in the twelfth century of the Common Era, it has been quite normal for the more famous Ṣūfī masters to have disciples in various regions of the Muslim world beyond their residential localities. It is a testimony to the global nature of Ṣūfī orders that most of them (or one or more of their branches) have created a presence and a spiritual history in different geocultural regions of the Muslim world. Modern communications have only made it easier for contemporary Ṣūfī masters to reach out to their globally scattered disciples, even if residing outside the Islamic world.

The Spiritual Descendents of the Prophet

The Muslim mind finds great satisfaction in discovering ideas or behavioral act as having a precedent in Prophet Muḥammad's life. It is the satisfaction of knowing that one is walking in the footsteps of the Prophet. As a popular traditional Muslim saying goes, that means one is "following the Prophet's *sunnah* (way of life)." It gives great solace to a Ṣūfī, knowing that the Ṣūfī way of thinking and the Ṣūfī way of life are modeled after the Prophet's inner *sunnah*. To Ṣūfī masters in particular, it is a matter of having the honor and privilege—as well as responsibility—to represent the Prophet on earth, insofar as continuing their esoteric function is concerned. This esoteric function makes every Ṣūfī master a shepherd of Muslim souls who safeguards the spiritual welfare of the community. This spiritual link, a functional one, between Ṣūfī masters and the Prophet is yet another argument in support of Sufism's orthodoxy. It also means that Ṣūfī masters are most deserving in being called the Prophet's spiritual descendents. We will discuss later in greater detail the nature of this spiritual link.

Sufism: A Reality Without A Name; A Name Without A Reality

There is an old Ṣūfī saying attributed to the eleventh century Ṣūfī, Hujwīrī (d. 1071 CE): "Sufism was once a reality without a name, now it is a name without a reality." This thoughtful remark on Sufism appears as a double critique when applied to contemporary Muslim society. The first critique—that Sufism was once a reality without a name—is directed at both modernist Muslims and the Salafists, who reject Sufism as un-Islamic on the grounds that it did not exist during the time of the Prophet, and that the term *taṣawwuf* was never used by him or by his companions. The second critique—that Sufism is now a name without a reality—is directed at contemporary Sufism itself for a number of obvious failings, particularly regarding the intellectual exposition of Ṣūfī doctrines.

In response to the modernist and Salafist argument that Sufism is un-Islamic, Ṣūfīs point out the need to carefully distinguish the "reality of a thing" from its "given name." There are many things in this world that existed long before being given a name—and Sufism is one of them. During the time of the Prophet, "Sufism was a reality without a name." Embodying the core of the Qur'ān, Sufism was a reality in the life of the Prophet who, according to tradition, "personalized" the holy book. On that account, Prophet Muḥammad may be regarded as the first Ṣūfī, even though he was never called by that name during his lifetime. As the embodiment of an ideal spiritual life, Prophet Muḥammad is the role model par excellence for all later Ṣūfīs—and even for every seeker of God in the Islamic world. Following the Prophet, many of his companions were leading a "Ṣūfī life."

Yet, the question remains of why such an important dimension of Islam as *taṣawwuf* (Sufism) had not been so named right from the beginning of the religion. Nasr answered the question by explaining that the need for naming it had not yet arisen in the Prophet's time. We name things in order to distinguish between them. But there was at that time no such need, precisely because the religion was still "fluid" in nature—as it was in the process of being revealed through to the end of Prophet Muḥammad's life. The religion of Islam had not yet solidified and crystallized into its constituent elements such as *sharī'ah* and *taṣawwuf*.[13] Thus, differentiation of its elements was unnecessary. Likewise, the Prophet's nascent community of Islam was still an "indivisible unit" that had yet to crystallize into socioreligious groups with well-defined distinguishing features in accordance with their religious and social functions. The unity of *taṣawwuf* and the *sharī'ah* was very much evident in the life of those in the new community.

On the criticism that there are failings in doctrinal expositions within contemporary Ṣūfī circles, Nasr can only agree. Many contemporary Ṣūfī masters in the Muslim world are respected by followers for their personal piety and knowledge of the practical aspects of Sufism. However, compared to Ṣūfī masters of the "golden era" (recalled by Hujwīrī), Ṣūfīs of our own day generally seem to lack depth in the understanding and exposition of Ṣūfī doctrines. This intellectual decline in doctrinal Sufism must be seen in the context of a larger historical picture—namely, the decline of traditional Islamic thought in the last one or two centuries, parallel with the growing influence of modern Western thought. Yet, thanks to the writings of some Western Ṣūfīs, intellectual Sufism is reasserting itself and beginning to have a significant impact on Western-educated Muslims. Among the reasons we selected Nasr as our major source of reference for our discussion on the role of a Ṣūfī master is that he is one of the world's best known expositors of Ṣūfī doctrines today.

Seyyed Hossein Nasr is a prolific scholar,[14] and his treatment of intellectual Sufism is extensive, covering the length and breadth of Ṣūfī doctrines. He sees these doctrines as embracing

> a metaphysics about the principle and nature of things, a cosmology concerning the structure of the Universe and its multiple states of being, a traditional psychology about the structure of the human soul to which is attached a psychotherapy of the profoundest order compared to which modern psychotherapy is but a caricature, and finally an eschatology concerning the final end of man and of the Universe and of man's posthumous becoming.[15]

Considering that Nasr has given scholarly treatment to all these intellectual domains, one can see how extensive his exposition of Ṣūfī doctrines has been. He has done that primarily to help open up the doors of the *ṭarīqah* to anyone who has both the interest and the qualifications. He insists that it is important in the present-day context for seekers of the *ṭarīqah* to have a sufficiently good understanding of Ṣūfī doctrines (although there can be exceptions). Without that understanding, the present-day potential seeker whose mind is usually cluttered with erroneous ideas will lack the necessary intellectual basis to pursue the Ṣūfī Path.

Barakah and the Saintly Function of Initiation

One of the most important functions of Ṣūfī masters is the saintly function of initiation. It is to initiate into the *ṭarīqah* those who aspire to become *faqīr* (disciples), and who pass the qualifications for initiation. Ṣūfī masters inherit the saintly function of initiation from the Prophet.[16] By virtue of inheriting that prophetic function, they have the right and the legitimacy to perform an initiation. As viewed within Ṣūfī tradition, only legitimate spiritual masters and their chosen representatives have the saintly initiatic power with the *barakah* to perform an initiation (*walāyah*) that is considered legitimate—as it is divinely blessed, and therefore promises the possibility of an efficacious spiritual transformation for the new initiates.

The Criterion of Legitimacy

The Ṣūfī tradition is very clear on the criterion used to verify who can and who cannot be considered as a legitimate Ṣūfī master. The criterion is purely spiritual: a Ṣūfī master is a person who is spiritually linked to Prophet Muḥammad through a chain of saintly initiations (*silsilah*). The spiritual link in question is itself invisible, and therefore likely to be questioned by people who are not in the Path. However, the existence of a spiritual link with the Prophet is acknowledged by the Ṣūfī community on the basis of an established *silsilah*. The chain has formal aspects that are verifiable. The most important of them is the record of a formal chain of spiritual masters linking each living Ṣūfī master to Prophet Muḥammad in his capacity as the first Ṣūfī master. The *silsilah* is available in written form.

All Ṣūfī masters and their disciples would be in possession of their own written *silsilah*, which they readily display when needed. It is for them a precious document since it shows the Ṣūfī master as having a spiritual ancestry traceable to the Prophet. That chain, once authenticated, is itself good enough a proof for them of the authenticity of the spiritual masters and the order they lead. It is a well-known fact in Ṣūfī circles that all existing Ṣūfī orders trace back the *silsilah* of their respective *shaykh*s to Prophet Muḥammad through ʿAlī ibn Abī Ṭālib (ca. 600–661), the fourth khalif (*khalīfa*) of Islam, who was his cousin and son-in-law. An exception is the Naqshabandīyah Order, which is linked to Prophet Muḥammad through ʿAbū Bakr (ca. 573–634), the first khalif of Islam.

The Process of Succession in the Spiritual Lineage

Ṣūfī masters become what they are after having risen through the ranks of disciples as determined and designated by their own spiritual masters, who have recognized their spiritual qualifications of leadership. But they can only assume the supreme title of Shaykh or Master upon the death of their own spiritual master. While their *shaykh* is still alive, they hold on to their highest designated rank among disciples in their order. This is as a *muqaddam* or a *khalīfah*, indicating one who already possesses the qualifications to fulfill the functions of the *shaykh* as a spiritual master. As a *muqaddam* or a *khalīfah*, the disciple might be entrusted by the *shaykh* with the authority to perform initiations in the latter's absence. Generally speaking, Ṣūfī masters appoint group leaders at several levels from among the disciples to assist them—eventually to succeed them when they are no longer alive. These disciples are to assist the living *shaykh*s in both spiritual and organizational matters of their Ṣūfī order.

It is normally the case that Ṣūfī masters appoint more than one *muqaddam* or *khalīfah*, especially when they have many disciples scattered in faraway places. Whether they will be succeeded as *shaykh* by just one *muqaddam* or by more than one depends very much on the individual spiritual standing of the *muqaddams*, and how they size up to each other in terms of knowledge, integrity, and reputation. If there is a *muqaddam* who far excels the other *muqaddams*, and is acknowledged as such by them, then it is possible that the disciple will become the sole inheritor of the title Shaykh, and the head of an undivided order. Otherwise, there will be several successor *shuyukh* (plural of *shaykh*), each leading a new branch of the order. The disciples who are not *muqaddams* are at liberty to choose from among the new *shuyukh*, and decide which will be their respective new spiritual master. From the perspective of the Ṣūfī community, when disciples become spiritual masters the traditional process that they must follow is a very clear matter, and one that is easily verifiable. In other words, it is fairly easy to distinguish between a legitimate Ṣūfī master and an illegitimate one.

Barakah, the Inner Reality of Succession

It is important to note that the "Path" to "shaykhship" that we have just described is not the only one known to the Ṣūfī tradition. Nasr has emphasized that

> many *faqirs* in various Sufi orders who were not designated as *muqaddams* or *khalifahs* later became shaykhs through the Will of Heaven. The history of classical Sufism is replete with such cases, especially in the earlier centuries when various functions prevalent in later Sufism did not as yet exist. In any case the veritable nature of any *shaykh* or *murshid* can only be gauged by the quality of his disciples. A tree is judged by its fruits.[17]

More important than the legitimacy of the formal aspects of the chain of initiations is the inner reality underlying that chain, namely, the *barakah* that in principle flows from Prophet Muḥammad to a Ṣūfī master. Such a flow is possible as a spiritual phenomenon because through the chain of initiations a spiritual master would be connected to the saintly function of initiation (*walāyah*) inherent in the prophetic mission itself.[18] As understood in Sufism, every major prophet has been sent by God to fulfill two functions, namely, to bring a religious law (*sharīʿah*) and to perform the saintly initiatic function. In other words, every prophet is also necessarily a saint. According to Ibn al-ʿArabī (1165–1240),[19] within each individual prophet it is the saintly function that takes precedence over the ethical-legal function. It is by virtue of being connected to the saintly initiatic function of Prophet Muḥammad that Ṣūfī masters carry within themselves the Muḥammadan grace (*barakah muḥammadīyah*)[20] that aids them in effecting a spiritual transformation in their disciples. The spiritual efficacy of spiritual masters depends primarily on the measure of *barakah muḥammadīyah* that flows in them.

Ṣūfī Masters as Guides to Perfection

In general terms, the fundamental role of a Ṣūfī master is to help "deliver man from the narrow confines of the material world into the illimitable luminous space of the spiritual life."[21] According to a *ḥadīth,* "The material world is a prison of the believer." Freedom in the ultimate sense means liberation from that prison to journey to God while still living on earth. In the Islamic universe, in order to realize this ultimate goal in life, one has to "return to the origin of the Islamic revelation itself and become in a spiritual sense both a companion and successor of the Prophet and the saints."[22] To be able to do that one has to participate in the *ṭarīqah*. But one cannot participate successfully in the Path without a teacher and a guide. In the light of our portrayal of Ṣūfī masters, it is clear that they are the best qualified to play the role of spiritual teacher and guide. With the spiritual asset of *barakah muḥammadīyah* at their disposal, they are in a position to effect a "spiritual rebirth and transformation" in the individual person who has made the choice to follow the *ṭarīqah*.

Ṣūfī masters are powerful spiritual magnets who continuously attract seekers of the Path to their circle of disciples of which they are the center. Thanks to their charismatic attraction, they usually live to see their circle of disciples growing bigger and bigger with time. It is their main duty to see that the spiritual welfare of every disciple and the integrity of their *ṭarīqah* as a whole is preserved. At the individual level their duty is to enable each disciple to experience a spiritual rebirth and to advance in spiritual transformation. Ṣūfī masters make it their task to frequently remind the new initiates that the formal initiation (*bay'ah*) of a seeker of God into the Path is only the beginning of a long spiritual journey, and not the end of it. Ṣūfī disciples have a tremendous responsibility, as Nasr emphasizes:

> Initiation into Sufism does not in itself guarantee realization. The disciple must be firm in his devotion to the master

> and in performing his religious and initiatic duties. He must love God more than the world, and be attached to Him not only through a theoretical comprehension of Sufi metaphysics but also by a total 'ontological' attachment. The Divine succour and aid (*tawfiq*) must also be present, without which nothing is possible. The gardener sows many seeds in the ground: not all of them grow to be plants that will bear fruit. [23]

The initiation entails profound obligations and responsibilities on the part of the disciple to lead a truly spiritual life dedicated to God.

Shaykhs know their disciples, and indeed know them only too well—better in fact than the disciples know themselves. They know the psychological state and the spiritual needs of disciples. In a sense, the *shaykhs* have conquered their disciples, since the disciples have surrendered themselves to their spiritual masters for the purpose of spiritual rebirth and transformation. As experienced spiritual psychologists, *shaykhs* know the elements and tendencies that can distract and derail disciples from the Path. They also know the elements and inclinations that need to be guided and developed to perfection. As accomplished travelers on the Path, Ṣūfī masters have experienced the ascensions of the spirit and passed through the stations of the heart, having been aware of the "pitfalls and dangerous passages of the Way."[24] Their role as guide is both to warn disciples of the dangerous obstacles they have to face along the Path, and to guide them to the stations of the Path while making clear that each accomplished station is in reality a divine gift or favor.

In concrete terms, Ṣūfī masters provide guidance and instructions to their disciples with two broad aims in mind: to enable disciples to achieve intellectual comprehension and clarity of spiritual doctrines; and to enable them to patiently and consistently observe spiritual acts whose primary aim is remembrance of God (*dhikr Allāh*) with actualization of the knowledge of God. A disciple must accomplish each of the above things individually; but there are also practices accomplished collectively with other disciples. Ṣūfī masters want disciples to lead lives impregnated with meanings contained in the spiritual formulae taken from the Qur'ān. Each formula prescribed for them refers back to the Divine Name *Allāh*.

In short, the lives of disciples are shaped, clothed, and penetrated by a host of Divine Names and litanies. A disciple is thereby intellectually and spiritually transformed into a man or woman of God who has attained a permanent state of God-consciousness, and who has realized proximity to the Divine Presence. The key spiritual act in a disciple's life is the invocation of the Divine Name (*dhikr Allāh*). In the Ṣūfī perspective, the goal of spiritual life is to have a heart that is constantly in the state of remembering God. Every act is done for the sake of God's remembrance. For this reason, Ṣūfī masters give the greatest possible attention to their disciples regarding the practice of *dhikr Allāh* to ensure that in form, technique, and spirit it is done in as perfect a way as possible. Advancement on the Path by disciples depends very much on the spiritual efficacy of their practice of invocation of the Divine Name.

Abū al- Ḥasan al-Shādhilī (1196–1258),[25] founder of the popular Shādhilīyah Order, through whom Nasr claims his initiatic link with the Prophet sums up the Ṣūfī spiritual Path as follows:

> The Sufi way is the holding of one's course toward God by four things. . . . The first of these four is remembrance (*dhikr*), the basis of which is righteous works, and the fruit of which is illumination. The second is meditation (*tafakkur*), the basis of which is perseverance, and the fruit of which is knowledge (*ʿilm*). The third is poverty (*faqr*) the basis of which is thankfulness, and the fruit of which is an increase of it. The fourth is love (*hubb*), the basis if which is dislike of the world and its people, and the fruit of which is union with the beloved.[26]

Ṣūfī Masters and Their Spiritual Assemblies

Insofar as Ṣūfī masters are the heads of organizations or brotherhoods that are spiritual in nature, they need to meet their disciples in groups regularly. Each Ṣūfī order usually has a center (*zāwiyah,* Persian: *khānagāh*) where the *shaykh*s can conduct their regular group meetings with the disciples, and where other spiritual activities can also be held. The most important activity to be conducted at the *zāwiyah* is the spiritual assembly (*majlis*) that the *shaykh*s themselves—or in their absence, one of their designated functionaries—lead. In such an assembly, the *shaykh*s clarify doctrinal matters appropriate for the moment, lead the disciples in spiritual acts, and usually conduct a spiritual concert (*samāʿ*). Nasr describes the symbolic significance of this spiritual gathering in these terms:

> The assembly (*majlis*) of the Sufi master is a terrestrial image of the heavenly assembly of the saints. The disciple (*faqir*)

> who gains the right of entry into this assembly by virtue of having been initiated by the master also gains for himself a place in the assembly of paradise, provided he remains faithful to the master and his instructions. Once he fulfills the conditions of discipleship and reaches perfection in the assembly, his station becomes of permanent importance and gains a significance beyond the life of this world and beyond the grave. The master leaves a permanent mark upon the disciple by virtue of which the disciple who has reached perfection again joins the assembly of his master in the other world. By the perfection gained in the *majlis* of the Sufis, the *faqir* gains access to the royal assembly of heaven and constructs for himself an exalted abode in the afterlife.[27]

Given the great significance that a Ṣūfī assembly has for disciples, it is perfectly understandable if a disciple places great priority in attending. It is a gathering from which disciples derive *barakah* from the master's presence, find peace and joy in sharing the master's intellectual and spiritual vision, and perform with the *shaykh* and fellow disciples the assembly's rituals. It is an occasion to which disciples wish to return again and again, for through the *majlis,* the most essential inner spiritual work is facilitated.

The Role of Ṣūfī Masters: The Future

In the foregoing pages we have presented the most important aspects of the role of spiritual masters as seen in the Islamic tradition. The discussion of these aspects was meant to clearly show that the passage of time has little changed that role. Seyyed Hossein Nasr is a contemporary Ṣūfī teacher. Yet the spiritual role he plays in relation to his disciples is hardly any different from the one played by Ṣūfī masters of the distant past. Nevertheless, many of the challenges Nasr has faced as a spiritual teacher are new, being unique to the contemporary world. His main challenge is one of articulating traditional Ṣūfī doctrines, and presenting the Ṣūfī spiritual life in a way that is comprehensible and appealing to the contemporary mind. In our view, given the traditional vitality of Sufism, the more than fourteen-centuries-old portrait of the Ṣūfī master will survive the challenges of the twenty-first century, God willing. As Nasr asserts:

The message of Sufism is timeless precisely because it speaks of truths which determine what one might call the pre-temporal existence of man in relation with God and which are based on elements of reality both transcendent and immanent within human nature which neither evolve nor decay.[28]

Notes

1. There are numerous works on the doctrines and practices of Sufism (known in Arabic as *taṣawwuf*), as well as on its manifestations in Islamic history. For works on Ṣūfī doctrines written by Westerners from within the Ṣūfī tradition see, for examples, Frithjof Schuon, *Sufism: Veil and Quintessence,* trans. William Stoddart (Bloomington, IN: World Wisdom Books, 1981); Titus Burckhardt, *An Introduction to Sufi Doctrine* (Lahore, Pakistan: Muhammad Ashraf, 1988); Martin Lings, *What is Sufism?* (Cambridge: Islamic Texts Society, 1999); William Stoddart, *Sufism: The Mystical Doctrines and Methods of Islam;* and William Chittick, *Sufism: A Short Introduction* (Oxford: Oneworld Publications, 2000). For an excellent work on the pervasive influence of Sufism on Islamic history and civilization see Seyyed Hossein Nasr, ed., *Islamic Spirituality: Manifestations* (New York: Crossroad, 1991), vol. 20 of *World Spirituality: An Encyclopedic History of the Religious Quest.*

2. The words *shaykh, murshid,* and *murād* are Arabic; *pīr* is Persian; and *tuan gurū* is Malay. In this essay, I will be using just the word *shaykh* to mean spiritual master. Note: Italicized foreign language terms in the essay, and in parentheses that serve as translations are Arabic, unless otherwise noted.

3. For an extensive discussion of this theme, see S. H. Nasr, ed., *Islamic Spirituality: Foundations* (New York: Crossroad, 1991), vol. 19 of *World Spirituality: An Encyclopedic History of the Religious Quest;* and S. H. Nasr, *Sufi Essays* (Chicago: ABC International, 1999).

4. To illustrate the role of a contemporary Ṣūfī master, we decided to concentrate on the intellectual thought and spiritual leadership of Seyyed Hossein Nasr, an Iranian-American scholar of Islam who has widespread influence in the Muslim world. We chose him partly because of his accomplishments as both a scholar and a Ṣūfī, and partly because we are more familiar with his "inner life" than with any other spiritual master. For the best single volume treatment of Nasr's life and thought, see Lewis E. Hahn, Randall E. Auxier, and Lucian W. Stone Jr., eds., *The Philosophy of Seyyed Hossein Nasr* (Chicago: Open Court, 2001).

5. Nasr, *Sufi Essays,* 30.

6. Ibid., 57. For a detailed contemporary discussion of the terms *walāyah* and *wilāyah,* see Vincent J. Cornell's introduction in *Realm of the Saint: Power and Authority in Moroccan Sufism* (Austin: University of Texas Press, 1998).

7. For one of the earliest rebuttals of this perception by a Western thinker, see René Guénon, "Islamic Esoterism," *Sophia: The Journal of Traditional Studies* 5, no.1 (1999): 10–14.

8. Interestingly, "Ṣūfī-ruled" Senegal is, at the time of writing, widely viewed as Africa's most politically stable and "democratic" nation. On the Mourides's political and economic domination of Senegal, see Leonardo A. Villalón, *Islamic Society and State Power in Senegal: Disciples and Citizens in Fatick, Senegal* (Cambridge: Cambridge University Press, 1995).

9. Nasr has dealt with the essential relationship between formal Islam and Sufism in a number of his works. See for example, *Sufi Essays; Ideals and Realities of Islam* (Chicago: Kazi Publications, 2000), and *The Heart of Islam: Enduring Values for Humanity* (New York: Harper San Francisco, 2002).

10. The six fundamental articles of Muslim faith are beliefs in: one God; angels; all divinely revealed books; all prophets and messengers of God; the Last Day, or Day of Judgment; and Divine decree and predestination. The five pillars of Islam are: testifying that there is no god but God, and testifying that Muḥammad is the (last) messenger of God; performing the five daily canonical prayers; fasting in the month of Ramadan from dawn to dusk; paying *zakāt* (personal and property taxes); and going on pilgrimage to Mecca once in one's lifetime, if possible.

11. According to a *ḥadīth*, differences of opinion among scholars are a blessing to the community.

12. The Ṣūfī path in its "organizational" aspects has developed to become a tree with roots sunk in the "substance of the Prophet," and numerous branches in the form of *turuq* (Ṣūfī orders) with their respective patron-saints and spiritual masters growing and spreading to every corner of the globe. On some of the major aspects of this institutionalization of Sufism in Islamic spiritual history on a global scale, see S. H. Nasr, *Islamic Spirituality: Manifestations.*

13. Nasr often touches on this theme in his works when legitimizing the integral role of fundamental components of Islam, such as *taṣawwuf* (Sufism), *sharīʿah* (Islamic law), and *kalām* (dialectical theology). See, for example, *Introduction to Islamic Cosmological Doctrines*, rev. ed. (Albany: State University of New York Press, 1993), and *Science and Civilization in Islam* (Cambridge: Islamic Texts Society, 1987).

14. For the most updated bibliography of Nasr's writings see Hahn, Auxier, and Stone, eds., *Philosophy of Seyyed Hossein Nasr,* 835–964.

15. Nasr, *Sufi Essays,* 17–18. For a summary of these doctrines see ibid., 45–47.

16. Ibid., 57. René Guénon asserts: "Tradition indicates expressly that the esoterism, as well as the exoterism, proceed directly from the Prophet and, in fact, any authentic *Tariqah* possesses a *silsilah* or "chain" of initiatic transmission going back definitively to that teaching through more or less large number of intermediaries" (Guénon, "Islamic Esoterism," 13).

17. S. H. Nasr, "Schuon and the Islamic Tradition," *Sophia: The Journal of Traditional Studies* 5, no. 1 (1999): 46.

18. Nasr, *Sufi Essays*, 57.

19. Ibn ʿArabī (born in Murcia, Spain) is regarded as the most influential expositor of Ṣūfī metaphysical doctrines in the history of Islam. Known especially in eastern Islam as the greatest master (*shaykh al-akbar*), he had given a treatment of incomparable depth on various aspects of the saintly function in relation to prophecy. On Ibn ʿArabī, see S. H. Nasr, *Three Muslim Sages* (Cambridge: Harvard University Press, 1964).

20. Nasr, *Sufi Essays*, 35–36.

21. Ibid., 57.

22. Ibid.

23. Ibid., 59, n.4.

24. Ibid., 62–63.

25. On this Ṣūfī master see Ibrahim M. Abu-Rabiʾ, ed., *The Mystical Teachings of al-Shadhili* (Albany: State University of New York Press, 1993).

26. Ibid., 109.

27. Nasr, *Sufi Essays*, 60.

28. Ibid., 35.

4

Hindu Spiritual Masters

Arvind Sharma

Introduction

The institution of the *gurū* occupies a key place in the Hindu scheme of things. In a famous verse from the *Devībhāgavata Purāṇa* (11.1.49) the *gurū* is identified successively with all the three gods of the Hindu trinity—Brahmā, Viṣṇu, and Śiva—and even described as the visible manifestation of the ultimate reality or *Brahman*. In another text, the *gurū* is described as Brahmā without his four heads, Viṣṇu without his four arms, and Śiva without his three eyes.[1]

The place of the *gurū* is so fundamental to Hindu tradition that one must begin by making a few distinctions. The word *gurū* tends to be used in Hinduism for both a secular and spiritual teacher. One's teacher at school, for instance, may be reverentially described as a *gurū*. More particularly, however, a *gurū* is one through whom a person receives sacred knowledge. The *Manusmṛti* (2.142), for instance, states that one who performs various sacraments is called a *gurū*. It provides various terms, such as *ācārya* or *upādhyāya* (2.140–41)[2] for those who give instruction in the Vedas. The sense of veneration associated with a teacher in general made it a trope, as when a father is described as a hundred times more venerable than a teacher, and a mother a thousand times more than the father (*Manusmṛti* 2.145). It is the word *gurū,* however, that gradually acquired the sense of a spiritual master of the kind with which this book is concerned—although in one of the earliest passages that highlights the need of a *gurū,* the word *ācārya* is used.[3]

> Just as, my dear, one might lead a person away from the *Gandhāras* with his eyes bandaged and abandon him in a place where there are no human beings, and just as that person would shout towards the east or the north or the south or the west, "I have been led here with my eyes bandaged, I have been left here with my eyes bandaged."
>
> And as, if one released his bandage and told him, "In that direction are the *Gandhāras,* go in that direction; thereupon, being informed and capable of judgment, he would by asking (his way) from village to village arrive at *Gandhāra;* in exactly the same manner does one here who has a teacher know, "I shall remain here only so long as I shall not be released (from ignorance). Then I shall reach perfection."[4]

The central role that the spiritual master plays in the context of a spiritual quest persists through all the major formations and transformations of Hinduism represented by Vedic Hinduism (up to ca. 400 BCE), classical Hinduism (ca. 400 BCE–1000 CE), medieval Hinduism (ca. 1000–1800), and modern Hinduism (ca.1800–present)—although the *gurū*'s role also acquires some special features in each of these phases.

The *Gurū* in Vedic Hinduism

The *gurū* came to be glorified in the Vedic period to the point where devotion for the master was placed virtually on par with God (*Śvetāśvatara Upaniṣad* 4.23).[5] However, spiritual circumspection accompanied such spiritual glorification. The qualifications a *gurū* should possess are carefully delineated in a famous passage in the *Muṇḍaka Upaniṣad* (1.2.12):

> For the sake of this knowledge, let him only approach, with sacrificial fuel in hand, a teacher who is learned in the scriptures and established in *Brahman*.[6]

This passage uses two expressions to describe the qualifications of the *gurū* or the spiritual master, stating that the *gurū* should be *śrotriya* and *brahmaniṣṭha*. The word *śrotriya* is derived from the Hindu word for revelation, namely, the *śruti*. It denotes a person well versed in the *śruti* (the Vedas) as the revealed scriptures of Hinduism. Thus, the *gurū* should be well versed in the scriptures. But the *gurū* must also be much more: the *gurū* should be *brahmaniṣṭha,* or one who is firmly established in the experience of ultimate reality. These dual qualifications become the hallowed *sine qua non* of a *gurū* in the tradition, and hang together. That is to say, the *gurū* must know both theory and practice; he or she should know how to talk about the ultimate reality, but the *gurū* should also have walked the talk.

The traditional discussion of requirements for qualification as a spiritual master contains an interesting wrinkle. The question is asked: Suppose a *gurū* possesses only one of the two qualifications—then what does one do? Curiously, the answer has been that a *gurū* who is a *śrotriya,* but not a *brahmaniṣṭha* should be preferred to one who is *brahmaniṣṭha,* but not a *śrotriya.* This is because the *śrotriya* will at least be able to pass on the tradition to the disciple even if not realized oneself. On the other hand, the *brahmaniṣṭha* may have had the experience of the ultimate reality, but would not possess the vocabulary to communicate it, due to lack of acquaintance with the Vedas.

The *upaniṣads* sometimes provide a list of the succession of teachers and disciples, which indicates that modes of transmission of the salvific teaching had become well established. How the pupil approached a teacher is well illustrated by the following account, which Śaṅkara (ca. eighth century CE) cites from an *upaniṣad,* but which is not found in the extant ones.

> Bāhva, asked by Bāṣkali to expound the nature of *brahman,* kept silent. He prayed: "Teach me, sir." The teacher was silent, and when addressed a second and a third time he said: "I am teaching but you do not follow. The self is silence!"[7]

In Vedic Hinduism, the moral qualifications required of a disciple were quite stringent. "Give it to none that is not tranquil," says one *upaniṣad,*[8] while another brings out the importance attached to truthfulness. When Satyakāma wished to be initiated, the master inquired about his lineage. He asked his mother "who replied: 'Son, I don't know what your lineage is. I was young when I had you. I was a maid then and had a lot of relationships. As such it is impossible for me to say what your lineage is. But my name is Jabālā, and your name is Satyakāma. So you should simply say that you are Satyakāma Jābāla.'"[9] The young boy related what he was told to his would-be teacher, who initiated him much impressed by his truthfulness.

The *Gurū* in Classical Hinduism

The spiritual master continued to play an important role when the Vedic tradition was transformed into classical Hinduism. By now Hinduism had come to be characterized by various schools of philosophy and religious sects, and this fact influenced the institution of the *gurū* by making it more diverse. However, the essential role of the spiritual master or the *gurū* remained the same—namely, to provide spiritual guidance to the pupil. The material from classical Hinduism enables one to actually specify the role of the spiritual master with more precision and depth, as one in which the master *assumes personal responsibility for* leading the pupil to the ultimate reality, whether conceived absolutistically or theistically. This is brought out vividly by the following account found in the *Viṣṇu Purāṇa,* which describes the interaction between the master Ṛbhu and the pupil Nidāgha.

> Although Ribhu taught his disciple the supreme Truth of the One Brahman without a second, Nidagha, in spite of his erudition and understanding, did not get sufficient conviction to adopt and follow the path of *jñāna,* but settled down in his native town to lead a life devoted to the observance of ceremonial religion.
>
> But the Sage loved his disciple as deeply as the latter venerated his Master. In spite of his age, Ribhu would himself go to his disciple in the town, just to see how far the latter had outgrown his ritualism. At times the Sage went in disguise, so that he might observe how Nidagha would act when he did not know that he was being observed by his Master.
>
> On one such occasion Ribhu, who had put on the disguise of a village rustic, found Nidagha intently watching a royal procession. Unrecognized by the town-dweller Nidagha, the village rustic inquired what the bustle was all about, and was told that the king was going in procession.

"Oh! It is the king. He goes in procession! But where is he?" asked the rustic.

"There, on the elephant," said Nidagha.

"You say the king is on the elephant. Yes, I see the two," said the rustic. "But which is the king and which is the elephant?"

"What!" exclaimed Nidagha. "You see the two, but do not know that the man above is the king and the animal below is the elephant? What is the use of talking to a man like you?"

"Pray, be not impatient with an ignorant man like me," begged the rustic. "But you said 'above' and 'below'—what do they mean?"

Nidagha could stand it no more. "You see the king and the elephant, the one *above* and the other *below*. Yet you want to know what is meant by 'above' and 'below'?" burst out Nidagha. "If things seen and words spoken can convey so little to you, action alone can teach you. Bend forward, and you will know it all too well."

The rustic did as he was told. Nidagha got on his shoulders and said, "Know it now, I am *above* as the king, you are *below* as the elephant. Is that clear enough?"

"No, not yet," was the rustic's quiet reply. "You say you are above like the king and I am below like the elephant. The 'king,' the 'elephant,' 'above,' and 'below,' so far it is clear. But pray, tell me what you mean by '*I*' and '*you*'?"

When Nidagha was thus confronted all of a sudden with the mighty problem of defining the "you" apart form the "I," light dawned on his mind. At once he jumped down and fell at his Master's feet, saying, "Who else but my venerable Master, Ribhu, could have thus drawn my mind from the superficialities of physical existence to the true Being of Self? O benign Master, I crave thy blessings."[10]

This assumption of the *personal* responsibility assumed by the spiritual master might explain the fervent devotion to the master elicited from the pupils.

The master assumes personal responsibility to save the disciple, but sometimes the disciples save the masters, as illustrated by the well-known account associated with Rāmānuja (1017–1137). His *gurū* whispered the super-secret *mantra* in his ear and forbade him to divulge it to anyone else. The next thing Rāmānuja did was to proclaim that sacred *mantra* to all and sundry from the top of the temple.

When asked to explain his impertinent conduct, Rāmānuja is believed to have asked the *gurū* whether it was true that whoever heard the *mantra* would be saved. Upon his confirming this he explained: "Look at it this way. I broke my promise to you and I will surely go to hell for doing so. But think of the hundreds who have been saved by hearing it." His *gurū* is believed to have acknowledged his disciple's greater insight by stating he had now become Rāmānuja's disciple.[11]

A well-known story from the *Mahābhārata* epic sheds some light on the role of the spiritual master in classical Hinduism, although its own context is more secular. Droṇācārya is depicted in the epic as the greatest master of martial arts of his times, who was grooming the Pāṇḍava prince, Arjuna, to avenge his insult at the hands of his former friend, Drupada. Ekalavya, a tribal boy also sought to be Droṇācārya's disciple on account of his reputation, but was turned down on account of his low birth. Time passed. Then one day Ekalavya bested Arjuna in a chance encounter in archery. Droṇa, shocked at the discomfiture of the favorite pupil, wanted to know who Ekalavya's *gurū* was. Ekalavya surprised Droṇa by telling him that after being rejected by Droṇa, he set up a replica of Droṇa and continued practicing archery by acknowledging Droṇa as his *gurū* in spirit. Upon hearing this, Droṇa demanded his *gurudakṣiṇā* (teaching fees) from the tribal lad, once he acknowledged Droṇa as his master. Droṇa cruelly demanded his thumb in fees, which meant that after its loss he would never be able to surpass Arjuna.

Although told in a secular setting, the story of Droṇa and Ekalavya also applies to spiritual masters. Droṇa's cruel treatment of Ekalavya points to the danger of an incapacitating exploitation of disciples by their masters. Hence, some texts add a third qualification for a spiritual master, beyond the criteria known to Vedic Hinduism: in addition to being a *śrotriya,* who is well-versed in scripture, and a *brahmaniṣṭha,* who is firmly established in the experience of ultimate reality, the teacher must be free from egoism. This resonates with the case of Droṇa who "was appointed to teach the art of warfare, how to fight and kill, *but not [to give] any moral lessons or war ethics,*" in which he obviously left something to be desired.[12]

The Ekalavya episode is instructive at three levels, moral, pedagogical, and spiritual: Its *moral significance* lies in the fact that just as Ekalavya was treated unjustly, Droṇa lost his life in an unjust manner and was killed on account of a lie uttered to him. Its *pedagogical significance* is illustrated by an incident in the life of Rāmānuja. Once when Rāmānuja was being instructed by Tirumālai Aṇṭān in the Tiruvāymoḷi of Nammāḷvar, his teacher hesitated "at a certain explanation, but Rāmānuja said that he was a disciple of Yāmuna's, like the legendary Ekalavya was a disciple of Droṇa's, a student who learnt from a master in spirit, without actually ever being in his presence."[13] Its *spiritual significance* indicates that ultimately there are no teachers, only disciples. That is to say, it is the faith of the disciple in the master that bears fruit—be it secular or sacred.

The *Gurū* in Medieval Hinduism

The medieval period of Hinduism is characterized by Hinduism's prolonged interaction with Islam—specifically Ṣūfī Islam, which has a tradition of *pīr-murīd* analogous to the *gurū-siśya* tradition in Hinduism. In a sense, however, the rise of Sikhism in north India offers the most obvious insights into the working of the *gurū* tradition during this period, as the Sikh religion takes its very name from the word *disciple*. These "disciples" were the followers of the ten Sikh *gurūs*, beginning with Gurū Nānak (1469–1539) and ending with Gurū Gobind Singh (1616–1708). The Sikh religion represents an extension of the Hindu *gurū* tradition in medieval India, in which both the spiritual and mundane dimensions of human existence came to be pervaded by the institution of guruship.[14]

Sikhism was only the most visible manifestation of the *gurū* phenomenon that characterized medieval Hinduism insofar as the attainment of liberation involved a complete devotion to the *gurū*. However, the Sant tradition of medieval India also focused on devotion to a deity with or without special characteristics (*saguṇa* or *nirguṇa*), and was characterized by the "acceptance of the sant as the teacher (*guru*)."[15] This emphasis on devotion was also true of classical Hinduism, but in that earlier historical context it was fully lodged in the textual tradition that accompanied it. By contrast, the newer Hindu *gurū* phenomenon gave rise to texts in medieval times that were not so much in Sanskrit, but rather in various regional languages of India, such as Hindi, Marathi, Tamil, and Telegu. This medieval cultural development surrounding the figure of the *gurū* was also highly theistic in its orientation, and centered on devotion to the name of God.

What need is there of a *gurū* if the religious emphasis is on an immediate apprehension of the divine? The *gurū* was needed to point to the pathway. The paradox of guruship here is similar to that in Hindu absolutism: If the *Brahman* is right here and now, what is the need for a *gurū*? The answer is similar: to make the obvious, obvious. George Orwell says somewhere that to see what is right in front of one's nose requires constant effort—one may even need someone to point it out. The *gurū* phenomenon continued to flourish in the absolutistic tradition as well. The following poem composed by Lallā (fourteenth century) from Kashmir provides a good example.

> "Think not on the things that are without:
> Fix upon thy inner Self thy Thought:
> So shalt thou be freed from let or doubt":—
> Precepts these that my Preceptor taught.
> Dance then, Lallā, clothed but by the air:
> Sing then, Lallā, clad but in the sky.
> Air and sky: what garment is more fair?
> "Cloth," said Custom—Doth that sanctify?[16]

Two other developments in medieval Hinduism are also worth noting. One is the tendency to identify the *gurū* and God. This tendency can already be seen in the *Śvetāśvatara Upaniṣad* (4.23) and the *Liṅga Purāṇa.* These and other texts teach that "the guru is identical with Śiva and the rewards of devotion to Śiva and to the guru are the same."[17] So the seeds of the identification between the *gurū* and God were already there in the earlier Hindu tradition, but it achieved remarkable extension during the medieval period. One wonders whether the tendency was not encouraged by the disruption of Hindu educational institutions during the medieval period, which might have given a more individualistic rather than institutional orientation to pedagogy. The devotional ethos that pervades medieval Hinduism may also have contributed to the tendency to divinize the *gurū*. In some circles the *gurū* was even given priority over God. A famous floating verse of this period captures the sentiment behind this: "Both God and guru stand in front of me, whose feet should I touch first. I shall touch the feet of the guru first, for it was he who led me to God."

Fervent exaltation of the *gurū* was also present in Tantrism, the other religious development worth noting during this period. Yet even tantric texts, noted for their liberality, warned against false *gurū*s (*Kulārṇavatantra* 13.128), and discussed the qualifications of *gurū*s and disciples (see *Śāradātilaka* 2.142–44; 3.145–52).[18]

The *Gurū* in Modern Hinduism

The modern period provides room for a fresh look at the role of spiritual masters in Hinduism because it presents a mixed picture. Some of the leading figures of modern Hinduism did *not* have spiritual masters in the traditional sense, including Rammohun Roy (1772/4–1833), Debendranath Tagore (1817–1905), Keshub Chunder Sen (1838–1884), Rabindranath Tagore (1861–1941), Śrī Aurobindo (1872–1950), and Mahatma Gandhi (1868–1948).

The case of Mahatma Gandhi is of special interest in this respect of not having a *gurū* in the traditional sense. He was almost under the spell of someone by the name of Raychandbhai, who was a jeweler by profession. Mahatma Gandhi regarded Raychandbhai as a spiritually distinguished person, but goes on to say:

> And yet in spite of this regard for him I could not enthrone him in my heart as my Guru. The throne has remained vacant and my search still continues.
>
> I believe in the Hindu theory of Guru and his importance in spiritual realization. I think there in a great deal of truth in the doctrine that true knowledge is impossible without a Guru. An imperfect teacher may be tolerable in mundane matters, but not in spiritual matters. Only a perfect *gnani* deserves to be enthroned as Guru. There must, therefore, be ceaseless striving after perfection. For one gets the Guru that one deserves. Infinite striving after perfection is one's right. It is its own reward. The rest is in the hands of God.
>
> Thus, though I could not place Raychandbhai on the throne of my heart as Guru, we shall see how he was, on many occasions, my guide and helper. Three moderns have left a deep impress on my life, and captivated me: Raychandbhai by his living contact; Tolstoy by his book, *The Kingdom of God is Within You*; and Ruskin by his *Unto this Last*. But of these more in their proper place.[19]

Mahatma Gandhi seems to represent the tenor of modern Hinduism in his wariness of imperfect *gurūs* and hesitation to enthrone one on his heart—although it must immediately be added that another famous modern Hindu, Swami Vivekananda (1824–1883) did have a *gurū*. One incident in this context is particularly revealing, in which Vivekananda (who was known as Naren before he became a monk) tested his master.

> Ramakrishna used to say to Naren, "You must test me as the money-changers test their coins. You mustn't accept me until you've tested me thoroughly." One day, Naren came

> out to Dakshineswar and found that Ramakrishna had gone into Calcutta. Naren was alone in the room, and suddenly he felt a desire to test the genuineness of Ramakrishna's often-expressed contempt for money. So he hid a rupee under Ramakrishna's mattress. Then he went to the Panchavati and began meditating. Presently, Ramakrishna returned and entered his room. No sooner had he touched the bed than he started back; he had felt actual physical pain. As he was looking around him in bewilderment, unable to understand what it was that had happened to him, Naren came in and stood watching him without saying a word. Ramakrishna called one of the temple attendants and asked him to examine the bed. The rupee was discovered, and Naren then explained what he had done. Ramakrishna fully approved.[20]

Another famous modern Hindu, Swami Dayananda Sarasvati (1824–1883), also had a *gurū* in Swami Virajananda; but this relationship involved more an intellectual than a spiritual sense.

Debate on the question whether a spiritual master is required to achieve liberation becomes particularly interesting in the context of Ramana Maharshi (1879–1950). Bhagavan Ramana Maharshi did not have a *gurū,* but paradoxically often insisted on the disciple's need for one in order to achieve liberation. This conundrum surrounding the role of a *gurū* is evidenced in the following conversation (recorded by S. S. Cohen) between him and Dilip Kumar Roy, the celebrated musician at Sri Aurobindashram:

> *Dilip*: Some people report Maharshi to deny the need of a Guru. Others say the reverse. What does Maharshi say?
>
> *B.*: I have never said that there is no need for a Guru.
>
> *Dilip*: Sri Aurobindo often refers to you as having had no Guru.
>
> *B.*: That depends on what you call Guru. They need not necessarily be in human form. Dattatreya had twenty-four Gurus—the elements, etc. That means that any form in the world was his Guru. Guru is absolutely necessary. The Upanishads say that none but a Guru can take a man out of the jungle of mental and sense perceptions, so there must be a Guru.

Dilip: I mean a human Guru. The Maharshi didn't have one.

B.: I might have had at some time or other. And didn't I sing hymns to Arunachala? What is a Guru? Guru is God or the Self. First a man prays to God to fulfil his desires, then a time comes when he does not pray for the fulfillment of a desire but for God Himself. So God appears to him in some form or other, human or non-human, to guide him as a Guru in answer to his prayer.[21]

Arthur Osborne notes after citing this passage that

> it was only when some visitor brought up the subject that Sri Bhagavan himself had not had a Guru that he explained that the Guru need not necessarily take on a human form, and it was understood that this referred to very rare cases. [22]

Modesty on the part of the spiritual master might complicate the situation further. Although Ramana Maharshi points to the need of a *gurū*, he would often disown that he had disciples. This sometimes led to comical situations such as the following with the English disciple, Major Chadwick:

> Ch. Bhagavan says he has no disciples?
>
> Bh. Yes.
>
> Ch. He also says that a Guru is necessary if one wishes to attain Liberation?
>
> Bh. Yes.
>
> Ch. What then must I do? Has my sitting here all these years been just a waste of time? Must I go and look for some Guru in order to receive initiation seeing that Bhagavan says he is not a Guru?
>
> Bh. What do you think brought you here such a long distance and made you remain so long? Why do you doubt? If there had been any need to seek a Guru elsewhere you would have gone away long ago.

The Guru or *Gnani* (Enlightened One) sees no difference between himself and others. For him all are *Gnanis*, all are one with himself, so how can a *Gnani* say that such and such is his disciple? But the unliberated one sees all as multiple, he sees all as different from himself, so to him the Guru-disciple relationship is a reality, and he needs the Grace of the Guru to waken him to reality. For him there are three ways of initiation, by touch, look and silence. (Sri Bhagavan here gave me to understand that his way was by silence, as he has to many on other occasions.)

> Ch. Then Bhagavan *does* have disciples!
>
> Bh. As I said, from Bhagavan's point of view there are no disciples, but from that of the disciple the Grace of the Guru is like an ocean. If he comes with a cup he will only get a cupful. It is no use complaining of the niggardliness of the ocean; the bigger the vessel the more he will be able to carry. It is entirely up to him.
>
> Ch. Then to know whether Bhagavan is my Guru or not is just a matter of faith, if Bhagavan will not admit it.
>
> Bh. (Sitting straight up, turning to the interpreter and speaking with great emphasis.) Ask him, does he want me to give him a written document?[23]

Sri Bhagavan taught in a subtle manner by silence, hardly admitting his role as *gurū*. Others go far in the direction of subtlety by mere looking. Huston Smith notes that "Professor Friedrich Spiegelberg, who taught philosophy at Stanford, used to tell his students that the forty-five seconds in which he gazed silently into Aurobindo's eyes were the most important in his life."[24] It is tempting to compare the silent, transformative look into Aurubindo's eyes to the initiation by look described in Hindu lore. "The guru can bestow his grace [give *dīkṣā*] either by thought, as the turtle hatches its eggs by merely thinking about them, or by look as the fish hatches its eggs by looking at them, or by touch as the hen hatches its eggs by sitting on them."[25] But *dīkṣā* by thought is said to be the best.[26]

What does the *gurū* do? Huston Smith was once asked, "What do you think of the *gurū* tradition?" and his response provides one answer:

> In principle, it is important. Basically, it's only a special case of having a role model—someone you look up to and

> try to imitate. Children couldn't develop if they weren't surrounded by people who have mastered life's basics and can show them the way. Language is a particularly obvious case. When it comes to how life should be lived, we are children to the end.
>
> The shadow side, of course, is that like every good it can be perverted. And, as the Latin warns us, *corruptio optimi pessima*—the corruption of the best produces the worst. We've had evidence to spare us of that in the last thirty years: shoddy gurus who let their power delude them into thinking that they were above the moral law. But abuses don't annul the principle, which remains valid. Christ was a guru, the Buddha, and Muhammad were gurus.[27]

The muted emphasis on the spiritual master among some of the leading figures of modern Hinduism can be attributed to the greater importance in modern times sometimes attached to social work, as opposed to soteriological work. It is apparent, however, that having a *gurū* remains a spiritual mode of choice among large numbers of Hindus. This betrays the deep roots of the *gurū* in India's history and culture.

Conclusion

What does the *gurū* ultimately accomplish? There seems to be an implicit recognition among Hindus that spiritual masters help dissolve the ego that comes between human beings and God. In fact, the boundaries between God, *gurū*, and the self only exist in ignorance. Ramana Maharshi equates the three and explains the relationship as follows:

> *Isvaro gururatmeti* (The Self is the God and Guru). A person seeks happiness and learns that God alone can make one happy. He prays to God and worships Him. God hears his prayers, and responds by appearing in human shape as a Master in order to speak the language of the devotee and make him understand the Reality. The Master is thus God manifest as human being. He gives out His experience so that the seeker might also gain it. His experience is to abide as the Self. The Self is within. God, Master and the Self are therefore seeming stages in the Realisation of the Truth.[28]

In Hindu tradition, the key role of the *gurū* is to teach the disciple that there is ultimately no distinction between the two of them and God. How the *gurū* does this may differ from case to case, but at least Ramana Maharshi leaves little doubt that this is what guru-hood is all about.

> The anecdotes differ in different books. We are not concerned with the names and the embellishments. The *tatva,* i.e., the moral, must not be lost sight of. The disciple surrenders himself to the master. That means there is no vestige of individuality retained by the disciple. If the surrender is complete all sense of individuality is lost and there is thus no cause for misery. The eternal being is only happiness. This is revealed.
>
> Without understanding it aright, people think that the Guru teaches the disciple something like "TATVAMASI" and that the disciple realizes "I am Brahman." In their ignorance they conceive of Brahman as something more huge and powerful than anything else. With a limited "I" the man is so stuck up and wild. What will be the case if the same "I" grows up enormous? He will be enormously ignorant and foolish! This false "I" must perish. Its annihilation is the fruit of Guru *seva*. Realisation is eternal and it is not newly brought about by the Guru. He helps in the removal of ignorance. That is all.[29]

Notes

1. P. V. Kane, *History of Dharmaśāstra,* 2nd ed. (Poona: Bhandarkar Oriental Research Institute, 1977), 5:2, 1072, n. 1735.

2. See Patrick Olivelle, *Law Code of Manu* (New York: Oxford University Press, 2004), 34. The tables are turned in the *Mahābhārata* wherein the *gurū* is described as superior to one's parents. See S. Radhakrishnan, ed., *Principal Upaniṣads* (1952; repr., Atlantic Heights, NJ: Humanities Press, 1996), 464.

3. *Chāndogya Upaniṣad* 6.14.1. See Radhakrishnan, *Principal Upaniṣads,* 463.

4. Ibid., 6.14.1–2. See Radhakrishnan, *Principal Upaniṣads,* 464.

5. *Śvetāśvatara Upaniṣad* 4.23. See Radhakrishnan, *Principal Upaniṣads,* 750.

6. *Muṇḍaka Upaniṣad* 1.2.12. See Radhakrishnan, *Principal Upaniṣads,* 679.

7. See Radhakrishnan, *Principal Upaniṣads,* 287.

8. M. Hiriyana, *Essentials of Indian Philosophy* (London: George Allen and Unwin, 1949), 27.

9. Patrick Olivelle, *Early Upaniṣads* (New York: Oxford University Press, 1998), 219.

10. As narrated in Joe Miller and Guinevere Miller, eds., *Spiritual Teachings of Ramana Maharshi* (Boston: Shambhala, 1988), 74–75.

11. For a fuller account see John Braisted Carman, *The Theology of Rāmānuja: An Essay in Interreligious Understanding* (New Haven: Yale University Press, 1974), 39–41.

12. Jonardon Ganeri, ed., *Collected Essays of Bimal Krishna Matilal: Ethics and Epics* (New Delhi: Oxford University Press, 2002), 96. Emphasis supplied.

13. Vasudha Narayanan, *Vernacular Veda: Revelation, Recitation, and Ritual* (Columbia: University of South Carolina Press, 1994), 103–4. This is reminiscent of Paul's discipleship of Jesus, whom he never met in person.

14. See Willard G. Oxtoby, "The Sikh Tradition," in *World Religions: Eastern Traditions*, ed. Willard G. Oxtoby, 2nd ed. (Toronto: Oxford University Press, 2002), 139–41.

15. Ainslie T. Embree, ed., *Sources of Indian Tradition,* 2nd ed. (New York: Columbia University Press, 1988), 372.

16. Cited in Louis Renou, ed., *Hinduism* (New York: Braziller, 1962), 209.

17. P. V. Kane, 5:2, 1072.

18. Ibid., 1071.

19. Mahadev Desai, trans., *Gandhi's Autobiography* (Washington, DC: Public Affairs Press, 1948), 113–14.

20. Christopher Isherwood, *Ramakrishna and His Disciples* (Calcutta: Advaita Ashrama, 1965), 209.

21. Arthur Osborne, ed., *Teachings of Bhagavan Sri Ramana Maharshi in His Own Words* (Tiruvannamalai: Sri Ramansramam, 1971), 117–18.

22. Ibid., 118.

23. Arthur Osborne, *Ramana Maharshi and the Path of Self-Knowledge* (1970; repr. York Beach, ME: Samuel Weiser, 1995), 141–42. He says elsewhere: "The person may call himself my disciple or devotee. I do not consider any one to be my disciple. I have never sought *upadesh* from any one nor do I give ceremonial *upadesh.* If the people call themselves my disciples I do not approve or disapprove. In my view all are alike. They consider themselves fit for being called disciples. What can I say to them? I do not call myself a disciple or a Guru" (Ramana Maharshi, *Talks with Sri Ramana Maharshi* [Tiruvannamalai: Sri Ramanasramam, 1984], 238).

24. Phil Cousineau, ed. *The Way Things Are: Conversations with Huston Smith on the Spiritual Life* (Berkeley: University of California Press, 2003), 80.

25. A. Devaraja Mudaliar, *My Recollections of Bhagavan Sri Ramana* (1960; repr. Tiruvannamalai: Sri Ramanasramam, 1992), 109.

26. Ibid., 110.

27. Coustineau, *The Way Things Are,* 75.

28. Maharshi, *Talks,* 570.

29. Ibid., 318–19.

5

Sikh Spiritual Masters

Mary Pat Fisher

Introduction

Although the central focus of Sikh faith is the One God—understood as formless, nameless, without any particular religion, pervading everywhere—the lineage of Gurūs is the definitive feature of Sikh history and spirituality. There were a total of ten extraordinarily enlightened and powerful Gurūs, providing a continuing heritage of visionary wisdom, compassionate and uplifting guidance, courageous revelation of truth, and union with God. The functions of these ten spiritual masters are still alive today, in the unique presence of the Gurū embodied in the holy scripture known as Gurū Granth Sāhib.

Sikhs are by definition oriented toward their Gurūs, for the word *sikh* means "disciple" or "student." But this is no academic orientation. Rather, it is an intimate spiritual relationship of deep love, faith, and reverence, as poetically described by Puran Singh:

> The title "Sikh," "The Disciple," was first given to us by Guru Nanak. We were mere corpses; he poured life into us. We were thus created anew by His love of us. He made us alive with our out-drawn love of Him and left us free. He freed us from the hatred of caste, colour and creed. He made us look straight at the sky towards the Infinite; he made us look upon the sun and the moon and stars as our kith and kin. He did knit us with the universe and he wove the design of the Infinite into the texture of our soul. He gave us then the universal music to sing; birds and animals to be our confidants, woods and rivers and hills to sing with us. This world that sat like a nightmare on us was thrown away: the new world was laid open before our eyes in His Vision. The veil was almost torn asunder and this spiritual universe of love was opened to our vision. And we were elevated from the valleys of darkness on to the sunlit heights. Peasants became poets by His touch. The enslaved womanhood was freed from its bondage of the soul. . . .
>
> This is the plain history. Our history is of the soul; all its events are of the soul. All truth for us is personal. We have not to prove it, we have to stand witness to it in our soul. By the title "Sikh," he linked us with Himself forever. And we cannot tear ourselves away from Him. It would be misery for us if we turn our backs on Him.[1]

History of the Gurūs

First in the series of Sikh Gurūs was the great mystic Gurū Nānak (1469–ca. 1539). He appeared in human form during very difficult times, in which Hindus were being brutally oppressed and massacred by misguided Muslim rulers. As a child in a Hindu family, Nānak was often lost in contemplation of the Divine. His sister Nānakī reportedly heard heavenly music surrounding him when he sat in prayer.[2] But he did not accept Brahmin ritualism. When a large ceremony was arranged in his childhood for him to be traditionally invested with the sacred thread, Nānak refused to wear it, explaining that he only wanted that sacred thread of praising God—the thread that would never wear out, never get dirty, never be lost. His preferred companions were the Hindu and Muslim ascetics who lived in the surrounding forest. Many days went by without his eating anything.

Many were the nights that he spent in deep meditation, with tears of *vairag* (detachment from the world) and great longing for God alone. When a doctor was called to cure him, young Nānak explained his condition by singing:

> Firstly I feel the pain of separation from God
> And another pain is of the hunger for His meditation. . . .
> O ignorant physician, minister thou not any medicine to me. . . .
> The pain persists and the body's suffering continues.
> Such a medicine produces no effect on me, O brother. (Gurū Granth Sāhib, 1256)[3]

At last, however, when he was about thirty years old, Nānak apparently met the One for whom he had been longing. According to stories told about his life, he had gone down to the river for his morning bath, but then did not reappear until three days later despite desperate attempts to locate him. When Nānak made his reappearance he seemed utterly transformed, with divine light shining in his eyes and a visible glow around his body. What had happened while he was missing? He had become Gurū Nānak. His explanation is preserved in Gurū Granth Sāhib:

> Me, the bard out of work,
> The Lord has applied to His service.
> In the very beginning He gave me the order
> To sing His praises night and day.
> The Master summoned the minstrel to His True Court.
> He clothed me with the robe of His true honor and eulogy.
> Since then the True Name has become my ambrosial food.
> They, who under the Guru's instruction,
> Eat this food to their satisfaction, obtain peace.
> By singing the Guru's hymns,
> I, the minstrel, spread the Lord's glory. (GGS, 150)

Soon after his mystical meeting, Gurū Nānak reportedly uttered the Mūl Maṃtar, which holds a central place in Sikh devotions and in Gurū Granth Sāhib:

> One God
> Named Truth
> Creator

Without fear
Without hate
Timeless, Immortal
Is neither born, nor dies
Self-existent
Is revealed by the grace of the Guru.
Truth in the beginning,
Truth through the ages
Truth now
Truth shall ever be. (GGS, 1)[4]

Taking his dear Muslim friend and early disciple, the rebab player Mardānā, with him to accompany his inspired singing, Nānak left his wife and sons for long years of traveling and spiritual teaching. According to God's command, Gurū Nānak journeyed extensively through India, the Himalayas, Afghanistan, Arabia, Sri Lanka—and perhaps Tibet and China. Wherever he went, he engaged Hindu and Muslim teachers in dialogues that contrasted the way of inner spirituality and kindness with that of outer rituals and religious barriers. When he dared to go on pilgrimage to Mecca dressed in pilgrim's garb—an act that to today is forbidden to non-Muslims—his spiritual wisdom drew a crowd of *mullah*s, *pīr*s, and *faqīr*s. They asked him:

> "Are you a Hindu or a Muslim?"
>
> "Neither," replied the Guru. "I am but a servant of God and a lover of man."
>
> The next question was, "Who is better and holier in your opinion—a Hindu or a Muslim?"
>
> Replied Guru Nanak, "Without good acts, the professors of both religions shall suffer; neither the Hindus nor the Muslims shall obtain entrance into God's court. All their devotions shall vanish like the fleeting dye of safflower. Both sects are jealous of each other. The Hindus insist on saying 'Ram' and the Muslims 'Rahim,' but they know not the one God."[5]

Many stories are told of Gurū Nānak's transformational effect upon those who encountered him. Once, for instance, he chose to eat in the home of Lalo, a carpenter, rather than attend the great feast organized for all the supposed holy people of the area by the wealthy chief of the town, Mālik Bhago. Outraged, Mālik Bhago ordered that

Gurū Nānak be produced before him. To explain why he had not accepted Mālik Bhago's invitation, Gurū Nānak reportedly asked that some of Lalo's food and of Mālik Bhago's food be brought. According to the story, when Gurū Nānak squeezed Mālik Bhago's rich food, drops of blood came from it; whereas when he squeezed Lalo's simple food, milk came from it. Mālik Bhago understood the point that his wealth had been gained by exploiting the poor, while Lalo's food offering was the result of his own honest labor. Mālik Bhago accepted the truth of Gurū Nānak's central teaching: that the way to God will be found only if one works hard to support oneself, and shares these honest earnings with others. The chief gave away everything he had to the needy and thenceforth dedicated himself to serving others.

In line with his emphasis on being self-supporting, rather than living on charity as many "holy people" were doing, Gurū Nānak ultimately settled on a piece of land at Kartarpur. He began farming there to feed not only his own family, but also the many devotees who came for guidance and blessings. Gurū Nānak himself worked in the fields. He and his devotees farmed collectively, sharing the food with those of all castes and creeds who visited the Gurū.

One who came was Lehna (1504–1552), a staunch Hindu devotee of the Goddess Durgā. When he arrived, Gurū Nānak greeted him by saying that he had been expecting him for some time. Lehna became such a devoted disciple that Gurū Nānak changed his name to "Aṉgad," or limb—meaning that he was an arm of the Gurū's own body. Then in front of a large group of devotees, Nānak transferred the guruship to Aṉgad, and made himself Gurū Aṉgad's disciple. Bhāī Gurdās, a contemporary chronicler of the Gurūs, explains the mystery of the transmission of guruship through the Sikh spiritual lineage:

> Before he died he [Gurū Nānak] installed Lehna and set the Guru's canopy over his head. Merging his light in Guru Angad's light the Sat Guru [True Gurū] changed his form. None could comprehend this. He revealed a wonder of wonders: Changing his body he made Guru Angad's body his own.[6]

A series of nine enlightened beings were eventually chosen as Gurū to follow Nānak as the key spiritual masters of the Sikh tradition. Each was empowered by his predecessor to carry on the Light (*jot*) of Nānak. Gurū Gobind Singh, the Tenth Sikh Gurū, explains the process in his autobiography:

> Nanak assumed the body of Angad and spread religion in this world. Then he was named Amar Das [the Third Gurū, who lived 1479–1574] as if a lamp was lit by the lamp. When the time of boon came, Ram Das [the Fourth Gurū, 1534–1581] became the Guru. Granting him the old boon Guru Amar Das left for his heavenly abode. Nanak was accepted as Angad Guru and (Guru) Angad was identified as (Guru) Amar Das. . . . This mystery was understood by the saints but the ignorant ones could not follow it. Ordinary persons considered them as different forms but some rare ones understood them as one. . . . When (Guru) Ram Das merged in the Lord he offered the seat of Guruship to (Guru) Arjan Dev [the Fifth Gurū, 1563–1606]. When (Guru) Arjan Dev went to the abode of the Lord, Hargobind [the Sixth Gurū, 1595–1644] was established in his place. When (Guru) Hargobind merged in the Supreme Reality, (Guru) Hari Rai [the Seventh Gurū, 1630–1661] sat in his place. His (spiritual) son was Hari Krishan [the Eighth Gurū, 1656–1664] from whom emerged (Guru) Teg Bahadur [the Ninth Gurū, c. 1621–1675].[7]

Throughout this process of developing an unbroken line of spiritual masters, all ten Sikh Gurūs continued to preach and practice the same simple and effective spiritual program begun by Gurū Nānak: devotion to God, *Nām* (continual repetition of and meditation on the Holy Name of God), reciting of sacred texts, *kīrtan* (singing sacred hymns in praise of God), working hard with one's own hands, and sharing the fruits of these efforts with others. Each of the Gurūs carried on the Light of Nānak in his own particular style, according to historical circumstances. In their inspired utterances, they often spoke of themselves as "Nānak." It was the Third Gurū, for instance, who sang, "Nanak, the Gurmukh [one whose face is always turned toward the Gurū rather than toward one's own thoughts] ever attains peace, and night and day remains imbued with the love of God" (Gurū Amar Dās, GGS, 590).

All of the ten Gurūs were remarkable spiritual masters. Several of them were installed as Gurū at a very young age. Har Rāi became the Seventh Gurū when he was only fourteen years old. When he was about to die, he appointed his five-year-old son, Harkrishan, as the Eighth Gurū. Gurū Harkrishan himself lived only to the age of eight, because he died of smallpox from attending the sick during an epidemic. Despite his youth and short tenure as Gurū, Harkrishan set a great example of self-sacrificial service, fearlessness, and truthfulness. Like the other Gurūs, he also had considerable mystical power. When Hindu pandits taunted him for being so young and carrying the great name of Lord Kṛṣṇa, Gurū Harkrishan merely touched a deaf and dumb Sikh water carrier with his staff, whereupon the water carrier expounded brilliantly on the subtleties of Kṛṣṇa's teachings in the *Bhagavadgītā*.

Gurū Gobind Singh became the Tenth Sikh Gurū at the tender age of nine. This was after his father, the Ninth Gurū, Teg Bahādur, was beheaded when he courageously and serenely stood up for freedom of religion of Hindus. From the beginning, young Gurū Gobind Singh was famous for his bravery, staunch determination, and spiritual power. In 1699, he dramatically created the Khālsā, a group comprised of those who were empowered to embody the Gurūs' teachings in their own lives, conquer their own inner evils, always stand on the front line against injustice to anyone, and remain solidly connected to God through *Nām*.

Before he died at the age of forty-two from stab wounds that reopened when he drew a stiff bow, Gurū Gobind Singh took a unique step: rather than naming a human successor to the lineage of Gurūs, he told his Sikhs that they were henceforth to consider the holy scripture compiled by the Gurūs as their Gurū—Gurū Granth Sāhib. This assignment of a sacred text to the role of spiritual master was a profound move in the history of religions, exhibiting the underlying mystical notion of how a Gurū functions in relation to disciples through the light (*jot*) of inspiration rather than through human form. The book is an extraordinary collection of mystical hymns by six of the Sikh Gurūs, and nineteen Hindu and Muslim holy people. It does not promote any particular religion but, rather, continually reminds devotees of the importance and blessings of continual remembrance of the One God, who is called by many names. In it, for instance, are songs of Kabīr, a spiritual master who was both Hindu and Muslim, who wrote, "Say not that the Vedas and revealed scriptures [Bible, Torah, Qur'an, and Zendavesta] are false. False is he who reflects not on them" (GGS, 1350).

Guruship Today

Because Gurū Gobind Singh did not continue the tradition of naming a human successor—and instead referred his devotees to Gurū Granth Sāhib—the mainstream Sikh tradition has not recognized any further

Gurūs. There have been groups who consider their teacher so enlightened that they treat him as a *gurū*, however. The Nāmdharis, for instance, recognize a line of living *gurūs* that started with Bābā Balak Singh (1799–1861) and is currently represented by Baba Jagjit Singh. They live simply, and seek to restore the feelings of devotion and moral purity that characterize the best of the Sikh tradition. Another lineage that insists on the presence of a living *gurū* is Radhasoami, which began with Shiv Dayal Singh, who in 1861 offered to serve as a spiritual savior who would carry his devotees into "Radhasoami," the Godhead. After his death, some thirty separate lineages ultimately developed from this root, each with its own succession of living spiritual masters. They are no longer formally identified as Sikhs.

Sikh spirituality is so universal, broad-minded, and powerful that it is capable of raising ordinary people to great spiritual heights—so long as they do not become egotistical when people recognize their genuine spiritual power and flock around them. But because Gurū Gobind Singh named Gurū Granth Sāhib as his successor, when a new true spiritual master arises from the tradition, Sikhs might not officially refer to him as Gurū, in the sense of recognizing him as a carrier of the *jot* of Gurū Nānak—for the guruship is now established in Gurū Granth Sāhib. People may gather around the new spiritual master, nonetheless, for the sake of his or her blessings and inspired wisdom. Sometimes their followers refer to them as *sant.*

The term *sant* does not mean the same thing as "saint" in English, in the Western sense of a very holy or kind person. It comes from the Sanskrit root *sat,* meaning "lasting, real, wise, and venerable." It has been used in India since ancient times as a reference to God, and was also associated with spiritual masters such as the *bhagats* of north India. Among the *bhagats* were fervent lovers of God such as Kabīr, Namdev, and Ravidas whose inspired hymns were incorporated into Gurū Granth Sāhib alongside hymns of the Sikh Gurus.[8]

In the twentieth century, one such revered spiritual teacher came up within the Sikh community, and attracted devotees from all castes and creeds. His name was Baba Virsa Singh (ca. 1934–2007). He himself never claimed to be a Gurū or even a *sant,* for he said that these are very great titles. His close assistant Gurdev Singh recalls:

> He always said, "I am only a farmer, the son of a farmer. I am just trying to be a better human being." Once when we were travelling back to India from the United States, a noted environmental scientist from the United Nations, Naresh Singh, sat with him on the airplane asking him questions for hours. When all his questions had been answered to

> his full satisfaction, Naresh Singh asked Baba Virsa Singh, "May I call you my guru?" Baba Virsa Singh Ji replied, "I am not a guru. It is your love. You may call me whatever you want." So some people out of their love and faith in Baba Virsa Singh called him their guru. But he sometimes said, "I am not even a Sikh. I am trying to become a Sikh. Still I am learning."[9]

Baba Virsa Singh's spiritual power began to manifest when he was a boy. His family members were farmers, and he had been sent out to cut fodder for their buffalos. When he cut a stalk and saw the sap oozing out, suddenly he was struck with the feeling that he was harming the plant and that it was in pain. He could not bear to cut any more plants, so he began praying that his father would excuse him from this duty. At once, sores appeared on the soles of his feet, so painful that he could not walk. He began to sit under a tree in meditation, calling out to he knew not whom. At last a being with long matted locks who was not visible to others appeared to him, but young Virsa Singh was very frightened by his ascetic appearance. That being kept appearing to him, and at last young Virsa Singh understood that it was Bābā Srī Chand, the elder son of Gurū Nānak, who did not become a Gurū, but rather was put in charge of the Udāsīs. This was a movement of spiritual masters who carried the teachings of Gurū Nānak as wandering ascetics.

Bābā Srī Chand instructed Virsa Singh to sit for many hours every day in intense meditation. Filled with spiritual longing, he disregarded things of the body and became very thin. Gurū Gobind Singh, the Tenth Sikh Gurū, also began appearing to him, and lovingly instructed him to eat, and to wear nice clothes. He had to reassure young Virsa Singh that doing so would not sever his connection with the One he loved. People began to bring their problems to Virsa Singh, calling him "Bābāji" (a respectful term used for an elder male) even though he was still beardless. Strange miracles began to happen around Bābāji, and people sought his visionary help in healing their sick and finding things they had lost. Bābāji's mother worried how to feed all the people who came, but Bābāji told her to keep taking flour for chapattis out of a ceramic urn without looking into it. Until the day that she peeked into it, there was always enough flour. For milk, many people were told in dreams to present a buffalo to Bābāji's family, so many buffalos came, and there was always enough milk for everyone.

After a period during which many people were miraculously healed, a wealthy aristocrat offered Bābāji his large estate as a place to settle—but Gurū Gobind Singh came to Bābāji at night and told him not to accept the offer. Bābāji immediately left with his followers the next morning, being ever obedient to his beloved Gurū. Eventually he was instructed in vision about a small piece of apparently worthless land on the outskirts of Delhi, and in 1968 he and a few followers began to develop it.

The land was very hostile—a barren, hot, dry, thorny, ravine-cut, treeless wasteland occupied only by wild animals and thieves. But in the midst of July's heat, obeying his Gurū's Hukam (spiritual command), Baba Virsa Singh and his followers began digging a well by hand, carrying on their heads baskets of stone and dirt from the hole. They slept in the open or in tents, and snakes often crawled over them at night. By great faith in God and extremely hard work, they turned that seemingly godforsaken land into flourishing, orderly fields and a first-class dairy where they produced the All-Asia prize cow. Over the years, some of the buffalos and pieces of this land were sold to buy more land in remote wastelands. These were also turned into record-breaking farms by faith and hard work, which seemed to invoke God's great blessings.

Bābāji settled in his community on the edge of Delhi, having shown by practical example the power of spirituality to transform barren wastelands. It is named "Gobind Sadan," which means "The House of God," and carries a reference to his beloved Gurū, Gurū Gobind Singh. For decades he was guiding and helping people of all social standings and religions, and thus furthering the nonsectarian mission of Gurū Gobind Singh, who said, "Let all humanity be recognized as one human race."[10] The profound impact that Baba Virsa Singh's teaching of unity has on disciples is explored by Major General Sujan Singh Uban, in *The Gurus of India*. There he describes personal meetings with various spiritual masters, including Baba Virsa Singh, whom he calls "the twenty-first Century Prophet." He explains:

> Dr. Arnold Toynbee has said in his debate on religion in the next [twenty-first] century that only that faith will endure which does not divide mankind on the basis of colour, caste, dogma, creed, sex, country or nationality but offers a quality of life which without distinction could be attained and shared by any one equally, all over. Guru Arjan Devji said, "*Sabhe Sanjhi wal sadain / tu kise na dise bahera jeo.*" (All are kinsmen—no one is an outsider. You shower Your grace on all alike.)
>
> Tremendous economic prosperity or intellectual attainments have failed to give satisfaction. On the contrary it

> has had just the reverse effect. . . . There is great hunger, therefore, for a highly satisfying spiritual experience throughout the world. The old shops run by Pandits, Mullahs and Padris are closing, being not in demand. The need is being felt to develop an entirely personal and intimate relationship with God through a system which does not advocate renunciation but active participation in the total activity of life without getting attached too much to it, and also sharing its fruits and joy with others. People are looking for realized souls who can teach through personal example and character and who have that unusual power to transform lives by their mere presence. . . .
>
> Baba Virsa Singh is a great advocate of constant remembrance of the Lord God. . . . His path is devotional. It is love and worship of the Lord, by dwelling upon the Name as enshrined in Guru's revealed Word. . . . The other two basics are hard personal labour to earn an honest livelihood and a life of caring and sharing. What could be simpler?
>
> The results of this become apparent very soon in one's own life. The purpose of one's life becomes clear and the life after seeking His blessings and meticulously following the path becomes interesting and joyful.[11]

Bābāji's instructions for the interfaith community continue to be followed now that he has left his physical body. Accordingly, the holy days of all the prophets are celebrated very enthusiastically at Gobind Sadan, with thousands of lights in the trees, sacred songs, talks about the teachings of each prophet, and big Laṉgars (free communal meals) for everyone. Baba Virsa Singh built sacred places devoted to the *avatāras* of Hinduism, a mosque for Muslim worship, a beautiful garden in which Jesus is lovingly worshipped by people of all religions, *havans* (sacred fire places, built according to ancient Indian tradition), a meditation pavilion devoted to Buddha and Mahavir, and Darbar Sahib where Gurū Granth Sāhib is read around the clock.

So powerful is the spiritual brew at Gobind Sadan, that many government leaders from all parties, scientists, scholars, religious leaders, and businesspeople, as well as working people of all sorts, would come to Gobind Sadan seeking spiritual solace and practical guidance. Surendra Nath, the late governor of Punjab, said of Bābāji, "The greatest problem in the world is solved easily by his words."[12] Bābāji often played the role of a peacemaker, helping to defuse communal tensions and insurgency movements to bring people back to harmony. At the same time, he regularly spoke out against hypocritical leaders of religious institutions, who chased sincere people away from God. Though illiterate, Bābāji habitually quoted from the scriptures of many religions. He told many stories of the prophets and holy people to illustrate the importance of having an inner connection with God, engaging in hard work through honest labor, and dedicating oneself to the service of others. Thus, he continually reiterated the main points of Gurū Nānak's simple path to God. Rather than claiming to be a Gurū in succession to Gurū Nānak and Gurū Gobind Singh, Bābāji said he was just trying to carry on their mission in practical form.

Qualities of the Gurū

The guidance and blessings of a true spiritual master are so important to the Sikh tradition that Gurū Granth Sāhib is filled with passages about the Gurū's greatness. It is the Gurū who gives the essential practice of reciting *Nām,* the precious Name of God—a short phrase that links a person with God. As Gurū Rām Dās said:

> The beneficent True Guru has implanted God's Name
> within me. . . .
> Through the Guru's word and the Guru,
> Love for Him is contracted. (GGS, 172)

Repetition of *Nām* makes a person courageous, fearless, strong, and unattached to worldly impediments; willing to serve others unselfishly; and faithfully devoted to God. Its power derives from its empowerment by the Gurū. Baba Virsa Singh had received the *Nām* "*Ik Ōnkār Sat Nām Srī Wāhe Gurū*" (There is one God, Who is Truth, Supremely Wonderful Teacher, beyond words) in a vision from Bābā Srī Chand and Gurū Nānak, who told him to give it to others. Accordingly, throughout his life Bābāji kept offering this *Nām* as a free spiritual gift to anyone who asked for it. He also authorized a few other people to give *Nām.* Thus, even though Bābā Srī Chand and Gurū Nānak, as well as their devotee Baba Virsa Singh, are no longer physically present, the spiritual transmission of *Ik Ōnkār Sat Nām Srī Wāhe Gurū* continues.

In addition to placing *Nām* in the hearts of devotees, the Gurū is a spokesperson for God. Gurū Gobind Singh said that before he took human birth, he was absorbed in meditation on God's "feet," but God sent him into the world to speak the divine message. In his autobiography, he makes these significant points about what the Gurū is and is not:

> The Timeless, Deathless One said,
> You are my chosen and cherished son
> Whom I have installed for strengthening faith and religion.
> Go down to earth and propagate righteousness
> and guide humankind away from wickedness.
> This is the purpose for which the Lord sent me
> and in consequence I took birth on this earth.
> I shall speak as directed by the Lord
> and shall not bear enmity to anyone.
> But any people who address me as God,
> will be consigned to the cauldron of hell.
> Regard me only as the humble servant of God,
> let there be no doubt or mystery on this score.
> I am the servant of the Supreme Lord,
> come on earth to watch His play.
> I shall utter on earth the word of the Lord,
> and shall not remain silent in this mortal world.[13]

In Sikh tradition, the Gurū is a servant of God, not an incarnation of God. He is an active agent, always working to link people with God. As such, Gurū Nānak likens the spiritual master to a boat that carries a person across the treacherous, stormy ocean of life: "Without the Guru, the world is drowned" (GGS, 138). "[Being proud] a person falls into the dreadful world-ocean. Without the Guru, no one is saved. Remembering the Lord, one is ferried across" (GGS, 1030). Guru Nānak sang:

> Thy Beloved is far off.
> Thou cannot meet Him. There is no boat nor a raft (to ferry thee across). . . .
> The Lord God's palace is beautiful.
> In it are studded stainless gems, rubies, pearls, and diamonds.
> It is a golden fort and is the home of nectar.
> How shall I scale the fortress without a ladder?
> By meditating on God, through the Guru, I shall behold it.
> The Guru is the ladder, the Guru the boat, and the Guru the raft. (GGS, 17)

The Gurū is likened not only to a boat and a raft, but also to water itself—specifically, to an ocean, a sea of wisdom and mercy with no limits. Gurū Nānak said, "The Guru is the ocean, and all his teachings are the river, by bathing wherein greatness is obtained" (GGS, 150). The Gurū is an ocean of jewels that can be reached when one churns the ocean by meditating deeply on the Gurū's inspired teachings. The Gurū is Amritsar, a pool of the ambrosial nectar of God's Name. The Gurū is a *sarovar,* a lake in which holy people swim like swans, eating the Gurū's pearls of wisdom as their food.

In the darkness of human ignorance, the Gurū awakens light. Gurū Rām Dās said, "When the Guru comes and kindles the lamp of the great divine knowledge in darkness, the mortal's attention is fixed on God" (GGS, 172). By the Gurū's effect, the disciple's spiritual vision is cleared, like collyrium put in the eyes. The Gurū is a lamp that illuminates all three worlds—the underworld, this one, and the upper world.

It is only by the spiritual master's grace that one can defeat the five evils: desire, anger, jealousy, attachment, and egotism. Gurū Nānak sang, "I have floored the five youths [wrestled with the five evils] for the Guru has patted me on my back" (GGS, 74). Our mind is like a mad elephant. Those inner evils have such a hold on our emotions and our mind that we cannot free ourselves without the powerful support of the Gurū.

The Gurū is like a mountain of ice, utterly cool emotionally, with no attachments, no enmity toward anyone. "No one now is my enemy, nor is anyone a stranger to me, and I am the friend of all" (GGS, 1299), said Gurū Arjun Dev, who remained calmly, lovingly concentrated on God through days of torture by heat. The Sikh Gurūs devoted themselves to the welfare of humanity, forsaking self-interest and the interests of their own families. Gurū Nānak traveled on four long journeys for twenty years of his life, despite his family's entreaties to come home. Gurū Gobind Singh knew and accepted that his entire family—father, sons, mother, and himself—would have to be sacrificed in the cause of God's mission.

All the Sikh Gurūs were known to have immense spiritual power. For instance, the story is told of Gurū Nānak's visit to the city of Sialkot. The inhabitants were in a panic because of the impending curse of a Muslim *pīr* (spiritual master). That *pīr* had blessed a childless Hindu couple with three sons, on the promise that the first son would be given to him. After the birth of the boys, the father could not bear to relinquish his son. The outraged *pīr* secluded himself in a domed room for forty days and let it be known that he was concentrating all his mental power in order to destroy the whole city. Gurū Nānak, a visitor to the city, sent a messenger to try to change the *pīr*'s mind and predicted that if he did not, God would thwart his threat to the city and end his retreat by noon of that day. The *pīr* did not relent. The Gurū sat under a tree and gazed with half-closed eyes at the dome of the *pīr*'s cell. Precisely at noon, it is said that the dome of the cell cracked with a loud sound, admitting rays of sunlight into the dark chamber, whereupon the *pīr* rushed out lest the dome fall on him.

After the incident, Gurū Nānak then chided the *pīr* for threatening to destroy the whole city over the mistake of one inhabitant. The *pīr* retorted that all the people were liars and should be punished. Gurū Nānak replied that God is love and that God's devotees should love and serve all the children of God, helping them to find the right path. In any case, he said, he could not believe that all the people of the city were spiritually dead. Thus saying, he sent his companion to the marketplace to purchase a *paisa*-worth of what is true and a *paisa*-worth of what is false. All the merchants were baffled by the request, except for one, who wrote on a piece of paper, "Death is true and life is false." Showing it to the *pīr,* Gurū Nānak explained that at least one person in the city was spiritually alive. The *pīr* succumbed to the teaching, bowed before Gurū Nānak, and committed himself to live thenceforth as a missionary for the Merciful, All-Loving God.

By his own great-heartedness, the Gurū is the one who can free disciples from their smallness, and the chain of births and deaths. "Without the Guru, how can there be emancipation? Without the Guru, how can the Lord's Name be meditated upon?" asks Gurū Nānak (GGS, 1041). Gurū Arjun Dev, the Fifth Gurū tells of the impact of a true spiritual master on a devoted disciple:

> He, whose disease of pride is cured by the grace of the Guru,
> Is always healthy and free from all diseases, says Nanak.
> As a pillar supports a house,
> So the Word of the Guru supports the mind.
> As the stone put into a boat swims across
> So the human by clinging to the Guru's feet swims across the world ocean.
> As the lamp throws light in the darkness,
> So a person shines on seeing the Guru.

> As a person finds the way in a great wilderness,
> So does the divine light shine within him when he joins
> the society of the Guru.
> I want the dust of the feet of such a Guru.
> O God: fulfill this desire, says Nanak.[14]

The spiritual lineage of human Sikh Gurūs was completed with the Tenth Master, Gurū Gobind Singh, who passed the guruship to Gurū Granth Sāhib, the holy scripture. The question now arises: How can a Sikh now have a personal relationship with the Gurū? On the one hand, many Sikhs have visionary experiences of the Gurūs. In their dreams, in meditation, and in visions they may experience the presence of one of the Gurūs. The feeling is that the Gurū never dies, but is eternally present. On the other hand, there is Gurū Granth Sāhib, the holy scripture that serves Sikhs as their Eternal Gurū. This mystery is explained by Baba Virsa Singh:

> In reality, what is the Guru? The words of the Master spoken through vision are the Guru. The Word of God passes through the body of the Master. It is the Word which is spiritual. Therefore you can refer to that Word as the Guru.
>
> The Master is respected and people prostrate before him because the Word of God has passed through him. Actually, why do we bow before the Gurus? They are like human beings. But the power of God—which we call *shabd* (the Word) or *gyan* (enlightened wisdom)—has passed through them. The Source from which the Word has come is worshipped, and that body through which it has passed is also worshipped. . . .
>
> Everything in the material world eventually comes to an end, but the Word will never end. The body passes away at a certain point, but the enlightened Word will never end.[15]

Ultimately, the True Gurū—the *Satgurū*—is God. Reverent references to *Satgurū* are found throughout Gurū Granth Sāhib. *Satgurū* may refer to a true spiritual master who can connect a person with God. However, many Sikhs understand this term as referring directly to God, the divine Preceptor. A more obvious reference to God as Gurū appears in the term *Wāhegurū* (Wondrous Gurū, also transliterated as *Vāhigurū*). *Wāhegurū* appears only a few places in Gurū Granth Sāhib, but is often given to Sikhs as the *Nām* (Name of God) that they are to recite over and over in remembrance of God. Thus, the word *Gurū* in Sikh tradition refers not only to a human spiritual master and a holy scripture, but also to God, nearness to whom is the most prized relationship.

The Role of the Gurū

The transformation of devotees is the most striking role of Sikh spiritual masters. In 1699, Gurū Gobind Singh waved his unsheathed sword before the congregated Sikhs and said that times were such that people must give their heads. Many thought him mad and ran away in fear. But slowly, one at a time, five came forward to offer their heads. They were from various levels of society, some of low caste—a warrior, a farmer, a washerman, a barber, and a water carrier. After a frightening drama in which Gurū Gobind Singh took each of the volunteers into a tent and seemingly beheaded them—for the sound of a sword blow was heard and blood flowed from under the tent—he brought them out together, dressed in the same glorious clothing as himself. He called them his Pañj Piāre (Five Beloved Ones) and said to them, "My brethren, you are in my form and I am in yours. He who thinks there is any difference between us errs exceedingly."[16] He baptized them with sweetened water stirred with a double-edged sword (*khaṇḍā*), to symbolize demolition of egotistic pride plus demolition of all barriers of caste, religion, and other social inequalities. Gurū Gobind Singh announced that by this initiation, "They who accept this *amrit* [nectar] shall be changed before your very eyes from jackals into lions, and shall obtain empire in this world and bliss hereafter."[17]

What is more, Gurū Gobind Singh had the Five Beloved Ones administer the same initiation to him, thus demonstrating his equality with them. When others were similarly baptized with *amrit*, all drank from the same bowl—something that caste-, hierarchy-, and contamination-conscious Indians had previously done only with intimate relatives. Gurū Gobind Singh named all the baptized men "Singh," meaning "lion," and all the women "Kaur," meaning "princess." From high to low, all were to be considered social equals. This transformation and empowerment of disciples had already been a hallmark of the Sikh spiritual masters, but Gurū Gobind Singh gave it especially dramatic form when he created the Khālsā. Those who were called Khālsā, according to Gurū Gobind Singh's code of ethics, not only observed strict disciplines such as abstention from drugs and alcohol, but also aimed to renounce anger and criticism. They were to vanquish the five inner evils in themselves, recite *Nām* perpetually, and always stand on the front line against injustice. They were to become *sant-sipāhīs*—combining the devotion and humility of a *sant* with the courage of a *sipāhī* (soldier)—to fearlessly resist evil, face difficulties, and help the poor with no sectarian divisions.

According to Sikh belief, to be transformed by the spiritual master, disciples must offer themselves totally in sacrifice. Halfhearted obedience is of little worth in the Gurū's court. Throughout Gurū Granth Sāhib, the Gurūs emphasize that a person who gives everything—*tān* (body), *mān* (mind) *dhan* (wealth)—to the Gurū wins the Gurū's great blessings and thence has no worry in this world or the next.

When disciples offer themselves fully, completely surrendering the ego, the Gurū takes on all responsibilities for taking care of them and their lineage. If the disciples seek union with God, the Gurū, being God-realized, can give that highest of rewards. The spiritual master becomes for sincere disciples a *paras,* the philosopher's stone that transmutes ordinary metals into gold. However, this process is not a painless one for them. Baba Virsa Singh explains:

> In order to be made into precious jewelry, gold must first be melted in the furnace. A washerman whacks and whacks clothes to clean them. It is not that God treats us unkindly; we are drubbed to cleanse our filth and to purify our mind. The filth will only leave us through constant pounding, pounding, pounding.[18]

Gurūs create tests for disciples that gradually wear down their egos. Recognizing the jewel that lies within the stone, the Gurūs keep cutting away extra material like a diamond cutter. By their vision, the Gurūs know their disciples better than the disciples know themselves, and yet keep forgiving their faults and bringing forth their virtues. Gurūs awaken their disciples from spiritual laziness, insisting on strict practice of meditation, devotions, and recitation of *Nām,* along with hard work in service to others, such that disciples can never become proud of their status or achievements. By personal example as role models, Gurūs teach the combination of immense spiritual power and utter humility. "I am not good and no one is bad," said Gurū Nānak (GGS, 728).

Gurū Aṉgad, the Second Gurū, was renowned for healing such incurable diseases as leprosy. And at the same time, he was so humble that when a proud swami who was jealous of his popularity challenged him to call in the long-overdue monsoon rains, he peacefully replied that rain would come when it was God's will. The swami turned the desperate villagers against Gurū Aṇgad, promising to magically bring the rains if they would drive the Gurū away. In their ignorance, the villagers did so. Gurū Aṇgad left without complaint. No one would give him shelter, so he settled in the forest. The swami's fasting and *mantra*s had no effect; the rains still did not come. When Amar Dās, who later became the Third Gurū, learned of this outrage, he chided the villagers for forsaking the light of the sun for a small lamp. They begged Gurū Aṇgad to return—and he did, to great rejoicing. The rains came.

Under the Gurū's tutelage, under the blessings of his *nazar* (merciful gaze), slowly, slowly, the dross of old *karma*s and self-pride is burned away, and the gold of true God-realization comes forth. Gurū Rām Dās speaks of this transmutation process:

> Hearing the Guru's word with the ears, glass is transformed into gold.
> Uttering the True's Guru's *Nam* with the mouth, poison is transmuted into nectar.
> When the True Guru casts his merciful glance, iron is turned into a jewel.
> When a person utters and reflects upon the Guru's wisdom, stone is turned into emerald.
> Eradicated are the pangs and poverty of those whom the True Guru has made sandal from wood.
> Whosoever touches the True Guru's feet, from beast and ghost he becomes an angelic person. (GGS, 1399)

The Gurū blesses disciples with the feeling of deep love for God. Without meeting the Gurū, human beings might otherwise remain unaware of the existence of the Unseen Power. Gurū Aṇgad sings:

> The Guru is drenched with the nectar,
> He showers handfuls of the nectar through the Holy Word, O King Divine!
> They whose hearts cherish the Guru's Word, ever drink the Nectar of God's Love.
> By the Guru's grace is the Lord attained; ended is all pushing and tossing about.
> The Lord's devotees become the Lord, God;
> Nanak, the Lord and His slave are one.[19]

Gurūs work very subtly, never calling attention to themselves, always referring only to God and their own Gurū as the great Powers at work. They do not reveal their own power outwardly; their disciples get glimpses of it only in dreams or visions. Ignorant people may try to judge the spiritual master's status; they will see nothing or may even draw negative conclusions, because the Gurū has not called them. Historian Giani Ishar Singh Nara tells a story about Gurū Gobind Singh, with the caveat that whereas Sikh Gurūs usually did not reveal miracles, Gurū Gobind Singh had to do so in order to get rid of a yogi's pride in doing magic. This proud yogi used to enchant people by showing miracles such as milking cows who were dry. When he first met Gurū Gobind Singh, the yogi said to him, "You are going around in the world calling yourself a Gurū. If you have any miraculous powers, show them to me; otherwise I cannot be satisfied." The Gurū promised to show him some miracles when he would visit the yogi's home. Later, according to Giani Ishar Singh Nara, Gurū Gobind Singh remembered his promise when he went to Thehri village, where the yogi lived.

At that time the yogi was sitting in meditation. The Gurū took out an arrow from his pouch, touched it to the ground and then to the yogi's head and spoke: "Hukam Nath, speak out your mind, are you alright?" The yogi replied, "My obeisance to Gurū Gobind Singh! I was happy with my power of performing miracles, but now that power has been withdrawn and I am bereft of all my strength."

> The Guru again spoke: "Hukam Nath, do you want to go to some other place? I will show you Delhi or Lahore as you may please and then bring you back here." The yogi recalled all that he had been wishing and boasting of earlier and replied, "All my desires have vanished. You have removed the very essence of my strength and left me like an empty shell."
>
> The Guru took pity on him and said, "You wanted to see miracles from me and you have seen them. Now rest here in peace; you have reaped the fruits of your desires."[20]

Recognizing the Gurū

Because the Sikh Gurūs tended to hide their power, how did Sikhs recognize them? Each Gurū was chosen by his predecessor through an enlightened vision. Some were relatives of the previous Gurū, but some were not. According to Sikh understanding, Gurū Nānak chose Aṉgad rather than either of his sons for the guruship because of his unselfish service. Gurū Aṉgad chose Amar Dās rather than his sons to succeed him because of his humble, selfless *seva* (volunteer service). Amar Dās was in his seventies, but he nonetheless had persisted in bringing jugs of fresh water on his head early every morning for the Gurū's bath. On one wintry morning, there was a cold wind and lightning; rain was imminent, but Amar Dās was still trying to fetch water. As he passed through a weavers' colony, he stubbed his toe on a weaver's loom, whereupon the weaver woke up and started yelling, "Thief, thief!" His wife chided him, "It's only old Amru, the homeless, who carries water for his Gurū daily, early in the morning. He slaves day and night for a good-for-nothing man." When Amar Dās heard his Gurū so insulted, he said, "Woman, you have gone mad!" whereupon she reportedly indeed went mad. According to the story, nothing could cure her madness until at last she was taken to Gurū Aṉgad, who forgave her. He told her, "Amar Das is not homeless; he is the shelter of the unsheltered. He is the strength of the weak and the emancipation of the slave!"[21]

After Gurū Aṉgad announced his choice of Amar Dās to succeed him in the spiritual lineage, the latter humbly went into retreat in his attic in his home at Goindwāl, meditating and praying for the grace and help of God, Gurū Nānak, and Gurū Aṉgad. Meanwhile, Gurū Aṉgad's son Dātū tried to set himself up as the Gurū. When no one came to see him, he reportedly went angrily to Gurū Amar Dās's place and kicked him, accusing him of being a mere servant who was trying to set himself up as a Gurū. The Gurū humbly rubbed Dātū's foot, lest it had been hurt in kicking him. He then left town so that Dātū could be the Gurū if he wanted. Gurū Amar Dās went to his home village, shutting himself in a small room with a notice on the door: "He who opens this door is no Sikh of mine, nor am I his Gurū." Not recognizing Dātū as their Gurū, and longing for Amar Dās, the Sikhs went to Bhāī Buddha, to whom Gurū Aṉgad had confirmed his choice of Amar Dās as his successor, and whose special duty it was to anoint each new Gurū (which he did, up to the sixth). He suggested that Amar Dās's horse would lead them to his hiding place, if they would let her loose. They did so and found his hiding place, but were stopped by the notice on the door. At Bhāī Buddha's suggestion, they entered not by the door but by breaking the back wall. There Bhāī Buddha requested Gurū Amar Dās, "Guru Aṉgad had tied us to your apron; where should we go now if you are not to show us the way?"[22] Deeply moved, the Gurū acquiesced and accepted his duty to the people.

Another crisis over the choice of Gurū arose when Gurū Harkrishan died of smallpox at the age of eight. Before he passed on, he said that his successor would be found in the town of Bābā Bakālā. This was an apparent reference to Gurū Teg Bahādur, fifth son of Gurū Hargobind. Being of a contemplative nature, Gurū Teg Bahādur was living quietly in seclusion in Bābā Bakālā. He continued to do so as the Sikhs looked for their new Gurū. Meanwhile, while some twenty-two would-be Gurūs set themselves up in Bābā Bakālā. The issue was not resolved until a wealthy trader, Bhāī Makhan Singh, came to town looking for the Gurū. When his ship was being threatened by a severe storm, he had prayed and offered to give five hundred gold pieces to the Gurū if he were saved. He reached Delhi after Gurū Harkrishan had died, but was told that his successor would be found in Bābā Bakālā. There he found many Sikhs in confusion, with self-styled *gurūs* abounding and demanding the people's allegiance and offerings. Bhāī Makhan placed two gold pieces in front of each one, but was still not satisfied that he had found the real Gurū. When he at last was told about Teg Bahādur, who was not inclined to meet many people, he placed two gold pieces in front of him as well. The Gurū remarked that he had pledged five hundred gold pieces. Bhāī Makhan Singh clasped his feet with delight and began shouting from the rooftop that he had found the true Gurū. Sikhs rushed to the place and cried, "Long live the Ninth Gurū!" The other pretenders were deserted. The story of Gurū Teg Bahādur shows that hallmarks of a true spiritual master—such as humility, equanimity, and enlightened wisdom—are always eventually recognized.

To publicly acknowledge a chosen Gurū in the spiritual lineage and avoid disputes over leadership, Sikhs gradually developed a symbolic ritual. Firstly, Gurū Nānak had worn a *seli,* a soft woolen cord like those used by Ṣūfīs as a symbol of detachment from worldly concerns. When he passed on the guruship to Gurū Angad, he gave him the *seli* to wear. This same *seli* was passed down to all the successors up to Gurū Hargobind, who preserved it for posterity. Instead, he donned a sword as a symbol of the need of the times after his predecessor, Gurū Arjun Dev, the Fifth Gurū, had been tortured to death under the authority of a misguided Mughal ruler. Sometimes five coins were placed in front of the new Gurū, symbolizing the five elements and also the creation of humans, indicating the Gurū's command over both. Sometimes a coconut was presented, representing the natural world. When Bhāī Buddha installed the third through sixth Gurūs, he put a *tilak* mark on their foreheads, symbolizing blessing in general and accession to the guruship in particular. The seat or *gaddi* of the Gurū became a symbol of his spiritual authority. Despite these powerful ritual symbols, the whole point of guruship in Sikh tradition was to bring forth the noble qualities in disciples rather than to make a show of hierarchy. Gurū Amar Dās said:

Guru's sikh and sikh's Guru, are one and the same
And both propagate Guru's mission.
The *mantra* of the Lord's Name
The Guru enshrines in the sikh's mind,
O Nanak, and he easily meets the Lord. (GGS, 444)

The Gurū-Disciple Relationship

The ideal Sikh is a person who has total faith in the Gurū. Such a person is called a *Gurmukh,* one who always turns his or her face toward his Gurū. This is in contrast to a *Manmukh,* one who is guided by his or her own thinking. Gurū Arjun Dev, the Fifth Gurū, sang that one who has even a glimpse of the Gurū will abandon all sins and find comfort in the Gurū's shelter. Therefore, he advises:

Leave all other cleverness
And attach yourself to the service of such a person.[23]

Gurū Amar Dās, the Third Gurū described the state of the *Gurmukh* in these mystical terms:

Immaculate is the golden body,
which is attached to the True Name of the True Lord.
Through the Guru, it obtains the pure Lord of bright Light,
and its fears and doubts are dispelled.
Nanak, the Gurmukh ever attain peace
and night and day they remain imbued with the love of the Lord. (GGS, 590)

The Sikh's love for the Gurū is based upon his or her profound love for God. One who loves God loves the spiritual master who unites him with God. Gurū Arjun Dev sang:

Let someone unite me with God.
I will cling to his feet,
With my tongue utter sweet words,
And make an offering of my very life. (GGS, 701)

So close is the relationship between God and Gurū in the disciple's mind that Sikhs tend to find them indistinguishable. Gurū Rām Dās, the Fourth Gurū sang, "Eternal and immortal is my True Gurū. He comes not, nor goes he. He himself is the Imperishable Lord Who is contained amongst all" (GGS, 759).

The Gurū's service is difficult, but so highly prized that some Sikhs willingly leave everything in order to serve the spiritual master. In the time of Gurū Gobind Singh, this meant offering their lives to serve in his small, always outnumbered, but exceptionally brave army—which was always under attack because both Hindu and Muslim rulers feared Gurū Gobind Singh's power. Hindu and Muslim armies besieged his citadel at Anandpur until the situation was so hopeless that several hundred Sikhs begged the Gurū's permission to escape with their lives. He told them they could go, on condition that they would write a statement admitting that he was not their Gurū and they were not his Sikhs. When forty of those deserters returned to their homes, the women were ashamed and refused to have anything to do with them. They told the men to either return to serve the Gurū or to stay home and be housewives, while the women would go to fight alongside the Gurū in their place. The forty deserters thus decided to return to Gurū Gobind Singh's service. Though few, they managed to hold off a large army pursuing Gurū Gobind Singh. All of them lost their lives in that battle. As Gurū Gobind Singh toured the battlefield afterward, he blessed each of the fallen, holding their heads in his lap and wiping their faces. When he came to the leader of the group, there was still enough life in his body that he opened his eyes and found his Gurū tenderly holding him. The Gurū asked him if he had any dying wish. Reportedly, the leader of the former deserters said:

> No father, I have seen you. I die for your cause, in your lap, and with your blessings. What else or more could I desire? But father, if you have taken compassion on us here, tear up our disclaimer, the paper on which we wrote, "You are not our Guru, and we are not your Sikhs."[24]

The Gurū not only tore up the disclaimer, but also gave the boon that all forty were saved forever from the chain of births and deaths. He granted them *mukti*, liberation from birth and death; the place where they lay down their lives for the Gurū has henceforth been called Muktsar, the "Pool of Salvation." The other leader of the group was a woman, Mai Bhago. Dressed in men's clothes, she had helped to rally the deserters; she fought alongside them and was wounded. Once she recovered, Gurū Gobind Singh allowed her to remain in his service, dressed like a man. To the end of his life, she was one of the ten sentries who stood around his bed at night to protect him from attack.

The Scripture as Gurū

Since Sikhs had such deep personal devotion to the Gurū, the living embodiment of Gurū Nānak's light—the light of God—what happened when there was no longer any Gurū in human form? How could this intense devotion and surrender be transferred to a book? We do not know and cannot speculate why Gurū Gobind Singh stopped the practice of naming a human successor. We know only that he ordered the Sikhs to henceforth regard the scripture, which had earlier been called "Granth Sāhib" or "Ādi Granth," as "Gurū Granth Sāhib," their revered Gurū. Before his passing, he told them:

> A Sikh who wants to see me should look at the Granth.
>
> One who wishes to talk to me should read the Granth and think over it. One who wishes to listen to my talk should read the Granth and listen to its recitation with attention.
>
> Consider the Granth as my own self, have not the least doubt about it.[25]

Thus, Gurū Granth Sāhib became an object of extreme devotion from that point forward in Sikh tradition. Sikhs never placed their holy scripture on the floor, but rather always on a raised place, usually under a beautiful canopy. Many Sikh families—no matter how poor—devote a separate room of their house to Gurū Granth Sāhib, calling the place *Darbar Sāhib,* "room of the revered court," a reflection of the court of those Gurūs who chose to live in regal style, such as Gurū Gobind Singh. Gurū Granth Sāhib is carefully wrapped in cloths and then in a beautiful outer fabric. Attendants often stand waving *Chaur Sāhib,* or sacred whisk over it, just as attendants used to wave *Chaur Sāhib* over the Gurū in human form. In the morning, Gurū Granth Sāhib is ceremoniously opened at random, and a passage is read from that page as instructions for the family or community. Sikhs are supposed to listen attentively and then contemplate the meaning of that passage as the Gurū's guidance for the day. Often this Hukam (divine order) is written on a blackboard so that anyone who passes by will be reminded of it.

Early every morning and evening, Indian time, many faithful Sikhs around the world also tune in by radio, television, or Internet for the live broadcast of *kīrtan* (singing of hymns from the Gurū Granth Sāhib) and Hukam from Gurū Granth Sāhib enshrined in the Golden Temple in Amritsar, the most revered Sikh holy place. At night, the scripture is closed, wrapped in fabrics, and carried on someone's head, with water sprinkled ahead of it to symbolically purify the way. It is then lovingly placed to rest for the night, as it were, on pillows in a specially constructed "bed." In the winter, it may be covered with a fine quilt so that the Gurū does not become cold. Gurū Granth Sāhib is also consulted for naming children or for important decisions, by the same method of opening at random, after standing in prayer before Gurū Granth Sāhib. The holy scripture also serves as the central affirmation of the Gurū's presence and blessings in a Sikh marriage ceremony. Whereas Hindu couples make four rounds around a sacred fire, Sikh couples circle Gurū Granth Sāhib four times while sacred hymns are recited and sung.

When Gurū Granth Sāhib is treated with such reverence, spiritually sensitive people can palpably feel and even see the glow of Gurū Gobind Singh's presence emanating from the scripture. A striking example of its blessedness occurred in Gobind Sadan's community north of Syracuse, New York, after the traumatic events of September 11, 2001. Misguided and drunken youths set fire to the building that Gobind Sadan devotees had been using for their interfaith gatherings, in the mistaken impression that the turbaned Sikhs were supporters of Osama bin Laden. Miraculously, even though the building was destroyed, Gurū Granth Sāhib—which is made of flammable paper—was totally untouched. Not a single word was damaged.[26] When devotees heard of the fire, their only concern was about Gurū Granth Sāhib. Even though they had a living teacher, that teacher himself continually taught them to revere Gurū Granth Sāhib and Gurū Gobind Singh as their eternal teachers.

As yet, the lineage of human Sikh Gurūs and Gurū Granth Sāhib are little known among non-Sikhs. Perhaps this is because Sikhs do not teach conversion of people away from their own faiths. But they have left us a vast spiritual treasure that may be plumbed in the years to come for authentic spiritual guidance and divine blessings that are freely offered to the whole of humanity.

Notes

1. Puran Singh, *Spirit Born People* (Amritsar: Singh Brothers, 2004), 9–10.

2. Traditional narratives about the life of Gurū Nānak are based on the *Janam Sākhīs*, collections of stories about the Gurū that seem to have been recorded from the late sixteenth century onward.

3. Hereafter, parenthetical citations from Gurū Granth Sāhib are referenced by the abbreviation GGS, followed by the page number on which the passage appears in the holy scripture. Gurū Granth Sāhib is standardized to a

length of exactly 1,430 pages, wherein passages are always found on the same page number regardless of the version. In this chapter, translations from Gurū Granth Sāhib are based on Manmohan Singh, trans., *Sri Guru Granth Sahib: English and Punjabi Translation,* 8 vols., 3rd ed. (Amritsar, India: Shiromani Gurdwara Parbandhak Committee, 1992). Generally, in this chapter, the word *gurū* is capitalized and set in roman typeface (viz., "Gurū") with reference to the Sikh Gurūs in accord with the Sikh custom of distinguishing them from other spiritual masters who might be called *gurū.*

4. Guru Nanak, *Mool Mantra,* in *The Wisdom of Sikhism,* trans. Charanjit K. AjitSingh (Oxford: OneWorld Publications, 2001), 15.

5. Bhai Gurdas, *Varan Bhai Gurdas,* 1.33 qtd. in Max Arthur Macauliffe, *The Sikh Religion: Its Gurus, Sacred Writings, and Authors,* 6 vols. (1909; repr. Delhi: Low Price Publications, 1998), 1:176.

6. Ibid., 1.45 (Guru Angad), in W. Owen Cole and Piara Singh Sambhi, *The Sikhs: Their Religious Beliefs and Practices,* 2nd ed. (Brighton, UK: Sussex Academic Press, 1995), 18.

7. Guru Gobind Singh, *Bachitra Natak,* 199.7–12, in *Sri Dasam Granth Sahib:Text and Translation,* 2 vols., trans. Dr. Jodh Singh and Dr. Dharam Singh (Patiala, India: Heritage Publications, 1999), 1:151–53.

8. Although some twentieth-century Western scholars presented Gurū Nānak himself as drawing ideas from the "Sant tradition" of north India, current scholarship tends to emphasize the independent origins of Sikhism. Professor Gurinder Singh Mann, Kundan Kaur Kapany Chair in Sikh Studies at the University of California, Santa Barbara, argued that W. H. McLeod (1932–2009), the influential scholar of Sikhism from New Zealand, argued in his *Guru Nanak and the Sikh Religion* (Oxford: Clarendon Press, 1968) "that Guru Nanak's writings can be understood within the paradigm of the 'Sant tradition,' which he defines as a synthesis of elements from Vaishnava Bhakti, 'hatha-yoga,' and 'a marginal contribution from Sufism.' [. . .] Within the context of the Guru Granth, it is fair to claim that there is a relative homogeneity of overall beliefs between the writings of the non-Sikh saints and those of Guru Nanak, and this is the reason why these people's compositions appear there in the first place. It is thus true that the compositions of these saints in the Guru Granth carry themes that align with those of Guru Nanak, and since these people came prior to the time of the Guru, it is reasonable to infer that he must have borrowed these ideas from them. But the initial difficulty that McLeod faced in reducing the writing of the non-Sikh saints into 'a coherent system' points to the complexity of their thinking and needs to be taken into consideration when arguing for their mutual influence upon one another.

"We know that the compositions of the non-Sikh saints that appear in the Guru Granth represent an edited version of their literary production and thus reflect what largely suited the Sikh religious and social thinking. [. . .] There is, however, no evidence to support the assumption that Guru Nanak knew or had access to the writings of Kabir or those of the other non-Sikh saints, and the manuscript evidence points toward the compositions of these poets entering the Sikh scriptural text during the period of Guru Amardas." Gurinder Singh Mann, "Guru Nanak's Life and Legacy: An Appraisal," *Journal of Punjab Studies* 17:1–2 (2011): 9–10.

9. Gurdev Singh, in discussion with the author, August 14, 2011.

10. Guru Gobind Singh, *Akal Ustat,* 86, in *Sri Dasam Granth Sahib,* trans. J. Singh and D. Singh; translation modified by Gobind Sadan, provided by the author.

11. Major General S. S. Uban, *The Gurus of India* (New Delhi: Allied Publishers Limited, 1992), 168–69.

12. "Surendra Nath's Praises," in *News from Gobind Sadan,* May 1994, 1.

13. Guru Gobind Singh, "Bachitr Natak," in *Dasam Granth,* as translated by Surendra Nath, introduction to *Jaap Sahib* (New Delhi: Gobind Sadan Publications, 1991), xvi.

14. Guru Arjun Dev, *Sukhmani Sahib,* 15.2–3, in *Guru Granth Sahib,* 282.

15. Baba Virsa Singh, "On the Guru Granth Sahib," *Gobind Sadan Times,* November 1999, International edition, 3.

16. Guru Gobind Singh, qtd. in Macauliffe, *Sikh Religion,* 5: 93.

17. Ibid.

18. Baba Virsa Singh, *Loving God* (New Delhi: Gobind Sadan Institute for Advanced Studies in Comparative Religion, 1995), 42.

19. Salok by the Second Guru (Guru Angad), *Asa di War,* Chant 1–4, in Dr. Santokh Singh, *Translation and Transliteration of Aasaa-Dee-Vaar: Sikh Holy Hymns* (Princeton, Ontario: Institute of Spiritual Studies, 1996), 64; translation modified by Gobind Sadan, provided by the author.

20. Giani Ishar Singh Nara, *Safarnama and Zafarnama,* trans. Joginder Singh (New Delhi: Nara Publications, 1985), 159; originally published in Punjabi as *Safar Nam ate Zafar Nama* (1971).

21. Qtd. in K. S. Duggal, *Sikh Gurus: Their Lives and Teachings* (New Delhi: UBS Publishers' Distributors, 1993), 68.

22. Qtd. in ibid., 76.

23. Guru Arjun Dev, Astpadi 17.10, in *Sukhmani Sahib,* trans. Harbans Singh Doabia (Amritsar: Singh Brothers, 1979), 179.

24. Qtd. in Kartar Singh, *The Story of Guru Gobind Singh* (Delhi: Hemkunt Press, 1983), 86.

25. Guru Gobind Singh, qtd. in Cole and Sambhi, *The Sikhs,* 105.

26. "Scriptures Survive Fire," *Gobind Sadan Times,* February 2002, International edition, 2.

6

Buddhist Spiritual Masters

Victoria Kennick

The Spiritual Master Says, "Work Out Your Salvation with Diligence."

In the novel *Siddhartha,* Herman Hesse explores the paradoxical nature of Buddhist spiritual masters. The book, whose title bears a name attributed to Buddha in his youth, revolves around the key question: What would happen if Prince Siddhārtha, the future Buddha, met the mature, enlightened Gautama Buddha? It makes us wonder whether Siddhārtha would have become a buddha's disciple, had he met one. Buddhist tradition says that Siddhārtha left home to seek enlightenment at the age of twenty-nine, and Hesse suggests that Siddhārtha would have carved out his own path—even *had he met* someone who was fully awakened. Hear these farewell words of the young seeker, spoken as Siddhārtha takes leave of Gautama:

> Not for one moment did I doubt that you were the Buddha, that you have reached the highest goal. . . . You have done so by your own seeking, in your own way, through thought, through meditation, through knowledge, through enlightenment. You have learned nothing through teachings and so I think, O Illustrious One, that nobody finds salvation through teachings. To nobody, O Illustrious One, can you communicate in words and teachings what happened to you in the hour of your enlightenment. The teachings of the enlightened Buddha embrace much, they teach much—how to live righteously, how to avoid evil. But there is one thing that this clear, worthy instruction does not contain; it does not contain the secret of what the Illustrious One himself experienced—he alone among hundreds of thousands. That is what I thought and realized when I heard your teachings. That is why I am going on my way—not to seek another and better doctrine, for I know there is none, but to leave all doctrines and all teachers and to reach my goal alone—or die. But I will often remember this day, O Illustrious One, and this hour when my eyes beheld a holy man.[1]

In this passage, Hesse exposes a paradox central to Buddhist tradition: On one hand, Gautama Buddha stands as the Buddhist spiritual master par excellence. On the other hand, he insisted that each disciple should discover the truth of his teachings personally. Gautama reportedly gave this admonition to disciples as he passed away in north India in the fifth century BCE,[2] a man of eighty years:

> And now, O priests, I take my leave of you; all the constituents of being are transitory; work out your salvation with diligence.[3]

Gautama's injunction "work out your salvation with diligence" indicates that waking up to the nature of reality depends on efforts of the individual, and not on a spiritual master. Walpola Rahula clarifies the point:

> [Buddha] admonished his disciples to "be a refuge to themselves." . . . He taught, encouraged and stimulated each person to develop himself and to work out his own emancipation, for man has the power to liberate himself from all bondage through his own personal effort and intel-

> ligence. The Buddha says: "You should do your work, for the Tathagatas [enlightened beings] only teach the way." If the Buddha is to be called a "savior" at all, it is only in the sense that he discovered and showed the Path to Liberation, Nirvana. But we must tread the Path ourselves.[4]

Regardless of the greatness of a spiritual master, disciples must come to their own realizations. For example, behind Gautama's monastery lived a butcher who was killing pigs for fifty-five days. Gautama heard the pigs squealing every day. Finally, the butcher committed suicide by pouring boiling water into his mouth. Even a buddha could not stop him. The butcher's own habitual performance of the act of killing moved him to do such an atrocious deed—even in the vicinity of a holy person. In a profound sense, as the butcher living next door to the monastery could not be saved by a buddha, no spiritual master can "teach" another person to become enlightened. A buddha's teaching, known as *buddha-dharma,*[5] is like medicine: to become effective, individuals must imbibe it.

Buddhists speak of three ways of taking the medicine of religious teachings: hearing, thinking, and meditating. Hearing or reading *buddha-dharma* is the preliminary level, after which one thinks deeply about what was heard or read. Thinking involves such analytical work as debating (identifying and resolving contradictions), and considering their application in various situations. Finally, for true mastery comes mixing one's mind with *buddha-dharma*. A spiritual master can be involved with disciples in all three activities—but in different capacities. Most obvious are the efforts of a spiritual master to educate disciples on the exoteric level by introducing the teachings, and promoting critical thought. The role of a spiritual master is both most limited and most profound when it comes to helping disciples mix their minds with *buddha-dharma*. Along these lines, Tenzin Gyatso, the fourteenth Dalai Lama notes:

> In my estimation, a general understanding of the framework of the Buddhist path that is common to the Great and Hearer vehicles [viz., all Buddhists] is something that we can develop quite clearly on our own by reading, introspective reflections, and so on. When practicing and developing the realizations of the Great Vehicle [Mahāyāna] path, however, we cannot always take the Great Vehicle sutras literally. There are various levels of meaning—the literal, the interpretable, and the final meaning. There are

> also many differences when we consider the traditions of the different monasteries.[6]

The above statement suggests that a spiritual master is most useful after students have already heard and thought about *buddha-dharma*. Reading and introspective reflections bring understanding that they can "develop quite clearly" on their own. But to go beyond that, generally help is needed. The Dalai Lama correlates each level of activity with a type of meaning: through reading, one gains access to literal meaning, and through introspective reflections one gains access to interpretable meaning. However, final meaning is only appropriated when the mind is mixed with *buddha-dharma*. Penetration into the deepest levels of *buddha-dharma* is harder to develop on one's own. Thus, a teacher is most helpful at the level of final meaning. Yet, as Hesse's Siddhārtha realized, a teacher cannot convey actual realization of the final meaning of *buddha-dharma*. To wake up and see things "as they are" (viz., *tathatā*, thusness), disciples must individually take the medicine of *buddha-dharma* and work out their salvation with diligence. At the deepest level of study, a teacher cannot teach.

Gautama Buddha: The Nonauthoritarian Spiritual Master

When Gautama emerged from his awakening under the Bodhi tree, he fasted and spent seven weeks there, by the Nairañjarā River in the middle Ganges basin of northern India.[7] This newly realized buddha balked at the thought of teaching.

> This Dhamma [Pali; Sanskrit: *dharma*] which I have realized is indeed profound, difficult to perceive, difficult to comprehend, tranquil, exalted, not within the sphere of logic, subtle, and is to be understood by the wise. If I . . . were to teach this Dhamma, the others would not understand me. That will be wearisome to me, that will be tiresome to me. . . . With difficulty have I comprehended [the Dhamma]. There is no need to proclaim it now. This Dhamma is not easily understood by those who are dominated by lust and hatred. The lust-ridden, shrouded in darkness, do not see this Dhamma, which goes against the stream, which is abstruse, profound, difficult to perceive and subtle.[8]

Buddhist tradition considers it fortunate that Gautama was urged to go out and teach by the god Brahmā Sahampati—one of a group of not yet enlightened subtle beings recognized in the Indian spiritual universe. Brahmā Sahampati, who attended Gautama after the awakening, requested the buddha three times to teach *buddha-dharma.* Considering this earnest appeal, Gautama surveyed the world with his buddha vision.

> [He] saw beings with little and much dust in their eyes, with keen and dull intellect, with good and bad characteristics, beings who are easy and beings who are difficult to be taught.[9]

Seeing that some could be taught, Gautama decided to go ahead. In the course of forty-five years between his awakening and the *parinirvāṇa* (passing away), Gautama had much time to teach, as he kept a rigorous schedule, usually sleeping just two hours per day.

Before Gautama adopted this vocation as a teacher, it is said that he felt the impulse to pay reverence to a spiritual master.

> On one occasion soon after his enlightenment, the Buddha was dwelling at the foot of the Ajapāla banyan tree by the bank of the Nerañjarā River. As he was engaged in solitary meditation the following thought arose in his mind: "Painful indeed is it to live without someone to whom to pay reverence and show deference. How if I should live near an ascetic or brahmin respecting and reverencing him?"[10]

Gautama's inclination to respect someone suggests the deeply satisfying role of having a spiritual master. Yet, after considering to whom he should defer, Gautama could not "see in this world any ascetic or brahmin who [was] superior" in emancipation to revere. In the absence of a superior master, Gautama came up with a brilliant solution: "How if I should live respecting and reverencing this very Dhamma which I myself have realized?"[11] This move on the part of Gautama to revere *buddha-dharma* had great implications for the tradition that followed in its name. Among the Three Jewels—*buddha* (awakened one), *dharma* (teachings), and *saṃgha* (spiritual community) in which disciples seek refuge—the *dharma* is called the true refuge, because it is directly experienced. The teachings always stand as the ultimate Buddhist spiritual master.[12]

Gautama discouraged people from naïvely following any of the Three Jewels—that is, himself, his teachings, and the customs of his spiritual community. "He told the bhikkhus that a disciple should examine even the Tathāgata [Buddha] himself, so that he [the disciple] might be fully convinced of the true value of the teacher whom he followed."[13] Gautama used the metaphor of a goldsmith who tests metal to see whether or not it is real gold by biting, scraping, and burning it. Like the smith who probes metal to determine its value, so a buddha's disciples should investigate *buddha-dharma* to determine whether or not the teachings are truthful and worthwhile. When disciples joined the *saṃgha,* Gautama received them with the words *ehi passiko* (Pali; Sanskrit: *ehi paśya*), meaning "come see." Gautama insisted that his disciples verify for themselves his authenticity, the rectitude of his teachings, and the utility of the *saṃgha.*

Once in a small town called Kesaputta (modern-day Kesariya, in Bihar) in the Kingdom of Kosala a group of people known as the Kalamas paid Gautama a visit and told him:

> Sir there are some recluses and brahmanas who visit Kesaputta. They explain and illumine only their own doctrines, and despise, condemn and spurn others' doctrines. Then come other recluses and brahmanas, and they, too, in their turn, explain and illumine only their own doctrines, and despise, condemn and spurn others' doctrines. But, for us, Sir, we have always doubt and perplexity as to who among these venerable recluses and brahmanas spoke the truth, and who spoke falsehood.[14]

In response to this, the Buddha advised:

> Yes, Kalamas, it is proper that you have doubt, that you have perplexity, for a doubt has arisen in a matter which is doubtful. Now, look you Kalamas, do not be led by reports, or tradition, or hearsay. Be not led by the authority of religious texts, nor by mere logic or inference, nor by considering appearances, nor by the delight in speculative opinions, nor by seeming possibilities, nor by the idea: "this is our teacher". But, O Kalamas, when you know for yourselves that certain things are unwholesome (*akusala*), and wrong, and bad, then give them up. . . . And when you know for yourselves that certain things are wholesome (*kusala*) and good, then accept them and follow them.[15]

Here again, we find the paradoxical nature of the Buddhist spiritual master: Gautama admitted that he had become a buddha—that is, he had awakened to reality as it is and was thus emancipated from the cycle of mandatory rebirths. Yet he plainly said that one must not listen to him as an unquestioned authority, merely because he was a buddha. Gautama reluctantly began to teach, but said that people must *ehi paśya*—come see, check out the nature of reality for themselves.

Women Buddhist Spiritual Masters

The tradition of wandering ascetics appears to be very old in Indian society. Reportedly, the young Siddhārtha's first teacher was a woman ascetic.[16] A century or so after Gautama passed away, the Greek traveler, Megasthenes (ca. 350–290 BCE) wrote of female ascetics in India who studied philosophy and abstained from sexual intercourse. The Jains, who lived alongside early Buddhists in the middle Ganges basin, may have been the first in India to establish a role for nuns. But the first concerted body of evidence indicating women's participation in the *pabbajita* (wandering) tradition is the collection of poems written by the Therī, women elders who had realized *buddha-dharma.* Gautama's aunt Mahāprajāpatī, who nurtured him after his mother's early death, became a prominent wandering ascetic. Reportedly, after her husband passed away, she went with five hundred women to Gautama, her sister's son, with the request that he found a *bhikṣuṇī saṃgha* (nun's community). In a mood reminiscent of his initial hesitance to teach, the Buddha agreed to start a nun's order—only after being asked three times.

"In one sense, all of the first Buddhist nuns were disciples of Mahāprajāpatī, as she was the first ordained nun, the founder of the order, and the first woman Buddhist teacher."[17] At least twelve women of Gautama's former harem (an ancient Indian institution of the rich and powerful) were among the many who originally joined Mahāprajāpatī's *bhikṣuṇī saṃgha.* Also among her numerous disciples was Gautama's beautiful looking half-sister, identified by him as the *bhikṣuṇī* foremost in meditative powers.

Normally, when female novices came to Gautama for ordination they had to make a request to both the *bhikṣu saṃgha* and the *bhikṣuṇī saṃgha.* There is record, however, of one woman who was ordained by Gautama himself according to his personal manner of ordination. He would simply say, "*Ehi!*" ("Come!"), and call the entrant by name. Her name was Bhadda Kuṇḍalakesa, and she was an avid debater.

Before her ordination, she had endured an unfortunate marriage and passed a number of subsequent years as a Jain nun. Eventually, she left the Jain order and wandered on her own.

> Whenever Bhadda arrived in a new village her method of announcing her desire to engage in religious debate was to stick a roseapple branch in a pile of sand. The village children kept watch on that branch to see if anyone would challenge her by knocking it down. If the branch withered while she remained at a village, she would procure a fresh one. After years of this kind of "dharma-encounter" Bhadda could find no equal.[18]

Finally, Bhadda was challenged by Sāriputta, one of Gautama's disciples. Reportedly, he defeated her in debate, and she was inspired to join Gautama's *bhikṣuṇī saṃgha*. "Even after her conversion, she seems to have kept her independent, wandering ways."[19] Her poem tells the story:

> I cut my hair and wore the dust,
> And I wandered in my one robe,
> Finding fault where there was none,
> And finding no fault where there was.
> Then I came from my rest one day
> At Vulture Peak
> And saw the pure Buddha
> With his monks.
> I bent my knee,
> Paid homage,
> Pressed my palms together.
> We were face to face.
> "Come, Baddha," he said;
> that was my ordination.
> I have wandered throughout
> Anga and Magadha,
> Vajji, Kasi, and Kosala;
> Fifty-five years with no debt,
> I have enjoyed the alms of these kingdoms.
> A wise lay follower
> Gained a lot of merit;
> He gave a robe to Bhadda
> Who is free from all bonds.[20]

Transmission of *buddha-dharma* was mostly in the hands of monks, but *bhikṣuṇīs* in Gautama's community were permitted to instruct other *bhikṣuṇīs*. Some nuns also assumed the responsibility for running the affairs of their *saṃgha*. Among Gautama's disciples, Therī Dhammadinna was considered to be the most gifted female teacher. One day, she was asked a host questions by her former husband, who had encouraged her to become a *bhikṣuṇī*. After she gave a series of lucid answers, he finally asked about *nirvāṇa*. According to Buddhist scriptures this was Dhammadinna's response:

> "You will never get to the end of your questionings. For in nirvana the higher life merges to find its goal and its consummation."
>
> And she told him that if he wanted to ask further, he should seek out Gautama. This he did, and, when he related the content of his exchange, the Buddha praised Dhammadinna saying, "Dhammadinna possessed learning and great wisdom. Had you asked me, I would have answered exactly as she did. Her answer was correct and you should treasure it accordingly."[21]

Susan Murcott in her study of the *Therīgāthā*, verses of women Buddhist elders, states:

> By virtue of having won his complete approval, Dhammadinna's response was declared *buddhavacana*, "the word of the Buddha." As such it is preserved in a discrete scriptural section of the *Majjhima Nikaya*. This is a rare example of *buddhavacana* uttered by a woman disciple. It indicates an equivalence between the Buddha's wisdom and her own.[22]

Qualities of Buddhist Spiritual Masters

Indian Buddhist commentators established criteria for judging both spiritual masters and disciples. Tibetan commentators inherited this concern for demanding high standards. Their tradition warns disciples to use discrimination to choose a teacher with suitable qualifications. Texts provide specific advice on "how to look for such qualities in a person who is a candidate for one's spiritual teacher;" specifically, Buddhist disciples must discern the mental qualities of the spiritual master "by examining his or her daily behavior, speech, and physical expressions."[23] Asaṅga's *Mahāyānasūtrālamkāra* (ornament for the Mahāyāna *sūtras*), a fifth-century CE Indian Mahāyāna Buddhist text, identifies ten qualities that a teacher should have: (1) moral discipline, which brings calmness, (2) mental quiescence, which brings inner peace, (3) pacification of the ten mental afflictions (*kleśas*): greed, hatred, delusion, conceit, speculative views, doubt, mental sloth, restlessness, shamelessness, and moral carelessness, (4) knowledge far greater than what the student has, (5) enthusiastic effort (*vīrya*) with willingness to teach, not succumbing to mental and physical fatigue, (6) full, rich knowledge of the scriptures, oral traditions, and initiations, (7) either complete intellectual knowledge or full intuitive understanding of emptiness (*śūnyatā*), (8) the skillful means (*upāya*) to explain *buddha-dharma* clearly and intelligently, (9) sincerity and compassion in guiding the disciples, without regard for fame, name, or salary, and (10) patience, with willingness to teach disciples of all levels of intelligence.[24]

The first six qualities are criteria by which to judge teachers. The remaining four bear on the teacher's relationship with disciples—and there is a sense in which compassion for students becomes an overriding factor. The Dalai Lama explains:

> As long as that person has that quality [compassion for students], even a single instruction that the teacher might give will be beneficial to the students. The other nine qualifications are necessary, but compassion is the principal quality required.[25]

The Tibetan yogi Milarepa (1040–1123) underscores this point about his *bla-ma* (Tibetan for *gurū*, spiritual teacher; Anglicized as *lama*):

> To serve a lama without compassion
> Is like worshipping a one-eyed demon;
> He and patron alike will misfortune meet.[26]

Milarepa says that the best remedy for the removal of the misery of life "is to realize the ultimate truth of reality under the direction of an enlightened lama."[27] This realization can begin with a seemingly minute step, as the spiritual master is not above working in tiny increments to lead the disciple. According to Tsongkhapa (1357–1419), to lay the foundation for all further attainments, an excellent teacher encourages students to produce good qualities of mind and reduce mental faults:

> The excellent teacher is the source of all temporary happiness and certain goodness, beginning with the production of a single good quality and the reduction of a single fault in a student's mind and eventually encompassing all the knowledge beyond that.[28]

Qualities of Buddhist Disciples

While disciples test their spiritual masters, the spiritual teachers also test disciples to determine their capacity to learn and grow spiritually. The third-century CE Indian Buddhist scholar Āryadeva sums up three qualities of favorable disciples in this verse from his *Catuḥśataka* (four hundred stanzas):

> It is said that one who is nonpartisan, intelligent, and diligent
> Is a vessel for listening to the teachings.[29]

Buddhists use the metaphor of a vessel to illustrate three additional good qualities of disciples, who should not be like an upside-down pot, a pot with a hole in the bottom, or a dirty pot: (1) Disciples who are close-minded about the religious teachings and practice are like upside-down pots. Such students will not be receptive to their spiritual masters, and thus cannot learn and make progress in spiritual development. (2) Disciples who do not remember what they learn are like pots with holes in the bottom. Thus, although students may learn some teachings, they do not retain the knowledge because the teachings are not contemplated and taken to heart. (3) Disciples who are polluted with wrong motivation for studying and practicing the religious teachings are like dirty pots. These may be students who wish to learn for the sake of fame or reputation, with no sincere interest in their own spiritual development or concern for others.

Buddhist tradition counsels that disciples should be as obedient to their spiritual masters as they would be toward their own fathers. The Dalai Lama emphatically states that such obedience is applicable only in cases where both the *bla-ma* and the student are *fully qualified*. Disciples are not to let their spiritual masters "lead them by the nose."[30] Disciples should avoid nonvirtuous acts, even if nonvirtuous acts are suggested or demanded by their spiritual masters. A *Jātaka* tale of one of Gautama's former lives illustrates the proper attitude for a disciple to take when faced with instructions to commit wrongdoing. Listen to this story.

Once upon a time in ancient India, long before the Buddha was born as Prince Siddhārtha, he was the *brāhmaṇa* (member of the priestly class) student of a *brāhmaṇa* teacher. The *gurū* complained of his financial problems, and asked his disciples to steal for him. The *gurū* justified this theft, claiming that it was virtuous to steal under such circumstances because Brahmā, the creator of the universe is the father of all *brāhmaṇas*. He reasoned that because Brahmā was their father, by extension *brāhmaṇas* actually own all the creations anyway. The *gurū* concluded that if his disciples took something on his behalf, they would actually not be stealing. Hearing of their teacher's plight and his justification for the proposed theft, most of the disciples agreed to steal for their teacher. But this one student remained silent. The teacher asked why he did not acquiesce, and the youth answered, "You, my teacher, have instructed us to steal. But according to the general teaching, stealing is completely improper. Although you have said to do it, it doesn't seem right." The teacher was pleased with this and said:

> I said this in order to test you all. He is the one who has actually understood my teaching. He has not been led foolishly anywhere like the front of a rivulet of water, but has examined what his teacher has said, and made his own determination. He is the best among my students.[31]

The *Jātaka* tale illustrates that both students and spiritual masters must exercise caution in their powerful and potentially disastrous relationship. A bad student would blindly follow egregious instructions, and a bad teacher could seriously mislead unwitting, inattentive, and undiscriminating students. A Tibetan maxim states, "If the fox tries to jump where the lion can jump, the fox will break its spine."[32] This means that disaster will follow when a disciple exercises unintelligent and unquestioned obedience to the spiritual master.

The Tibetan Buddhist Experience of Discipleship

Tibetan Buddhist tradition celebrates the spiritual master's role to the extent that the *bla-ma* is counted as a fourth "Jewel" along with the *buddha, dharma,* and *saṃgha.*[33] Tibetan tales of liberation (Tibetan: *rnam-thars*) often magnify the qualities of disciples to offer them as role models. Milarepa's life story is preeminent among the *rnam-thar* in this regard. It depicts four stages of the master-disciple relationship:

a great yearning to find a teacher, a momentary depth encounter of aesthetic shock with the spiritual master, the long work of a disciple's purification, and recognition of the spiritual master.

Great Yearning

Milarepa developed a force of great yearning after he realized the harmful acts of magic he committed in a family squabble. He felt acute remorse for the destruction he caused through creating a hailstorm, greatly feared the consequences of his acts, and developed an unbearable longing for an opportunity to practice *buddha-dharma* under the guidance of a qualified *bla-ma*. Milarepa became obsessed with the wish to procure corrective teachings, and could only think of how to amend his wrongdoings.

> I was filled with remorse for the evil I had done by magic and hailstorms. My longing for the teachings so obsessed me that I forgot to eat. If I went out, I wanted to stay in. If I stayed in, I wanted to go out. At night sleep escaped me. . . . I asked myself unceasingly, and passionately by what means I might practice the true teachings.[34]

There is a striking resemblance between Milarepa and Sadaprarudita, the "ever-weeping" disciple of the Buddha whose story is told in the *Lotus Sūtra*, a key Mahāyāna Buddhist scripture. Sadaprarudita, likewise filled with self-reproach, describes his intense longing to hear *buddha-dharma*:

> Therefore, O Lord, I used to pass day and night in self-reproach. . . . When I was taking my daily recreation or was walking in woody thickets, when betaking myself to the roots of trees or to mountain caves, I indulged in no other thought but this: "O how I am deluded by vain thoughts!" . . . And when I had perceived thee, so benign and merciful to the world, and was lonely walking to take my daily recreation, I thought: "I am excluded from that inconceivable, unbounded knowledge!" Days and nights, O Lord, I passed always thinking of the same subject.[35]

Notice that in both cases the ultimate spiritual master—the object of longing—is the *buddha-dharma*. A *bla-ma* or a buddha serves as a doorway to the teachings, but ultimately the teaching is the focus of a disciple's yearning. This is consistent with Gautama's reverence for the *buddha-dharma,* in the absence of any superior human master.

Aesthetic Shock

In the absence of great yearning, even if disciples encounter great religious teachers, they are unlikely to recognize the greatness. By contrast, in the presence of great yearning, first encounters with spiritual masters tend to be of unusual intensity. The disciple is awestruck or in some way aesthetically shocked by a glimpse of a long-sought spiritual master. This penetrating experience makes a lasting impression that cements the bond between them. An aesthetic shock might occur as a spiritual master comes in a dream or contemplative vision. The mere hearing about the teacher through a casual mention by a third party can precipitate an aesthetic shock; or a face-to-face encounter could set it off.

In Milarepa's case, just hearing the name "Marpa" made a shocking and indelible impression upon him that increased his already intense yearning for religious teachings. Milarepa was struck with an aesthetic shock of recognition that revolutionized his spiritual career.[36] He said:

> Hardly had I heard the name of Marpa the Translator than I was filled with ineffable happiness. In my joy every hair on my body vibrated. I sobbed with fervent adoration. Locking my whole mind in a single thought, I set out with provisions and a book. Without being distracted by any other thought, I ceaselessly repeated to myself, "When? When will I see the lama face to face?"[37]

Purification

Spiritual masters might appear in the form of animals, ordinary human beings, inanimate objects (such as a broken pot that gave Milarepa a teaching on impermanence), or subtle beings in dreams or meditations. As progress on the spiritual path is made, disciples begin to see their spiritual masters as buddhas, and teachings on *tathatā* in all things. However, before the disciples are purified, the masters tend to appear in much cruder form. For example, when Marpa's Indian teacher, Nāropa was endlessly seeking his *gurū,* Tilopa, he came to a point of utter despair at not finding him. Here again, we see the force of great yearning and its fruit. Just when Nāropa was at an extremely low point of despair, Tilopa appeared, saying:

> You and I have been inseparable like body and shadow from the time you first saw the leprous woman. . . . Many impure visions came because you were defiled through bad karma, therefore I could not be seen.[38]

Geshe Rabten, a contemporary Tibetan Buddhist commented:

> Gurus act as a mirror of your mind. When you see them as having faults, these flaws are projections of cloudy delusions obscuring the pure nature of your own mind and mirror back to you what you must work on and learn about in order to gain liberation.[39]

The form of a spiritual master varies greatly according to the inner level of preparation of the disciple and circumstances of the encounter. Through efforts made by disciples, spiritual masters appear as increasingly pure. There is a saying in the Kagyu lineage, to which Milarepa belonged, about this correlation between the appearance of the spiritual master and the quality of the disciple's perception:

> If you see your Guru as a Buddha you will receive a Buddha's blessing. If you see him as a Bodhisattva, you will receive a Bodhisattva's blessing. If you see him as a siddha you will receive a siddha's blessing. If you see him as an ordinary person—a good spiritual friend—such is the blessing you will receive. If you feel no devotion or reverence for him, you will receive absolutely no blessing.[40]

An initial aesthetic shock in contacting the spiritual master strikes a disciple with an indelible impression. But depending on the heaviness of mental defilements, it may take years of purification before a disciple fully realizes the spiritual master's true nature. The disciple should eventually realize that the master is none other than himself or herself.[41]

Recognizing the Spiritual Master

Eventually, disciples must be weaned from attachment to the outward form of their spiritual master. They take leave, and might eventually become great spiritual masters themselves. Often the disciple does not feel ready to take leave; but an accomplished master knows when to cut the cord, however painful the spiritual surgery might be. For example, after several years with his *bla-ma*, Milarepa was sent away for solitary meditation in caves. Lama Marpa told him to

> go first and meditate in these foreordained sacred places. If you meditate, you will serve your lama, you will show your gratitude to your father and mother, and you will achieve the aims of all sentient beings. If you cannot meditate, there will only be an increase in evil actions during a long life.[42]

Though Milarepa bid farewell, and received his last human blessing from the *bla-ma,* he never lost sight of his beloved Marpa. He was beset with profound sadness on leaving Marpa, knowing they would not meet again in the present life. Yet he had already endured severe trials and tribulations that gave him the confidence to carry out his *bla-ma*'s instructions, no matter how demanding they might be. The prospect of never seeing his spiritual teacher again was terrible for Milarepa.

After many desperate moments while separated from his *bla-ma,* Milarepa learned that Marpa was actually with him. This realization came to Milarepa when he encountered a visionary form of his *bla-ma* in response to an intense, heartfelt longing to be with Marpa. One day, when Milarepa was on the brink of an emotional breakdown—weeping from the grief of separation and petitioning his *bla-ma* for help—Marpa appeared in a vision, riding a lion "on a cluster of rainbow clouds resembling a robe of five colors."[43] As the radiance of the vision increased, Marpa asked his disciple to assess the cause of his despair and great yearning:

> "Great Sorcerer, my son, why with such deep emotion," he asked, "did you call to me so desperately? Why do you struggle so? Have you not an abiding faith in your Guru and Patron Buddha? Does the outer world attract you with disturbing thoughts? . . . Do fear and longing sap your strength? Have you not continuously offered service to the Guru and to the Three Precious Ones above? Have you not dedicated your merits to sentient beings in the Six Realms? . . . No matter what the cause, you may be certain that we will never part. Thus, for the sake of the Dharma and the welfare of sentient beings, continue your meditation."[44]

Milarepa was comforted by the speech of his *bla-ma,* and gradually became accustomed to solitude. He increasingly understood that the spiritual bond with his *bla-ma* would not be broken. He sustained contact with Marpa due to his faith and meditative practice. During some twelve years of strict seclusion, Milarepa never ceased to call upon Marpa and remember his kindness. His songs customarily open with expressions of gratitude, appeals for guidance, and prayers never to be separated from his spiritual master.

Through prayer and tantric visualization the yogi Milarepa maintained a vision of his *bla-ma,* radiating light at the *cakra* (energy center) on the crown of his head. Thus Marpa became Milarepa's constant companion as an extraordinary ornament of his subtle body. Far away from Marpa's abode, Milarepa sang:

> I have finally obtained complete instruction. I will never again have anything to do with profane deeds. I need never be separated from my lama, so long as I can visualize him in meditation above the crown of my head.[45]

Even after Marpa passed away from earthly life, Milarepa felt that his *bla-ma*'s subtle spiritual body (*saṃbhoga-kāya*) continued to offer spiritual guidance. He also realized that Marpa was none other than a buddha with whose formless *dharma* body (*dharma-kāya*) he could identify.

Zen Buddhist Teacher-Student Encounters

Gautama Buddha had pointed to *buddha-dharma* as the embodiment of himself. K. Sri Dhammananda of the Theravadan tradition expounds on this pan-Buddhist idea:

> It is through the practice of Dhamma that the real Buddha can be known. The Buddha has said, "He who *sees* the Dhamma *sees* me." The Dhamma is not a set of teachings for us to accept and believe in, but to try out and *see* for ourselves. Our Enlightened Master himself said: "*Ehipassiko,*" that is, "Come and See!" If we accept the Dhamma as our refuge and guide, we will need no other authority.[46]

On the other side of the Buddhist spectrum, Yasutani-roshi, a spiritual master in the Japanese Zen (Chinese: Chan, Korean: Sŏn, Vietnamese: Thiền) tradition discloses the same point:

> In Buddhism, "Buddha-nature" is an intimate expression and "Dharma-nature" an impersonal one. But whether

> we say Buddha- or Dharma-nature, the substance is the same. One who has become enlightened to the Dharma is a Buddha; hence, Buddha arises from Dharma. The Diamond sutra says that all Buddhas and their enlightenment issue from this Dharma. Dharma, it follows, is the mother of Buddhahood. Actually there is neither mother nor son, for as I have said, it is the same whether you say Buddha or Dharma.[47]

Thus it was that upon passing away, Gautama could veritably instruct disciples to work out their own salvation. He left them with a dharma that was truly indistinguishable from himself, and ultimately from their own *buddha-dharma* minds. At this point the paradox of the Buddhist spiritual master is resolved. The teacher can rightly say: "Work out your salvation with diligence!" Why did Gautama Buddha throw disciples back on themselves with these words? Because in the deepest study, a teacher cannot teach.

At the point of nonduality there is no longer any teacher, and there is no longer any student. When the mind mixes with Gautama's teachings, the teacher is none other than the student—and both are *buddha-dharma.* And while the Tibetan poet Milarepa resolved the separation from his *bla-ma* through tantric meditation, disciples in the Zen Buddhist tradition often realize nonduality through encounter dialogues (Japanese: *kien mondō*) with the spiritual master (Japanese: *rōshi*).

Paradox as the Seed of Nondual Identity

An authentic Zen *rōshi* is one who acts from deep personal experience of the *buddha-dharma* identity.

> In the person of a genuine roshi, able to expound the Buddha's Dharma with a conviction born of his own profound experience of truth, is to be found the embodiment of Zen's wisdom and authority. Such a roshi is a guide and teacher whose spirit-heart-mind is identical with that of all Buddhas and patriarchs, separated though they be by centuries in time. . . . Like sound imprisoned in a record or tape, needing electrical energy and certain devices to reproduce it, so the Heart-mind of the Buddha, entombed in the sutras, needs a living force in the person of an enlightened roshi to re-create it.[48]

One Zen method of recreating the "Heart-mind of the Buddha" is through *kōans*, which are anecdotes derived from the *kien mondō* genre. Encounter dialogues were based on spontaneous interactions with spiritual masters.

> From the appearance of the *Platform Sūtra* in 780 to the beginning of the Song dynasty in 972, the term *classical Chan* refers first and foremost to a particular style of behavior displayed by Chan masters in the course of their interactions with students and other masters. Rather than explaining the Dharma in a straightforward expository language, such masters are depicted as being more inclined to demonstrate it by means of paradoxical replies and inexplicable counterquestions, gestures and physical demonstrations, and even the shocking and painful tactics of shouts and blows.[49]

A number of these paradoxical exchanges were formalized into *kōans*, with the idea that by contemplating them, disciples could gain glimpses of the nonduality that collapses all student-teacher-*buddha-dharma* barriers. Take for example the first *kōan* from the famous *Mumonkan* collection, entitled "Joshu [on the inherent nature of a] dog":[50]

> A monk in all seriousness asked Joshu: "Has a dog Buddha-nature or not?" Joshu retorted "Mu!"

Mu! means "no!" The traditional verse of Mumon's that encapsulates the issue of master Joshu's negative answer to the monk's question goes:

> A dog, Buddha-nature!—
> This is the presentation of the whole, the absolute imperative!
> Once you begin to think "has" or "has not"
> You are as good as dead.[51]

Mumon's own comment on the case of *Mu!* illumines the paradox embedded in *Mu!*

> In the practice of Zen you must pass through the barrier gate [like a toll station] set up by the patriarchs. To realize this wondrous thing called enlightenment, you must cut off all [discriminating] thoughts. . . .

> What then, is this barrier set by the patriarchs? It is Mu, the one barrier of the supreme teaching. Ultimately it is a barrier that is no barrier. One who has passed through it cannot only see Joshu face to face, but can walk hand in hand with the whole line of patriarchs. Indeed, he can, standing eyebrow to eyebrow, hear with the same ears and see with the same eyes.[52]

Yasutani-roshi's contemporary commentary on Mumon's insights makes plain that the spiritual master of Chan Buddhism is none other than *buddha-dharma*. The disciple comes to hear with the same ears, see with the same eyes as every buddha of the spiritual lineage. Master Joshu conveys Gautama's *dharma*, which is none other than *buddha* mind.

> "One who has passed through it cannot only see Joshu face to face . . ." Since we are living in another age, of course we cannot actually see the physical Joshu. To "see Joshu face to face" means to understand his Mind. ". . . can walk hand in hand with the whole line of patriarchs." The line of patriarchs begins with Maha Kashyapa, who succeeded the Buddha, it goes on to Bodhidharma, the twenty-eighth, and continues right up to the present. ". . . eyebrow to eyebrow . . ." is a figure of speech implying great intimacy. ". . . hear with the same ears and see with the same eyes" connotes the ability to look at things from the same viewpoint as the Buddha and Bodhidharma. It implies, of course, that we have clearly grasped the world of enlightenment.[53]

Although Zen encounter dialogues are seed capsules of *buddha* mind, they also dig into everyday life. Paradoxically, the enlightened mind is both rarified and earthy. Monks wandering on alms rounds could easily receive a dog bite. Seeing the dog, they should ask themselves the profound but simple question, "Is a dog Buddha or not?"

> The monk and the dog have been associated in a strange way from the early days of Chan history in China. The koan "Mu!" or "Wu!" which is the "iron bull" given to all the Zen monks to chew thoroughly, is no other than Chao chou's . . . answer to the question: "Is the dog endowed with Buddha-nature?" Even when out in the collecting tour, the monk is accosted by the dog.[54]

Chan tradition uses the image of a hen who pecks the outside of her egg, while the chick pecks from the inside. In this simile, the spiritual master is the hen; the disciple is the chick. The hen alone cannot bring the chick to enlightenment from the darkness of the egg's interior. Likewise, the chick benefits from the hen's focused and powerful, yet gentle help.

> All the roshi's unique skills and compassion come into full play once he senses that the student's mind is ripe, that is, barren of discriminating thoughts and clearly aware—in other words, in a state of absolute oneness—revealed variously in how the student strikes the dokusan bell, how he walks into the dokusan room, how he makes his prostrations, and the way he looks and acts during dokusan. In a variety of ways the roshi will prod and nudge this mind into making its own ultimate leap to awakening.[55]

Joshu shouting *Mu!* was the hen pecking the egg—as was Gautama, silently lifting up a flower in front of Mahākāśyapa.

Chan Spiritual Masters as Role Models

The origin of Chan traces back to a silent sermon in which Gautama Buddha held up a flower. Thereupon, a single disciple, Mahākāśyapa, became enlightened. That Flower Sermon stands as the prototypical encounter dialogue for Chan practitioners, and all subsequent encounter dialogues boil down to the same nondual recognition had by Mahākāśyapa. Yet each teacher-student exchange is embedded—or should we say, encoded—in a specific cultural context.

The story of Huineng (638–713), the sixth Chan patriarch of China's home soil, provides an encounter dialogue embedded in the critical East Asian ethic of filial piety. Hence, this Chan figurehead is offered as a role model of the filial son, in conformity with the core value of a Confucian culture.

> The legendary Huineng depicted in the *Platform Sūtra* is an illiterate layman from the far south of China. His, whose family had been reduced to such poverty that he had been making his living gathering and selling firewood. Although of humble origin, this Huineng is blessed with the highest of all Chinese moral qualities: he is a filial son taking care of his widowed mother. This image of the humble, unas-

> suming paragon is clearly developed from the hagiography previously associated with [the spiritual master] Hongren, who was supposed to have sat in meditation by day and minded the cattle at night. In all these qualities, Huineng is the very antithesis of the highly cultured and socially advantaged monks who dominated the Chinese Buddhist *sangha* at the time.[56]

The presentation of spiritual masters as embodiments of filial piety are seen throughout Chinese culture, be it Buddhist, Confucian, or Daoist. The primary impact of the *Platform Sūtra* was felt through the "image [of Huineng] rather than through doctrines per se,"[57] or even through his actual status in Chinese society—and a key part of that image is the filial piety of Huineng.

The story of Huineng from the *Platform Sūtra,* is a microcosm of Chan Buddhist values and teachings. Beyond establishing a role model for filial piety, it gave a quintessential illustration of the depth of the Chan master-disciple connection. Here, Huineng tells of his first encounter with the Chan master Hongren:

> Good friends, listen quietly. . . . While I was still a child, my father died and my old mother and I, a solitary child, moved to Nan-Hai. We suffered extreme poverty and here I sold firewood in the market place. By chance a certain man bought some firewood and then took me with him to the lodging house for officials. He took the firewood and left. Having received my money and turning towards the front gate, I happened to see another man who was reciting the Diamond Sutra. Upon hearing it my mind became clear and I was awakened.
>
> I asked him: "Where do you come from that you have brought this sutra with you?"
>
> He answered: "I have made obeisance to the Fifth Patriarch, Hung-jen, at the East Mountain."
>
> Hearing what he said, I realized that I was predestined to have heard him. Then I took leave of my mother and went to [East Mountain] . . . and made obeisance to the Fifth Patriarch. . . .
>
> [Hung-jen asked me]: "Where are you from that you come to this mountain to make obeisance to me? Just what is it that you are looking for from me?"
>
> I replied: "I am from Ling-nan, a commoner from Hsin-chou. I have come this long distance only to make

> obeisance to you. I am seeking no particular thing, but only the Buddhadharma [or only to become a Buddha]."
>
> The Master then reproved me, saying: "If you're from Ling-nan then you're a barbarian. How can you become a Buddha?"
>
> I replied: "Although people from the south and people from the north differ, there is no north and south in Buddha nature."[58]

Thus, the *Platform Sūtra* teaches devotion to both biological and spiritual lineages. This twin relationship to family and spiritual master grows from the Confucian soil of social responsibility, so important to Chan ethics. The story is so rich that its cultural bed supports universal Buddhist teachings and profound insights into human nature. On the side of Buddhist teachings is the paradoxical conundrum that caps Huineng's story: "there is no north and south in Buddha nature." This strikes the nonduality of *buddha-dharma*. On the side of human nature, the *Platform Sūtra* exposes Huineng's great yearning to connect with a spiritual master and the *buddha-dharma*—a yearning seen in Sadaprarudita, Milarepa, and even Gautama Buddha himself, whose thought after awakening was to find someone to revere.

Contemporary Buddhist Role Models

"Engaged Buddhism" is a term coined by the Vietnamese Thiền master, Thich Nhat Hanh, with reference to socially responsible Buddhist practice. These days, among Buddhist spiritual masters there is a trend toward social engagement that reaches across the Buddhist cultural spectrum. Those who are engaged Buddhists serve as strong role models for the application of Buddhist ethics in the twenty-first century.

Theravadan Social Engagement

Ayya Khema (1923–1997) was among the first women to be fully ordained in the Theravadan tradition. Born in Germany to Jewish parents, she escaped the Nazis in a group of some two hundred children, and wound up with her family in a Japanese prisoner of war camp during World War II. Ilse Ledermann became a wife and mother of two children, traveled widely, and in her mid-fifties became a *bhikṣuṇī* at a time (1979) when becoming a Western nun was still a very rare feat. Under the name Ayya Khema, she worked through obstacles to pave the way for other women by helping to establish forest monasteries in Australia and Germany; forming the International Women's Buddhist Center in Sri Lanka; coordinating the first International Conference of Buddhist Nuns, from which issued "Sakyadhita," a global Buddhist women's association; and writing more than two dozen books on *buddha-dharma,* with a focus on meditation. She provided immense moral support for women pathfinders and ordained several of them into the *bhikṣuṇī saṃgha.*

Indo-Tibetan Social Engagement

Tenzin Gyatso (b. 1935), the fourteenth Dalai Lama, was awarded the Nobel Peace Prize in 1989 based on his work for a nonviolent solution to the problem of China's occupation of the Tibetan cultural region, and Five Point Peace Plan that called for Tibet to be a "zone of peace." On March 10, 2011 the Dalai Lama relinquished his role as a political leader of the Tibetan people. This was a remarkable act in the context of the "Arab Spring," a revolutionary sociopolitical movement, sparked by the self-immolation of a Tunisian vegetable vendor on December 17, 2010, in which people across large swaths of the Arab culture zone took to the streets, demanding that their leaders step down.[59] Tenzin Gyatso—not an Arab leader—stands as a Buddhist role model, showing nonattachment to political power.

The Dalai Lama champions the right of a woman to receive full Buddhist ordination. His adamant support of women's rights will help Buddhists to revive the *bhikṣuṇī saṃgha,* an institution that had become nearly defunct around the globe due to crippling lineage breaks. In 2007, he addressed representatives from nineteen countries, gathered at the University of Hamburg to discuss the possibilities for full ordination of women in the Tibetan Buddhist tradition, as follows:

> The Buddha taught a path to enlightenment and liberation from suffering for all sentient beings and people in every walk of life, to women as well as men, without discriminating class, race, nationality, or social background. For those individuals who wished to dedicate themselves fully to the practice of his teachings, he established a monastic order that included both a Bhikshu Sangha (an order of monks) and a Bhikshuni Sangha (an order of nuns). The Buddhist monastic order has thrived throughout Asia ever since and has been essential for the development of Buddhism in all its various dimensions—in the fields of philosophy,

> meditation, ethics, religious ritual, education, culture, and social transformation.[60]

Tenzin Gyatso noted that a *saṃgha* for monks is found in almost all Buddhist countries, while a *saṃgha* for nuns is limited to a few—some of which are incomplete, as in Tibetan traditions. He argued that as modern women are thoroughly involved in secular vocations, they should likewise have full access to religious activities available to men "by receiving a spiritual education and training, by serving as role-models, and contributing to the well-being of society."[61]

> Full ordination will enable nuns to pursue their aims wholeheartedly by learning, contemplating, and meditating [viz., appropriating *buddha-dharma* on all three levels]. It will enhance their opportunities to benefit society in research, teaching, counselling, and other activities that help disseminate the Buddhadharma. With these thoughts in mind and having carried out extensive research and consulted leading Vinaya and Tibetan scholars around the world—backed by all members of the Tibetan traditions since the 1960s—I express my full support for the establishment of the Bhikshuni Sangha in Tibetan Buddhism.[62]

The Dalai Lama thereby recognized as fully ordained the nuns in the Tibetan traditions "who have received full Bhikshuni ordination according to the Dharmagupta lineage."[63]

Thiền Social Engagement

Thich Nhat Hanh (b. 1926), known to disciples as Thây, is a Vietnamese Thiền monk who lived through the crisis of the Vietnam War. He founded the School of Youth Social Service in Saigon, whose mission in the thick of war was to rebuild villages and resettle families, as well as run schools, medical centers, and agricultural cooperatives. He also founded the Van Hanh Buddhist University in Saigon; the Unified Buddhist Church in France; and Plumb Village, the monastic and lay retreat center in France dedicated to promoting peace and healing where Thây is now based. In the spirit of engaged Buddhism, he developed retreats for Vietnam War veterans and is fond of teaching children.

Thây posts a caption on the Plum Village home page that says, "Breathe, you are online." This is just one among many simple teachings that encourage disciples to mix the mind with *buddha-dharma.*

The nudge to make a sudden connection between everyday life and an awakened mind is characteristic of the Thiền (Chan) tradition to which he belongs. For Thây, profound Buddhist practice is as direct as answering the telephone with a smile or "deep listening" to someone. This deep listening is among the most profound teachings of engaged Buddhism today, with applications stemming from personal relationships to international relations. In the following interview transcript, Thich Nhan Hanh speaks of the practice in response to Anne A. Simpkinson, who asked what he might have said to Osama bin Laden after the 9/11 attacks:

> If I were given the opportunity to be face to face with Osama bin Laden, the first thing I would do is listen. I would try to understand why he had acted in that cruel way. I would try to understand all of the suffering that had led him to violence. It might not be easy to listen in that way, so I would have to remain calm and lucid. I would need several friends with me, who are strong in the practice of deep listening, listening without reacting, without judging and blaming. In this way, an atmosphere of support would be created with this person and those connected so that they could share completely, trust that they are really being heard.
>
> After listening for some time, we might need to take a break to allow what has been said to enter into our consciousness. Only when we felt calm and lucid would we respond. We would respond point by point to what had been said. We would respond gently but firmly in such a way to help them to discover their own misunderstandings so that they will stop violent acts from their own will.[64]

Conclusion

An ethos of equal opportunity for participants in *buddha-dharma* is manifesting in contemporary Buddhist institutions—as intended by Gautama Buddha. This comes in the form of a strong representation of laymen and laywomen in the *saṃgha,* as well as in a growing *bhikṣuṇī saṃgha*. With a vital fourfold *saṃgha* of monks, nuns, laymen, and laywomen, the Buddhist tradition is coming full circle. Yet, this abundance of opportunity comes with the multiplication of exotic cultural displays that have nothing to do with *buddha-dharma*. The situation, thus, brings an acute need for disciples to discern who is an authentic spiritual master. Theravada monk K. Sri Dhammananda advises:

> One must try to follow the guidelines given by the Buddha without mistaking cultural traditions for the Dhamma. . . . Devotees should guard themselves against being emotionally manipulated by various individuals and groups who try to win converts or to gain some personal benefit. We must develop confidence in the Dhamma which shows the way to cultivate ourselves to the highest level by practicing all the good qualities and avoiding human weaknesses. . . . The best advice that we can give to beginners who have problems choosing which tradition to follow is to study the basic teachings of the Buddha first-hand before they attempt to follow any religious master from a particular school of Buddhism.[65]

Now, finding "the basic teachings of the Buddha" is not always easy because *buddha-dharma* comes filtered through the lens of culture. At the levels of hearing and thinking the variation is great—as seen in the wide variation of Theravada, Indo-Tibetan, and Chan material presented in this chapter. In accord with historical circumstances, these first two ways of taking *buddha-dharma* medicine are modified by cultural imprints.

Despite inevitable cultural modulations, the activities of authentic Buddhist spiritual masters of any time and place should reflect a deep realization of *tathatā*—thusness—things just as they are. This profound Buddhist insight into *tathatā* at the core of Gautama's teaching was the basis of his nonauthoritarianism, which stands as the touchstone for evaluating the authenticity of Buddhist spiritual masters. This is because at the deepest level of mixing the mind with *buddha-dharma*, buddha is not the property of anyone, and no authority can either take it from anyone or give it to anyone.

Notes

1. Herman Hesse, *Siddhartha*, trans. Hilda Rosner (New York: Bantam Books, 1981), 33–34. According to Buddhist tradition, Gautama had, in the hoary past, prostrated at the feet of the previous buddha, and determined

that he would follow the *buddha-dharma*. He proceeded to practice the perfections of patience, morality, effort, etc. for aeons, and thus work out his own salvation.

2. Dates for the birth and death of Gautama the Buddha have been under review by scholars; and despite some difference of opinion, it appears safe to locate the time of his passing in the fifth century BCE. In his review of *The Dating of the Historical Buddha, Die Datierung des Historischen Buddha, ed. Heinz Bechert, 2 vols (of 3),* L. S. Cousins concluded: "From the point of view of reasonable probability the evidence seems to favour some kind of median chronology and we should no doubt speak of a date for the Buddha's Mahāparinibbāna of *c.* 400 B.C.—I choose the round number deliberately to indicate that the margins are rather loose." "The Dating of the Historical Buddha: A Review Article," *Journal of the Royal Asiatic Society,* 3rd series, 6, no.1 (April 1996): 63, http://www.jstor.org/stable/25183119. Paul Dundas states, "A re-examination of early Buddhist historical material . . . necessitates a redating of the Buddha's death to between 411 and 400 BCE." *The Jains,* 2nd ed. (London: Routledge, 2002), 24. For more on the murky problem of Gautama's dates, see the fifteen articles gathered in A. K. Narain, ed., *The Date of the Historical Śākyamuni Buddha* (Delhi: B. R. Publishing Corp., 2003).

3. Henry Clarke Warren, *Buddhism in Translations* (Delhi: Motilal Banasidass Publishers Pvt. Ltd., 1992), 109. Walpola Rahula translates this as: "Then, Bhikkhus, I address you now: Transient are conditioned things. Try to accomplish your aim with diligence." *What the Buddha Taught* (New York: Grove Press, 1974), 138.

4. Rahula, *What the Buddha Taught,* 1–2.

5. *Buddha-dharma* is a Sanskrit term. South Asian Buddhist scriptures are written in two languages, Pali and Sanskrit. Terms in this chapter are given in Sanskrit, unless in a direct quotation or otherwise noted. The Theravāda (Sanskrit: Sthaviravāda) tradition of South Asia has a Buddhist canon preserved in Pali, while India's Mahāyāna tradition recorded theirs in Sanskrit. Subsequently, in the course of Buddhist history, the scriptures were translated into other languages, including Chinese, Tibetan—now coming more fully into English. Gautama himself probably spoke Māgadhī Prakrit, a language of the Magadha kingdom.

6. Tenzin Gyatso (Dalai Lama), *Snow Lion Newsletter and Catalog* 12, no.4 (Fall 1997) (Ithaca, NY: Snow Lion Publications), 1.

7. Tradition states that the first week after awakening Gautama sat in a single posture under what later became known as the Bodhi tree in the bliss of emancipation; the second week, he stood before the same tree with motionless eyes; the third week, he paced up and down a jeweled staircase created by psychic powers; the fourth week, he dwelled in a jeweled chamber pondering the higher teachings and emanating six rays of colored light from his body; the fifth week, he sat in one posture by the nearby Ajapala Banyan tree in the bliss of emancipation, spoke for the first time (to a *brāhmaṇa*), and withstood temptations of Mara's daughters; the sixth week, he sat under the Mucalinda tree in the bliss of emancipation, sheltered from cold winds and rain by a serpent who coiled around him seven times. He then gave spiritual

refuge to the serpent king who took on the guise of a boy; the seventh week after enlightenment, he again sat in the bliss of emancipation—this time under the Rajayatana tree.

8. Mahathera Narada, *Buddha and His Teachings,* 2nd, rev. ed. (Kandy, Sri Lanka: Buddhist Publication Society, 1988), 35.

9. Ibid., 36.

10. Ibid., 33.

11. Ibid., 34.

12. Buddhists teach that Gautama had more than one body (*kāya*). The theory of two or three buddha bodies (*buddha-kāya*) found among various branches of Buddhism supports this view. The historical body (*nirmāna-kāya*) of a buddha can be seen by some, and a visionary buddha body (*saṃbhoga-kāya*) can be seen by some. But one never truly sees a buddha until one actualizes in himself or herself the buddha mentality, which is the formless subtle body of the teachings (*dharma-kāya*).

13. Rahula, *What the Buddha Taught,* 3. Although Buddhist schools normally link themselves to the Buddha through an unbroken spiritual lineage, Gautama named no successor when he passed away.

14. Ibid., 2.

15. Ibid., 2–3.

16. Susan Murcott, *First Buddhist Women* (Berkeley: Parallax Press, 1991), 41. Feminine gender terms in Sanskrit and Pali for unconventional Buddhist women of ancient India include: *manavika* (student in an ascetic order), *samani* (renunciate), *cariki* (wanderer), *brahmacarini* (student under brahmanism), *sikkhamana* (probationary Buddhist), *bhikkhuni* (Buddhist nun who completed twelve years in the order), *therī* (Buddhist elder), *paribbajika* (ascetic), *molibaddha-paribbajjika* (ascetic who has her hair bound in a top knot), and *komara-brahmacariya* (woman who practices the vow of celibacy).

17. Ibid., 19.

18. Ibid., 45.

19. Ibid., 46.

20. Ibid., 46–47.

21. Ibid., 63. Dhammadinna's discourses are preserved in the *Culla Vedalla Sutta* section of the *Majjhima Nikaya* (Middle length sayings) of the Buddhist Pali canon.

22. Ibid., 63.

23. Gyatso, *Snow Lion Newsletter,* 8. The Dalai Lama summarizes the nature and importance of these criteria: "Since reliance on a lama is a very important factor in spiritual practice, there are detailed presentations of the qualifications that are necessary for such teachers. . . . The import of doing this is to emphasize the point that the spiritual teacher should be someone who will not mislead the students. Particularly, in tantric practice it is explained that the lama and disciple should examine each other for up to twelve years before adopting a teacher-disciple relationship" (Ibid.).

24. The ten qualities of a spiritual master are reduced to three categories: mental purification, religious experience, and favorable relationship to disciples. Mental purification pertains to moral discipline and pacification of

the *kleśas* (negative emotions); religious experience includes rich knowledge of scriptural texts, accomplishment in the two branches of meditation (viz., quiescence and special insight), and energetic enthusiasm for religious practice. Favorable relationship to disciples involves having more knowledge than the disciple, the ability to express oneself well and clearly explain the teachings, and compassionate motivation to teach disciples of all levels of intelligence. See Tsongkhapa, *The Great Treatise on the Stages of the Path to Enlightenment,* comp. Joshua W. C. Cutler, ed. Guy Newland, trans. The Lamrim Chenmo Translation Committee (Ithaca, NY: Snow Lion Publications, 2000) 1:70–71. Regarding communicative skill, Asaṅga says that a teacher's preaching should be "sweet, free of conceit, without fatigue (sadness) . . . gentle, clear (intelligible), spreading among people, pure, without allurement . . . without bait . . . and heard." Asaṅga, *Mahāyānasūtrālamkāra,* trans. Surekha Vijay Limaye (Delhi: Sri Satguru Publications, 1992), 228–29.

25. Gyatso, *Snow Lion Newsletter,* 8.

26. Garma C. C. Chang, trans. *The Hundred Thousand Songs of Milarepa,* 2 vols. (Secaucus, NJ: University Books, 1962), 2: 559. On the *bla-ma* as *gurū,* see note 33.

27. Lobsang P. Lhalungpa, trans., *Life of Milarepa* (New York: E. P. Dutton, 1977), 163.

28. Tsongkhapa, *Great Treatise,* 70.

29. Āryadeva qtd. in Tsongkhapa, *Great Treatise,* 75. These three qualities can be explained as follows: (1) Disciples should be upright, meaning to be unbiased in consideration of friends and enemies, and honest, with no attempt to gain something for oneself based upon special influences and privileges. (2) Disciples should possess intelligence, meaning they should have the ability to understand the subject and exercise discriminative powers of analysis. (3) Disciples should take interest and care in what they do, meaning they should not be careless, sloppy, and forgetful.

30. Gyatso, *Snow Lion Newsletter,* 8.

31. Ibid.

32. Ibid., 15. Some Tibetan spiritual biographies present radical examples of the teacher-disciple relationship in which a disciple does whatever the teacher orders. Such appears to be the case of Nāropa with his teacher Tilopa. However, one must keep in mind that Nāropa was a preeminent Buddhist scholar before he took up tantric yoga, and his story is an esoteric teaching for highly qualified students and disciples. On the surface level as a popular tale, Nāropa's spiritual biography teaches the positive quality of devotion to a religious quest.

33. Tibetan Buddhists added the spiritual master to the formulaic Three Jewels of the Refuge prayer. Thus, the central prayer that initiates any Tibetan Buddhist meditation or ritual session involves taking "refuge" in the *bla-ma* or *gurū,* in addition to the *buddha* (awakened one), *dharma* (teachings), and *saṃgha* (spiritual community). The *bla-ma* is beloved by Tibetans for introducing them to the *buddha-dharma.* Yet the teachings always remain the actual object of Refuge. Tibetans translate *gurū,* the basic Sanskrit term for spiritual

master, as *bla-ma* (pronounced *laa-mah*). *Bla* means a condition that is above or higher than something else; thus, *bla-ma* means the higher one, hence an upper monk. *Bla-ma* can be applied loosely to all fully qualified members of a monastery—but more correctly to the head monk, chief teacher, or learned monks.

34. Lhalungpa, *Life of Milarepa,* 41.

35. H. Kern, trans., *Saddharma-Pundarika, or the Lotus of the True Law* (New York: Dover, 1963), 61–62. On Sadaprarudita see also Conze, Edward, trans., *The Perfection of Wisdom in Eight Thousand Lines and Its Verse Summary* (Bolinans: Four Seasons Foundation, 1973), 294–97.

36. On "aesthetic shock" see Ananda Kentish Coomaraswamy, *Christian and Oriental Philosophy of Art* (New York: Dover Publications, 1956).

37. Lhalungpa, *Life of Milarepa,* 43.

38. Freidrich Wilhelm, *Prufund Und Initiation im Buche Pausya und in der Biographie Des Naropa* (Wiesbaden: Otto Harrassowitz, 1965), 70–71. (Passage translated by Elsie Becherer for the author.)

39. Geshe Rabten and Geshe Ngawang Dhargyay, *Advice from the Spiritual Friend: Tibetan Teachings on Buddhist Thought and Transformation* (New Delhi: Publications for Wisdom Culture, 1977), xvi.

40. Jamgon Kongtrul, *The Torch of Certainty,* trans. Judith Hanson (Boston: Shambhala Publications, 1977), 128.

41. This is the lesson of the Ṣūfī tale, *Mantiq-ut-tayr,* a classic of Persian mysticism. The story goes that a flock of birds set out with great longing to find the king of birds, called Simurg, meaning "thirty birds." After devastating trials and tribulations, only thirty birds make it to their destination where "the Sun celestial began to shine forth in front of them, and lo! how great was their surprise! In the reflection of their faces these thirty birds of the earth beheld the face of the Celestial Simurg. When they cast furtive glances towards the Simurg, they perceived that the Simurg was no other than those self-same thirty birds." R. P. Masani, *Conference of the Birds, A Sufi Allegory: Being an Abridged Version of Farid-ud-din Attar's Mantiq-ut-tayr* (New Delhi: Asian Educational Services, 2003), 118.

42. Lhalungpa, *Life of Milarepa,* 94.

43. Chang, *Hundred Thousand Songs,* 1:3.

44. Ibid., 3–4.

45. Lhalungpa, *Life of Milarepa,* 100.

46. Dhammananda, *Practical Buddhism* (Taipei, Taiwan: Corporate Body of the Buddha Educational Foundation, 1987), 43–44.

47. Yasutani-roshi quoted in Philip Kapleau, *Three Pillars of Zen* (Garden City, NY: Anchor Press, 1980), 78.

48. Kapleau, *Three Pillars,* 95–96.

49. John R. McRae, *Seeing Through Zen: Encounter, Transformation, and Genealogy in Chinese Chan Buddhism* (Berkeley: University of California Press, 2003), 76. McRae notes that "written transcriptions of encounter dialogue do not appear until the compilation of the *Anthology of the Patriarchal Hall* in 952—around a century and a half after encounter dialogue was supposedly first

practiced" (79). They are a genre unto themselves, consisting of a core story that is presented as having actually happened. "I must emphasize that these qualities of apparent historical realism are literary effects, characteristics of the genre, and not facts about the dialogues and their participants. . . . Whether or not the dialogues ever happened the way they are recorded is of course highly questionable." The point is that the anecdotes were paradoxical seeds intended to elicit flashes of insight. Teachers and students improvised on them, coming up with their own views. "The issue of whether or not animals possessed the Buddha-nature, the potentiality or actual presence of enlightenment within the ordinary psychology of illusion, was in fact hotly debated in late-eighth and ninth-century Chinese Buddhism" (75).

50. Kapleau, *Three Pillars,* 76.

51. Ibid., 77.

52. Ibid.

53. Ibid., 83.

54. Daisetz Teitaro Suzuki, *Training of a Zen Buddhist Monk* (New York: Cosimo Classics, 2007), 26.

55. Kapleau, *Three Pillars,* 97.

56. McRae, *Seeing Through Zen,* 68.

57. Ibid.

58. Philip B.Yampolsky, trans., *Platform Sutra of the Sixth Patriarch* (New York: Columbia University Press, 1967), 126–27. See also John R. McRae, trans., *The Platform Sutra of the Sixth Patriarch* (Berkeley: Numata Center for Buddhist Translation and Research), 27–28. Here is the core of Huineng's account: "On my way out [of] the gate I saw someone reciting a sutra, and as soon as I heard the words of the sutra my mind opened forth in enlightenment. I then asked the person what sutra he was reciting, and he said, '*The Diamond Sutra.*' . . . My hearing this was through a karmic connection from the past" (28).

59. See interactive timeline of events of the Arab Spring, accessed September 15, 2011, http://www.guardian.co.uk/world/interactive/2011/mar/22/middle-east-protest-interactive-timeline.

60. Tenzin Gyatso, "His Holiness the XIVth Dalai Lama: Full Ordination of Women in Tibetan Buddhism," accessed September 15, 2011, http://www.Rinpoche.com/teachings/hhdlwomen.htm.

61. Ibid.

62. Ibid.

63. Ibid. Full ordination of women is controversial in Tibetan Buddhist tradition, but even more so in countries where Theravadan tradition prevails. In September 2009 the ordination of Buddhist nuns in Perth, Australia was conducted with a controversial result. A prominent, American-born Theravadan monk and scholar, Bhikkhu Bodhi, who attended the 2007 Hamburg Conference at which the Dalai Lama spoke, publicly stands in support of full Theravadan ordination of women. Yet he sees the potential schism among members of the Bhikkhu *saṃgha* precipitated by such progressive actions. Here is an excerpt of one of two letters he wrote to Ajahn Sujato in Perth,

Australia, about the controversial full Theravadan bhikkhuni ordination. Bhikkhu Bodhi's first letter, dated November 3, 2009 (of which the following is an extract), lent full support, while a second letter, issued three days later, retracted a measure of his support—not, however, in contradiction to the following statement:

Though the conservatives in the Sangha will balk and attempt to create obstructions, the movement towards the full emergence of a Theravada Bhikkhuni [nuns] Sangha is now, I believe, inevitable in all the countries with major Theravadin constituencies. I remember in the early 1980s, and even the 1990s, how we were all convinced the rejuvenation of a Bhikkhuni Sangha was a legal impossibility. Yet, as Bob Dylan used to sing, "the times they are a-changin." Sri Lanka already has a strong Bhikkhuni Sangha, which, however, has not yet been officially acknowledged by the Government or the chief authorities in the Bhikkhu Sangha. The buds of a Bhikkhuni Sangha have been quietly germinating in Thailand, right beneath the noses of the Chao Khuns and Phra Khrus, though they try not to—or pretend not to—notice it. It is likely that women in the other SE Asian countries will soon be taking full ordination; perhaps some have already done so. Indian and Nepali Buddhist women have become bhikkhunis, and in the U.S. a few Burmese women have taken this step, considered strictly illegal within Myanmar itself, where it is even punishable by imprisonment. "Bhikkhu Bodhi's Letters on the Nun's Ordination in Perth," November 11, 2009, http://BuddhistChannel.tv/index.php?id=70,8683,0,0,1,0. The letters were first published at http://sujato.wordpress.com/.

64. Anne A. Simpkinson, "What I would say to Osama bin Laden: Zen monk Thich Nhat Hanh talks about how listening is the first step towards peace," accessed September 15, 2011, http://www Beliefnet.com/Faiths/Islam/2001/10/What-I-Would-Say-To-Osama-Bin-Laden.aspx?p=1#ixzz1Ua8fH0TI.

65. Dhammananda, *Practical Buddhism*, 38, 31, 39.

7

Confucian Spiritual Masters

Simon Man Ho Wong

Introduction

For long, Confucianism has been misconstrued as an ethical, social, and political system that lacks a spiritual dimension. As a result of research worked out by scholars in the last few decades, this misconception has gradually been revised.[1] However, we should still admit that the prevalence of this misconception in the past decades is not without reason. I believe that, despite other important factors, it has something to do with the immanent character of Confucian spirituality—a kind of spirituality that does not emphasize a distinct other world or an absolute transcendence of a God or Creator, as it does in many other religions. The immanent character of Confucian spirituality and its impact on the role of spiritual masters becomes the foundational issue of this chapter.

The Notion of a Confucian Sage

A spiritual master, in the broad sense of the term, can be viewed as *sheng* or sage in the context of Confucianism.[2] To understand the notion of a Confucian sage, we may begin by examining the etymological meaning of the Chinese character *sheng*. According to the *Shuowen jiezi* (An explanation of words and terms), the standard etymological dictionary composed in the Eastern Han dynasty (25–220 CE) of China, *sheng* is defined as *tong*, a word meaning "penetrate" or "pass through."[3] The commentary on this definition suggests that a sage is one who understands things thoroughly.[4] The dictionary further states that the character *sheng* is composed of two parts: the phonetic *cheng* and the signific *er*, which means "ear." The commentary quoting the *Fengsu tong* (Comprehensive meaning of customs), a text of the Eastern Han, explains that the ear as signific expresses the idea that a sage understands the reality of things in hearing their sound, namely, through the sage's ear.[5] This corresponds to the definition *tong*, since both "penetrate" and "ear" here bear the implication that a sage thoroughly understands things. Some scholars, however, go farther to suggest that the sage hears and understands the voice of spirits.[6] This suggestion enables the word *sheng* to convey a sense of transcendence. However, this departure from a sense of Confucian immanence may need more justification if we confine the original meaning of *sheng* strictly to what is stated in the *Shuowen jiezi* and its commentary. A sage is one who hears and understands the reality of things—but not the voice of spirits.

The fact that a sage thoroughly *understands* the reality of things instead of *hearing* the voice of spirits does not preclude the notion that a sage has a spiritual dimension. If we extend our investigation to some ancient Confucian texts, we will find that a transcendent realm is clearly present in their descriptions of a sage. Julia Ching observes:

> Some texts use words like "heavenly" and "godly" to describe the sages. The *Book of History* ("Counsel of Great Yü [Yu]") associates the sage with the word *shen* (godly), and its commentary describes him as one whose virtue comes naturally, or as one who possesses a penetrating (*t'ung* [*tong*]) understanding of all things. In the Elder Tai's version of the *Book of Rites* (ch. 40), the sage is said to be someone "whose wisdom penetrates the great Way, who can respond to change without loss, and who fathoms the nature and feelings of the myriad things." In the *Book of*

> *Rites* itself, the word is given the meaning of "producing" or "giving life to the myriad things." And the *Doctrine of the Mean* calls the sage a man "co-equal with Heaven" (ch. 31).[7]

The Chinese classic texts open up a wider vision for the definition of a sage. We have already seen that a sage understands things thoroughly. Here we see that sages understand *all* things thoroughly—and their understanding of the nature of things is so penetrating that they produce or give life to the myriad things. In this way, a sage is described as "godly" and "co-equal with Heaven." A description from a commentary on the *Book of Changes* best summarizes the notion of a sage:

> The character of the great man is identical with that of Heaven and earth; his brilliance is identical with that of the sun and the moon; his order is identical with that of the four seasons, and his good and evil fortunes are identical with those of spiritual beings. He may precede Heaven and Heaven will not act in opposition to him. He may follow Heaven, but will act only as Heaven at the time would do.[8]

This comment should not be taken merely as a literary expression; it means what it says and vividly presents the sage in active relationship with a transcendent realm. To use a statement frequently mentioned among Neo-Confucians in the Song (960–1279) and Ming (1368–1644) dynasties, a sage "regards Heaven and Earth and the myriad things as one body."[9] In other words, a sage is one with the universe. This is a kind of transcendence that is cosmologically oriented, in which the sage as the microcosm is one with the macrocosm of the universe, and participates fully in the ever-producing process of the universe.

The exaltation of the state of a sage may raise the question of its accessibility: Is sagehood naturally endowed or can it be attained through learning and efforts? For a long period in the Wei (220–265) and Jin (265–420) dynasties, sagehood was generally regarded as a distant goal almost impossible for ordinary people to achieve. It is not until the Song dynasty that the Neo-Confucians explicitly declared the accessibility of sagehood through self-cultivation.[10] This is actually a revival of the notion of classical Confucianism in the ancient period that every individual can become a sage.[11] That sagehood is attainable is guaranteed by self-cultivation, which is essentially moral. Thus, a sage can be viewed as having cultivated the state of moral perfection of a human being. Wang Yangming says:

> The reason the sage has become a sage is that his mind has become completely identified with the Principle of Heaven [*tianli*] and is no longer mixed with any impurity of selfish human desires.[12]

Moral perfection is marked by selfish desires being eradicated completely, so that the human mind is completely identified with the Principle of Heaven.[13] Accomplishing such moral perfection, one thereby becomes a sage.

By now, we can see that there are two aspects of a sage. On the one hand, a sage regards all things as one body; on the other hand, a sage is one who has completely wiped out selfish desire. These two actually represent the spiritual and the human aspects of a sage, which are not incompatible in the context of Confucianism, and can be linked together. In other words, a sage completely destroys selfish desire. This reveals a universal loving-kindness (benevolence or humanity, *ren*) that enables the sage to understand and penetrate into all things in themselves, and see them as nothing but the manifestations of Heaven or the Principle of Heaven. Identifying the mind with the Principle of Heaven, the sage gains insight into the oneness of all things in the universe. This assertion may require much detailed elaboration. However, despite the historical complexities of its interpretations, suffice it to say at this point that a Confucian sage can be defined simply as a person who has eradicated selfish desire completely, and thereby penetrates into all things and regards all things, immanent and transcendent, as one body.

The Characteristics of a Confucian Sage: Confucius

In Confucian tradition, figures such as Yao, Shun, Yu, Tang, King Wen, King Wu, and the Duke of Zhou had been singled out for praise as the ancient sages.[14] Yet we do not know much about them—and some of them, such as Yao and Shun, are even viewed by critical historians as legendary figures.[15] It is Confucius (551–479 BCE), an actual historical figure, who was commonly agreed to be the preeminent sage in the history of China. That Confucius possessed human qualities is clearly shown in the *Analects*, a record of his sayings and behavior by his disciples. In it we observe how Confucius described himself:

> The Governor of She asked Tzu-lu [Zilu] about Confucius. Tzu-lu did not answer. The Master [i.e., Confucius] said,

"Why did you not simply say something to this effect: he is the sort of man who forgets to eat when he tries to solve a problem that has been driving him to distraction, who is so full of joy that he forgets his worries and who does not notice the onset of old age?"[16]

Confucius viewed himself as a common person who worked very hard and was happy even in his old age.

If human beings can be classified into three types according to their quality—those who are born with knowledge, those who attain knowledge through study, and those who turn to study only after having been vexed by difficulties[17]—Confucius would consider himself as belonging to the second type. He plainly admitted that he was not born with knowledge, but only sought earnestly the ancient teaching that he loved.[18] And whatever he learned, he shared with his friends and disciples. He said:

> My friends, do you think I am secretive? There is nothing which I hide from you. There is nothing I do which I do not share with you, my friends. There is Ch'iu [Qiu, Confucius's name] for you.[19]

As an authentic person, Confucius disclosed all he had. Sometimes he even considered himself a learner, for he said:

> Even when walking in the company of two others, I am bound to be able to learn from them. The good points of the one I copy; the bad points of the other I correct in myself.[20]

Therefore, as a teacher he never adopted a lofty position but instead interacted openly with his disciples in the context of his genuine life experiences. Furthermore, Confucius was not authoritarian as a teacher. For example, when his disciple was displeased with his visiting Nanzi, the notorious wife of Duke Ling of Wei, he swore an oath saying that he would be cursed by Heaven had he done anything improper.[21]

With regard to the things that concerned Confucius, there is no doubt that he paid much attention to human affairs. It seems he "never discussed strange phenomena, physical exploits, disorder or gods."[22] He told his disciples to devote themselves earnestly to the duties due to human beings, and respect spirits of the dead and gods—but keep them at a distance.[23] When a disciple asked about serving spirits of the dead, Confucius said, "If we are not yet able to serve man, how can we serve spirits of the dead?" Having been asked about death, he answered, "If we do not yet know about life, how can we know about death?"[24] That Confucius was not interested in discussing issues on spirits of the dead, gods, and life after death is quite obvious.

Seeing Confucius as one who viewed himself as a common person and paid attention to human affairs instead of supernatural things, we may have the impression that he was a humanistic and nonreligious thinker. Yet, this would be a one-sided observation. We must acknowledge that although Confucius did not dare to discuss spirits of the dead and gods and kept them at a distance, he did respect them:

> When Confucius offered sacrifice to his ancestors, he felt as if his ancestral spirits were actually present. When he offered sacrifice to other gods, he felt as if they were actually present. He said, "If I do not participate in the sacrifice, it is as if I did not sacrifice at all."[25]

Confucius was well known for his inheritance of the traditional religious rites, including sacrificial rites. In performing sacrificial rites, he was always dignified with deep respect to the spirits of the dead and gods. It has been argued that Confucius sacrificed "as if the gods were present," meaning that he did not really believe in the existence of the spirits of the dead and gods; and the stress for funeral and sacrificial rituals by the Confucians reflects only a sentiment of respect towards their departed forbears.[26] However, what may be closer to the truth is that though Confucius did not explicitly assert the existence of spirits of the dead and gods, neither did he deny it.[27] If a Confucian sage penetrates into all things in the universe, then death, spirits of the dead, and gods (if they exist) should be among the constitutive elements of the Confucian reflection on life and human beings. That Confucius did not overtly discuss questions about death, spirits of the dead, and gods does not mean that he was simply unmindful of them. Rather, it was because life and human beings were his central concerns, and were of primary importance in his teachings.[28]

Whether Confucius believed in the existence of spirits of the dead and gods is still a subject of controversy. Yet, that he had a genuine belief in Heaven is something beyond question. He said:

> The gentleman stands in awe of three things. He stands in awe of the Mandate of Heaven [*tianming*]; he stands in

> awe of great men, and he stands in awe of the words of the sages. The inferior man is ignorant of the Mandate of Heaven and does not stand in awe of it. He is disrespectful to great men and is contemptuous toward the words of the sages.[29]

Traditionally, Heaven was regarded as the supreme Lord on High—that is, the origin and governor of all things in the universe. Confucius inherited this notion of Heaven, and had an existential feeling of awe toward it. He noticed that most people did not have this feeling because of their ignorance of Heaven's Mandate. Not only did he stand in awe of Heaven, but also he had connection with Heaven:

> Confucius said, "Alas! No one knows me!" Tzu-kung [Zigong] said, "Why is there no one that knows you?" Confucius said, "I do not complain against Heaven. I do not blame men. I study things on the lower level but my understanding penetrates the higher level. It is Heaven that knows me."[30]

Here, the higher level refers to the Mandate of Heaven and the lower level refers to mundane matters.[31] Confucius was able to understand the Mandate of Heaven through his study of mundane matters. This was a vision that few people—perhaps, no other person—could achieve at his time. It seems that Confucius adopted a high position here in the sense that he thought nobody but Heaven understood him, because only he could understand Heaven. And since he understood the Mandate of Heaven, he had deep faith in Heaven. When Huan Tui, a military officer in the state of Song, attempted to kill Confucius by felling a tree, he had no fear and said, "Heaven produced the virtue that is in me; what can Huan T'ui [Huan Tui] do to me?"[32] He made a similar point on another occasion:

> When under siege in K'uang [Kuang], the Master said, "With King Wen dead, is not culture (*wen*) invested here in me? If Heaven intends culture to be destroyed, those who come after me will not be able to have any part of it. If Heaven does not intend this culture to be destroyed, then what can the men of K'uang do to me?"[33]

This incident happened when Confucius and his disciples arrived at Kuang. The people of Kuang mistook Confucius for their enemy, Yang Hu, and surrounded him.[34] Again, Confucius was without fear even in time of danger, since he had deep faith that he had received the Mandate of Heaven for his mission to preserve traditional culture.

Perhaps it was the close connection between Confucius and Heaven—something others did not have—that made Confucius unfathomable to his disciples, and others. Yet, from time to time, a wise person was able to conceive the extraordinary qualities of Confucius:

> The guardian at I [Yi] (a border post of the state of Wei) requested to be presented to Confucius, saying, "When gentlemen come here, I have never been prevented from seeing them." Confucius' followers introduced him. When he came out from the interview, he said, "Sirs, why are you disheartened by your master's loss of office? The Way has not prevailed in the world for a long time. Heaven is going to use your master as a bell with a wooden tongue [to awaken the people]."[35]

The guardian at Yi discerned that Confucius had received the Mandate of Heaven to awaken people from chaos and confusion of immorality at his time. This was a mission of which only Confucius was capable. Confucius was also admired by his disciples, who compared him to the sun and moon in the sky:

> Shu-sun Wu-shu [Shusun Wushu] slandered Chung-ni [Zhongni] (Confucius). Tzu-kung said, "It is no use. Chung-ni cannot be slandered. Other worthies are like mounds and small hills. You can still climb over them. Chung-ni, however, is like the sun and the moon that cannot be climbed over. Although a man may want to shut his eyes to the sun and the moon, what harm does it do to them? It would only show in large measure that he does not know his own limitations.[36]

Zigong was one of Confucius's very intelligent disciples, and this is how he described his master. When someone said that Zigong was actually superior to Confucius, Zigong responded,

> Let us take outer walls as an analogy. My walls are shoulder high so that it is possible to peer over them and see the beauty of the house. But the Master's walls are twenty or thirty feet high so that, unless one gains admittance through

> the gate, one cannot see the magnificence of the ancestral temples or the sumptuousness of the official buildings. Since those who gain admittance through the gate are, shall we say, few, is it any wonder that the gentleman should have spoken as he did?[37]

In Zigong's view, Confucius was far superior to him. Not only Zigong, but even Yan Yuan, who was commonly agreed to be the best of Confucius's disciples, held the same opinion:

> Yen Yuan [Yan Yuan], heaving a sigh, said, "The more I look up at it [the Way of Confucius] the higher it appears. The more I bore into it the harder it becomes. I see it before me. Suddenly it is behind me. The Master is good at leading one on step by step. He broadens me with culture and brings me back to essentials by means of the rites. I cannot give up even if I wanted to, but, having done all I can, it seems to rise sheer above me and I have no way of going after it, however much I may want to."[38]

It seemed to Yan Yuan that the Way of Confucius had a quality that was inaccessible to him. From our understanding of Confucius's philosophy, the Way of Confucius is the Way (*dao*)—the Way of Heaven (*tiandao*)—which is not impossible to attain through intense moral self-cultivation. Yet, it is a goal so difficult to achieve that perhaps only a sage such as Confucius could achieve it. And it is because Confucius fully embodied the Way of Heaven that he can be called a sage.

The Unity of Heaven and Man (*tian ren heyi*) in Confucius

We have already seen the human and spiritual aspects of the sage Confucius. Confucius was a human teacher who possessed a heavenly quality that was virtually inaccessible to other people of his time. One may wonder how these two aspects can actually combine to form a unity in a person. In other words, how could a humble person who worked hard to learn from others be at the same time somebody confident enough to claim that nobody understood him, and that he was able to enlighten people from spiritual darkness? The answer to this question leads us to probe the subject of Confucian spirituality in greater depth. We should first pay attention to the fact that despite Confucius's belief that Heaven is the supreme Lord on High, he seldom discussed it:

> Tzu-kung said, "We can hear our Master's [views] on culture and its manifestation, but we cannot hear his views on human nature and the Way of Heaven."[39]

Given Confucius's faith in Heaven, it would be unreasonable for some historians to attribute Zigong's stating his unwillingness to discuss Heaven to agnosticism. A possible explanation of his silence on the subject of Heaven is that the subject (as well as the subject of human nature) is beyond the comprehension of most people.[40] However, was it not Confucius's mission—or the mission of any Confucian sage—to manifest Heaven to people, no matter how difficult it is for people to comprehend? It is exactly because of his silence on the matter that Confucius receives the following comments by H. H. Rowley in his comparative work on the subject of prophecy:

> His confidence in the power of Heaven to preserve him, and his sense of a mission to men appointed by Heaven, is as strong as that of the prophets of Israel. Where he falls short of them is in the remoteness of God, and in the littleness of the place that God had in his teaching. While for him God was real and His purpose clear, his unwillingness to talk about Him meant that he did little to make Him real for his followers. There might be a will of God for him, but he said nothing to make men feel that there was a will of God for them, and worship was but the offering of reverence and not the receiving of grace. Hence, in effect, his teaching was reduced to ethics, instead of the communication of the religion which he himself had.[41]

This comment seems very forceful because it provides an essential reason for asserting the spiritual dimension of Confucius's teaching on the one hand, and explaining why Confucianism was sometimes misinterpreted as a mere ethical system on the other. It nevertheless gives us the impression of the inferiority of Confucianism as a religion because of its spirituality being weakened; Rowley has adopted the Hebrew tradition as the standard of religion in judging the teaching of Confucius. Hans Küng, however, criticizes Rowley's comment:

> Rowley had to develop a skewed perspective because he did not seriously take into account the religious type and the literary genre that had little to do with the Israelite prophets, but a great deal to do with Confucius and even

> the ancient Chinese tradition: this is the religious type of the *sage* and the literary genre of *wisdom literature*.[42]

According to Hans Küng, Confucius's silence on the subject of Heaven does not shatter the spirituality of Confucianism; it only reflects that Confucianism belongs to a religious type different from that of some others—the religious type of the sage. Yet Hans Küng did not go into the details of this religious type in his book. To explore the meaning of this religious type, in which the subject of the sage becomes the focus, it is necessary to look at the following conversation between Confucius and his disciple:

> Confucius said, "I do not wish to say anything." Tzu-kung said, "If you do not say anything, what can we little disciples ever learn to pass on to others" Confucius said, "Does Heaven (*T'ien* [*tian*]) say anything? The four seasons run this course and all things are produced. Does Heaven say anything?"[43]

This is one of the few statements about Heaven by Confucius in the *Analects*. Shu-hsien Liu thinks that this passage has a very important implication. For Liu, Confucius "never for a moment doubted the existence of Heaven, and he did inherit the traditional faith in Heaven as the Lord on High." However, in Confucius's creative interpretation of the traditional belief, "he made a smooth transition from the traditional belief in Heaven to his own understanding of Heaven," and this understanding is shown in the conversation. Heaven here becomes "the transcendent creative power working unceasingly in the universe." It "does not show any personal characteristics and does not intervene in the natural state of affairs."[44] This means that the bearing of Heaven as the Lord on High had begun to be transformed into the transcendent creative power in Confucius's teaching.

Confucius had his reasons for not talking about Heaven. His silence gives us a deeper understanding of the relationship of a Confucian spiritual master with the transcendent realm. In fact, it is more important for us to know why Confucius refrained from talking about Heaven than to speculate what he might have said about Heaven. Because he did not speak of Heaven, such speculation becomes irrelevant. Confucius refrained from talking about Heaven not because it is incomprehensible to most people. On the contrary, as implied in Shu-hsien Liu's argument, Confucius was imitating Heaven. Heaven does not say anything in running the seasons and producing all things—and thus benefiting all things in the universe.

Perhaps the profound implication of Confucius's "non-saying" of Heaven is that Heaven—without being the object of saying—is not a supreme Other influencing the mundane world with commands or supernatural powers. Rather, Heaven (viz., the Way of Heaven or Mandate of Heaven) is completely embodied in and manifested through the ever-producing process of all things in the mundane world. This ever-producing process appears as the unceasing process of self-cultivation in human beings. For a human being, it is only through incessant moral self-cultivation that one can realize the Way of Heaven. Confucius was silent about Heaven because he was identified with Heaven. Thus it is no surprise that Confucius said, "It is man that can make the Way great, and not the Way that can make man great."[45] The Way of Heaven is totally immanent in the world, and within the world only a human being is able to broaden or manifest the Way to its completion by means of their moral activities.

The seeming inconsistency found in the qualities of Confucius—that he was humble and worked hard to teach and learn from others on the one hand, and was confident and became a sage or a great spiritual master on the other—can be resolved by an appreciation of the immanent character of Confucian spirituality. This also explains the following passage:

> The Master said, "How dare I claim to be a sage or a benevolent man? Perhaps it might be said of me that I learn without flagging and teach without growing weary." Kung-hsi Hua [Gongxi Hua] said, "This is precisely where we disciples are unable to learn from your example."[46]

What is interesting here is that Confucius did not dare to claim himself a sage; he thought he was an ordinary person working unceasingly to teach and to learn. However, for his disciple Gongxi Hua, it is precisely the quality of unceasingness in his teaching and learning that is fathomless and unattainable. Zigong even declared that learning without flagging was wisdom, and teaching without growing weary was benevolence—and since Confucius was wise and benevolent, he was a sage.[47] Here we see how the human and spiritual aspects were combined seamlessly together in Confucius, who practiced human virtues incessantly and thereby revealed the spirituality that was present in him. As Tu Weiming observes,

> Confucius certainly did not "set the limits beforehand," but he fully acknowledged his inability to attain sagehood. In

> this peculiar way he was a sage to his followers but not to himself, and for that reason he became the exemplar of sagehood itself.[48]

Confucius "perceived himself as a person who was as yet on the way to 'giving his body complete fulfillment.'" "Thus Confucius, the sage, serves as an exemplary teacher of humanity, not only because of the extraordinary accomplishments that establish a distance between him and the rest of us, but because of those aspects of his humanity that bring him near to us and make him accessible."[49] For Confucianism, a sage is inaccessible only in the sense that the achievement of sagehood is extremely difficult, but never impossible. Confucianism is after all a kind of spirituality completely embodied in unceasing moral human activities.

The Process of Attaining Sagehood

Since sagehood is accessible, the process of attaining it becomes a significant issue.[50] For Confucianism, the path by which one comes to be a sage may vary according to different personalities and environmental factors. And though there is no absolute standard process or set of stages for self-cultivation to be found in the tradition, the spiritual progress of Confucius provides a general picture of the steps that one may go through in morally transforming oneself. Confucius described his own spiritual evolution as follows:

> At fifteen my mind was set on learning. At thirty my character had been formed. At forty I had no more perplexities. At fifty I knew the Mandate of Heaven (*Tien-ming*). At sixty I was at ease with whatever I heard. At seventy I could follow my heart's desire without transgressing moral principles.[51]

Confucius at Fifteen

For all Confucians, setting one's mind on learning is a crucial point of departure for becoming a sage. The *Analects* tells us that Confucius did this at age fifteen. But what is meant by learning? It is not just the increase of knowledge as we usually mean it nowadays. The increase of knowledge is definitely part of learning, but the major concern in Confucian learning always pertains to the Way. As Confucius said, "I set my mind on the Way, base myself on virtue, lean upon benevolence for support and take my recreation in the arts."[52] He also said, "One has not lived in vain who dies the day he is told about the Way."[53] Thus, the Way (*dao*) is the ultimate goal of learning, the understanding of which will enable one to transform and elevate his or her mind. From the fact that Confucius compared the Way to benevolence (*ren*), we see that the learning of the Way bears a moral sense. The purpose of learning for Confucianism is therefore to acquire the Way whereby one becomes a moral or authentic human being, the perfection of which is the sage. Setting the mind on this purpose of learning is the starting point of the entire moral enterprise of Confucian self-cultivation.

Confucius at Thirty

The meaning of "at thirty my character had been formed" is actually not very clear in the Chinese original. It can be translated literally as "at thirty I could stand [*li*]."[54] Confucius said, "Take your stand on the rites," and "one has no way of taking his stand unless he understands the rites."[55] These statements have been explained as indicating that Confucius was able to understand the true meaning of the rites and behave properly at the age of thirty. However, taking one's stand on the rites, and behaving properly can be extended to mean the establishment of one's unbending character. Confucius said,

> Those sufficiently good [*ke*] to be participants [*yu*] in their studies may not be sufficiently good to be participants in pursuit of the Way; those sufficiently good to be participants in pursuit of the Way may not be sufficiently good to be participants in a common stand; those sufficiently good to be participants in a common stand may not be sufficiently good to be participants in the exercise of moral discretion.[56]

"In a common stand" here implies people having a strong will and unbending character. Yet the "exercising moral discretion" is higher still—and a requirement of *ren* (benevolence). Confucius admired people having strong will and unbending character. He said, "The Three Armies can be deprived of their commanding officer, but even a common man cannot be deprived of his will."[57] He thought that strength, resoluteness, simplicity and reticence are close to *ren*, which is the highest virtue one can possess.[58] Yet, Confucius admitted that being unbendingly strong is not easy to achieve:

> The Master [Confucius] said, "I have never met anyone who is truly unbending. Someone said, "What about Shen Ch'eng [Shen Cheng]? The Master said, "Ch'eng is full of desires. How can he be unbending?"[59]

Confucius's answer shows that being unbending is possible only when people get rid of their desire, so that they will not betray their own personality in return for any sensual pleasure. This idea was succeeded by later Confucians who claimed that a great person is "one whose heart cannot be dissipated by the power of wealth and honors, who cannot be influenced by poverty or humble stations, who cannot be subdued by force and might."[60]

Confucius at Forty

Having an unbending character—and thereby not subjecting one's will to favorable or adverse circumstances—is not an easy achievement. However, a person with unbending character with strong will does not necessarily always make a correct judgment in dealing with the external world. Recall, Confucius said that "those sufficiently good to be participants in a common stand may not be sufficiently good to be participants in the exercise of moral discretion." The "exercise of moral discretion" is more difficult to attain than being "participants in a common stand."

It was not until the age of forty that Confucius was able to free himself from any misguided judgment on human affairs. He said, "At forty I had no more perplexities [*huo*]." Perhaps Confucius could be called a man of wisdom at this stage since he also said, "The man of wisdom has no perplexities."[61] Obviously, a man of wisdom can be defined as a man having no perplexity. But what is the exact meaning of having no perplexity? Some Confucians of later ages interpreted it as "having no doubt about the oughtness [*dangran*] of things" or "understanding the principles of things."[62] This explanation may give us an impression that "having no perplexity" is related to the increase of knowledge, which is compatible with Confucius's teaching. Yet, from the *Analects* we find that its meaning actually is concerned more with morality than with knowledge. Confucius said:

> When you love a man you want him to live and when you hate him you want him to die. If, having wanted him to live, you then want him to die, this is perplexity.[63]

Elsewhere, he said, "To let a sudden fit of anger make you forget the safety of your own person or even that of your parents, is that not perplexity?"[64] Here, "perplexity" refers to the state of being emotional that impedes one to see things as they are and deal with them appropriately. A person of wisdom is one who does not indulge in excessive love or hate that becomes an obstruction from seeing the reality of things. This, of course, does not mean that the person has no love or hate. Confucius said, "It is only the benevolent man who is capable of liking or disliking other man."[65] A benevolent person is often a wise person, who, without being emotional, is able to make correct moral judgment—liking those who really deserve to be liked, and disliking those who really deserve to be disliked.

Confucius at Fifty

Confucius attained a higher state of self-cultivation when he knew the Mandate of Heaven at the age of fifty. As we mentioned already, Heaven was traditionally regarded as the supreme Lord on High that governs the universe. Since Confucius was in awe of Heaven, the idea of Heaven as the Supreme Lord must be present in his thought. However, as we have seen, there is a second perspective of viewing Heaven that is also present in Confucius's thought: this is Heaven as the transcendent creative power working unceasingly in the universe, which Confucius was able to recognize at age fifty. Because he had reached a high state of self-cultivation, the moral creativity of his mind was in total conformity with the transcendent creative power of Heaven. With this conformity, I would suggest that Confucius had attained the state of experiencing the universe as one body. Since he recognized the oneness of the universe, he was fully aware of his exact position, and in turn his mission in the universe—this is what Confucius meant by knowing the Mandate of Heaven. Forming one body with the universe may correspond to what we today call religious mystical experience. Based on this, some scholars draw a line between Confucius at the age of fifty and before, claiming that at the younger age Confucius was conscious only of moral values, while beyond the age of fifty he was also conscious of super-moral or religious values.[66] In fact, it is important to admit the presence of religious values in Confucianism. But it is not necessary to separate moral from super-moral or religious values, since in Confucianism all religious values are revealed through moral transformation in its perfection. For Confucianism, Heaven, whether it is the Supreme Lord on High or the transcendent creative power, is always the moral Heaven.

Confucius at Sixty

Experiencing all things as one body enables the Confucian spiritual master to penetrate into all things and understand them in themselves. This accounts for Confucius being at ease with whatever he heard at the age of sixty. Whatever Confucius heard may be extended to mean whatever he encountered in his daily life. Whatever kind of situation Confucius encountered—whether good or evil, happy or sad—he simply accepted them without any feeling of disgust or confrontation. This can be compared with the state of having no perplexity at the age of forty, in which Confucius still had discrimination against things or people who deserved to be disliked. At sixty, however, he was able to accept all things as they were peacefully, because he was able to see (or hear) the goodness of all things in themselves. In this, Confucius was acting in accord with Heaven, as all living beings exist and grow under Heaven, without any one of them being expelled or discriminated against by Heaven.

Confucius at Seventy

"At seventy I could follow my heart's desire without transgressing moral principles." From accepting all things in themselves, Confucius moved farther, and at seventy he elevated himself to the state of following his desire spontaneously without any transgression. This means that not only his behavior, but also his thoughts and ideas were nothing but pure manifestations of Heaven; his way was the Way of Heaven. As Fung Yu-lan correctly described, "Confucius allowed his mind to follow whatever it desired, yet everything he did was naturally right of itself. His actions no longer needed a conscious guide. He was acting without effort."[67] In fact, he had fully actualized his vision of the oneness of the universe into his life and practice. And "this represents the last stage in the development of the sage."[68]

The Authentic Confucian Sage: Criteria and Contributions

As far as I can see, there are no standard criteria for determining the authenticity of a sage in the Confucian tradition. But searching for criteria reminds us of Zhang Zai (1020–1077), an important Neo-Confucian in the Northern Song dynasty (960–1126) who proclaimed what he believed to be the ideal Confucian:

> To establish the heart [*xin*] for Heaven and Earth;
> To establish the Mandate [*ming*] for the living people;
> To inherit the lost learning of the past sages;
> To open [the way to] peace for the ten thousand ages [in the future].[69]

We may conveniently treat these four statements as criteria based on the contributions of a sage.

To Establish the Heart (xin) *for Heaven and Earth*

For the first statement, the philosophical meaning of "Heaven and Earth" can be regarded as an extension of the transcendent Heaven. The images of sky (Heaven) and earth (Earth), signifying the two functions of the transcendent Heaven, do nothing but give a more detailed explication of the meaning encompassed in Heaven. Therefore, "Heaven and Earth" in this context is philosophically the same as the transcendent Heaven. While the "heart" (or "mind") may have a profound meaning according to the Neo-Confucian tradition, it is enough for us to explain it as "essence" here. This establishment of the essence is crucial for the manifestation of Heaven, or even for sustaining Heaven as Heaven. So what is the essence of Heaven that has to be established? The answer is: there is a common agreement in Neo-Confucianism that the heart for Heaven and Earth is the human being. Thus, to establish the heart for Heaven and Earth means to try to live as a human being, or to be a moral and authentic human being. Once again we observe the humanistic and immanent character of Confucian spirituality, in which the essence or core of Heaven lies in the incessant effort of being human.

To Establish the Mandate (ming) *for the Living People*

In the second statement, the Mandate refers to Heaven's Mandate. To establish the Mandate of Heaven for people means to let people live in accord with the Mandate of Heaven, or the Way of Heaven. This implies helping them to live as moral and authentic human beings. The ideal of a Confucian is not only to accomplish oneself, but also to accomplish others morally—a task that only a sage can completely achieve. This may be inferred to mean that a sage develops a cultural environment through the impact of which people will be refined and promoted spiritually.

To Inherit the Lost Learning of the Past Sages

The third statement depicts the transmission of the Way of Heaven. As we have seen, Confucian learning is not just the increase of knowledge; it is the learning of the Way that will easily be lost even with subtle carelessness. The Way is in the teachings of the sages, and the teachings are preserved in the Confucian classics. Thus, to succeed the sages and transmit their teachings means to study and teach the classics. This had developed into the scholastic and academic tradition in Confucianism.

To Open [the Way to] Peace for the Ten Thousand Ages [in the Future]

The last statement may have a political and social bearing. It suggests that a Confucian gentleman is expected to become a political or social leader who works out various kinds of institutions, policies, and measures to foster peace and prosperity in society that lasts for generations to come. The ideal in this sense is that a sage is at the same time a ruler. The sage is perfect in virtue or moral self-cultivation, and also in having talent for politics; the Confucian spiritual master should therefore be a spiritual leader as well as a political leader.

Using Zhang Zai's four statements on the ideal Confucian as the criteria for determining the authenticity of a Confucian spiritual master, we see that a sage is one who should have great achievements in spiritual cultivation, creating a cultural environment for the spiritual growth of people, transmitting the Way preserved in the classics, and developing a political and social order for the benefit of humankind. However, the fundamental criterion of a Confucian spiritual master remains the high level of attainment of virtue or spirituality. This is because the achievements in areas of culture, scholarly studies, politics, and so forth can be viewed as nothing but manifestations of—and the eventual completion of—the virtue of the sage. Yet, these areas are no less important, because for Confucianism all spiritual values are fully embodied in the world of humanity.

Was Confucius a Sage?

Judged by the four criteria for determining the authenticity of a sage, Confucius, indeed, is entitled to be regarded as the exemplar of the spiritual master in Confucianism. Traditionally, he was praised as the "greatest sage and foremost teacher" (*zhisheng xianshi*) in China. This title does capture his most prominent achievements. A more detailed reflection enables us to see that he made significant contributions to the four aspects that just enumerated.

Firstly, *Confucius achieved extensive self-cultivation*. There is no doubt that Confucius attained the highest level of spiritual or moral self-cultivation. This accomplishment indicates a state deemed to be that of a sage, which Confucian tradition claims only a few figures before Confucius were able to attain.

Secondly, *Confucius achieved extensive learning*. In addition to self-cultivation, Confucius emphasized extensive learning. He said, "The gentleman [is] widely versed in culture."[70] One of his contemporaries said, "Great indeed is Confucius! He has wide learning but has not made a name for himself in any field."[71] Confucius considered himself to be a learner and perpetuator of ancient culture. The extensive knowledge of ancient culture that he possessed included mastery of the most basic six arts of ritual, music, archery, charioteering, calligraphy, and arithmetic. Obviously, the six arts are not only physical; they include mental and spiritual disciplines as well. Taking the art of archery as an example, Tu Weiming gives a vivid explanation of its function:

> The training [of the six arts] represents a concerted effort to transform the body into a fitting expression of the mental and spiritual resources within. . . . The art of archery, for example, is intended at once to improve one's skill as an archer and to discipline one's mind so that it is constantly tranquil. Furthermore, archery requires self-examination: if we fail to hit the mark, we must first search for the fault within ourselves. The archer tries to produce a finely tuned disposition that informs every gesture of the body. Thus one becomes thoroughly familiar with one's mental states while learning to do the kinds of things archers do. Yet for all this mental discipline, the bodily form remains the basis of the enterprise, and is acknowledged as such in traditional Confucian education. After all, the body so conceived is no purely physical entity; it is inseparable from the mind and spirit.[72]

The cultural knowledge of the six arts enables one to develop physically, mentally, and spiritually. They are considered as "elementary learning" (*xiaoxue*) in the Confucian tradition, partly because they were emphasized by Confucius.

Thirdly, *Confucius engaged in transmission of the Way of Heaven.* Another contribution made by Confucius is that he taught the classics, which are supposed to contain the Way of the past sages. He was the first one who taught not only nobles, but also the common people of his time. For this reason, he was called the foremost teacher. As for the content of the classics, Rodney L. Taylor has a brief summary of them:

> The most essential collection, the Five Classics, includes: the *I-Ching* [*Yijing*], *Classic* or *Book of Changes,* a divinatory work with philosophical commentaries which explain the patterns of change inherent in the universe; the *Shih-ching* [*Shijing*], *Classic* or *Book of Poetry* or *Odes,* a collection of some 300 poems thought to exemplify the quintessential expression of poetic beauty and moral virtue; the *Shu-ching* [*Shujing*], *Classic* or *Book of History,* a record of the deeds of the early sage-kings; the *Li-chi* [*Liji*], *Book of Rites,* detailed accounts and philosophical meanings of the rituals of the ancient sage-kings; and the *Ch'un-Ch'iu* [*Chunqiu*], *Spring and Autumn Annals,* a record of the events in the state of Lu, native state of Confucius.[73]

There is another work added to these five to comprise the Six Classics, "the *Yüeh-Ching* [*Yuejing*], *Classic of Music,* which purportedly discussed the philosophical meaning of music."[74] This classic is no longer extant. Confucians believe that through the study and assimilation of the classics one will act according to the Way of Heaven, and develop one's spirit and moral nature. For instance, Confucius suggested that "the salient and overriding meaning of the *Book of Poetry* is its purity and uncorruptedness." He said:

> The *Odes* are three hundred in number. They can be summed up in one phrase, "Swerving not from the right path."[75]

Rodney L. Taylor explains:

> Confucius believed in the oral and spiritual purity of this collection of poems. This is based upon the presupposition that the age out of which this poetry emerged was itself an age of purity, for it was the period of the founding sage kings of the Chou [Zhou] dynasty [1111–247 BCE]. . . . Thus,

> from the Confucian point of view these poems embody the very spirit of their age. In turn, if one thoroughly studies such works, they will have nothing short of a transforming effect on the individual. This approach to the *Book of Poetry,* which will be mirrored by later Confucians with this Classic as well as other Classics, is the very seed from which the Confucian scriptural tradition developed.[76]

Ever since the official establishment of Confucian tradition in the Han dynasty (206 BCE–220 CE), the classics—having a strong spiritual dimension—assumed the status of scripture. They became authoritative texts that represented the state orthodoxy for about two thousand years. Confucius was purported to have edited or contributed to the formation of the Six Classics. Even if the participation of Confucius in editing the classics is doubtful to some modern historians, it is certain that Confucius inherited and transmitted the classics from the ancient past, and thereby helped to establish them as the core literature of Chinese civilization.

Lastly, *Confucius opened the way to peace for the ten thousand ages.* Although Confucius did not in his lifetime succeed in finding an opportunity to implement his political and social reform, he was glorified in the Han dynasty as a ruler without a crown or a government. This was feasible for the Han Confucians who interpreted the *Spring and Autumn Annals* as a work written by Confucius who conferred esoteric meaning on the work to express his ethical and political ideas and to establish political institutions and disciplines for the Han dynasty. Confucius was even described as a divine being who received the Mandate of Heaven, knew that the Han dynasty would come, and therefore set forth a political ideal that would be complete enough for the people of Han to realize. But soon this kind of interpretation of Confucius was declared heterodox. Throughout Chinese history, Confucius, though celebrated as a sage, remained to be honored as a human being. At the end of the nineteenth century, however, there was a brief revival of the theory that Confucius had been divinely appointed to be a ruler, but this lasted for only a very short period.[77] In short, Confucius had been revered as a ruler who brought order to the Chinese Han Empire—though not totally without basis, however. It seems that this view largely reflects the subjective interpretation of some Confucians rather than a reality in history.

If the Confucian ideal of having a sage as the political leader was not fulfilled by Confucius, it was claimed to have been realized by the sage-kings in the ancient Golden Age before Confucius's day. For example, Confucius often expressed his admiration for Yao and Shun, whom he considered as sages as well as model rulers. Yao was venerated especially for his yielding the throne to his wise minister, Shun, showing that he did it without any selfish desire. Shun was praised not only for his political wisdom, but also for filial piety toward his wicked father, stepmother, and half-brother who all wanted to murder him.[78] And Yu, the successor of Shun, was well-known for selfless devotion to his work of controlling the flood. It took him away from home for eight years—during which time he passed his house three times, but did not dare to enter.[79]

Besides political and social administration, the ancient sages were also exalted for their advancement of material culture. Julia Ching describes the work they did:

> In the *K'ao-kung chi* [*Kaogong ji*], a work thought to be of the Warring States period [403–222 BCE], the wise men who invented tools and implements and transmitted the skills they acquired in using these were called *kung* [*gong*] (artisans), but the tools and techniques themselves were attributed to the invention of the original "sages" (*sheng*): "Making carts to travel on land and boats to travel on water, these were all the creations of the sages."
>
> The "Great Appendix" to the *Book of Changes* mentions Fu-hsi [Fuxi] ["Animal-Tamer"] or Pao-hsi [Baoxi] as the inventor of the eight trigrams, as well as nets for hunting and fishing, and of Sheng-nung [Shennong] ["Divine-Farmer"] as the maker of ploughs and shares for tilling the soil. They were followed by the Yellow Emperor, Yao and Shun, who allegedly built canoes and oars, used oxen to draw carts and yoked horses to chariots, built double gates for defence and made bows and arrows.[80]

Thus, according to the Confucian ideal, a sage can make contributions in different areas of culture. What is essential about Confucian spiritual masters is their virtue—that is, the moral and spiritual values that they manifest through themselves and their activities in the mundane world. We say *moral* and *spiritual* because for Confucianism, something moral must be spiritual, and vice versa; whereas to some people something moral may not be spiritual, and something spiritual may not be moral. In fact, for a Confucian, all kinds of activities—be they cultural, academic, political, social, or technical—are laden with spiritual values as long as they are the genuine expressions of one's nature which is endowed with the Way of Heaven.

A Traditional Confucian Spiritual Master: Wang Yangming

It seems that after Confucius, not even one Confucian was generally accepted to be a sage. The Confucian list of sages includes the ancient sage-kings and Confucius only.[81] Yet, throughout the history of the tradition there were many Confucian gentleman and virtuous persons who perpetuated the teaching of Confucianism, and continued to strive for realization of the Confucian ideal. Among them was Wang Yangming (1472-1529) in the Ming dynasty, a renowned Confucian who deserves to be called a spiritual master in Confucianism. If *spiritual master* in Confucianism is defined as a sage, then Wang Yangming cannot be called a spiritual master. However, here I am using the term in a broader sense.

Wang Yangming's outstanding quality appeared when, at the age of ten, he asked his teacher what the greatest thing to do in life was. The teacher's reply was that it was to study and pass examinations. On hearing this, Yangming was dissatisfied, and said that the answer should be to become a sage. When he learned that to become a sage one had to investigate all things in the world, he began by trying to investigate bamboos. From morning till night, he was unable to find the principle of the bamboos. On the seventh day, Yangming became sick because he had contemplated very hard. He sighed, thinking that it was impossible for him to be a sage, since he did not have the tremendous energy to investigate things that becoming a sage required.[82] Yangming then underwent a period of interest in the art of letters, and of being absorbed in Daoism and Buddhism. Eventually, he returned to Confucian tradition and understood the meaning of the Confucian Way.[83]

Yangming's well-known experience of enlightenment happened when he was exiled to Longchang, Guizhou, where the living conditions were extremely difficult. There Yangming came to realize that he was able to be free from the influence of honor or disgrace, success or failure—but he was still puzzled by the problem of life and death. He made a stone coffin for himself, and spent days and nights sitting in silent meditation seeking for pure tranquility. He asked himself what a sage would do in such circumstances. Then one night Yangming suddenly got enlightened. Being filled with joy, he thoroughly understood the meaning of the "investigation of things" (*gewu*) and the "extension of knowledge" (*zhizhi*). He knew that his mistake in the past was seeking to realize the principle from external things and events, while the Way of the sage was actually present in his own nature. It was the year 1508. Yangming was thirty-six years old.[84]

From the age of thirty-six years on, Yangming began to advocate his own teaching, which sprang from his enlightenment experience. As a spiritual master, however, he did not assume a position high above his disciples, or impose his teaching on them. In this way, Yangming resembles Confucius. Together they reflect the characteristic of Confucian spirituality that manifests through intimate interaction between authentic personalities and inspiration from the life experiences of teacher and disciples. We have a record of an incident about Yangming in the *Wang Yangming quanji,* which says:

> In the autumn of 1524 [when he was fifty-two and in retirement from public office], he prepared a banquet for his students on the night of the Mid-Autumn Festival. The tables were set outdoors, at the Pi-hsia [Bixia] Pond near the T'ien-ch'üan [Tianquan] Bridge. Over a hundred persons were present. Wine was served, after which the students enjoyed themselves by singing, pitching darts, beating drums, or boating. Pleased and a little gay himself, Yang-ming composed poems to honor the occasion.[85]

Yangming wrote two poems regarding the festival banquet incident. These final lines of Yangming's two poems encapsulate the amicable relationship between a Confucian spiritual master and his disciples:

> (1) Old as I am, I sing wild songs tonight; to be transformed into heavenly music, filling up the Great purity [i.e., the sky].
>
> (2) Setting aside the lute while the notes are still vibrating in the spring breeze, Tseng Tien [Zeng Dian], the ardent and eccentric, understands my mind best.[86]

These verses present a lively picture of how Yangming enjoyed life happily and harmoniously with his students. But, this intimacy by no means diminished the degree of respect the students had for Yangming. Xu Ai, a devoted disciple of Yangming's, had this to say about him:

> The master is naturally intelligent and perceptive. But he is also serene, joyful, straightforward, and easygoing. He pays no attention to his appearance. People who knew how impatient of restraints and conventions he had been as a young man, and how he was once absorbed with the writing of artful prose and poetry, and with the teachings of Buddhism and Taoism [Daoism], regarded his new theories as novel doctrines, unworthy of careful study. They did not realize that his three years of exile among barbarians, and his efforts to keep [his mind] at peace while in the midst of difficulties, had brought him a degree of discernment and of single-mindedness that indicates his penetration into the state of sagehood, and his attainment of supreme harmony and truth.[87]

While acknowledging the serene and easygoing character of his master, Xu extolled him as having entered the sphere of sagehood. From this we see how venerable Yangming was in the eyes of his disciples.

The immanent character of Confucian spirituality is revealed in Yangming's teaching. According to a record by his disciple, Yangming changed three times in the development of his teaching. First, he taught the doctrine of "unity between knowledge and action;" second, he propounded quiet meditation; and finally, he recognized the defect of quiet sitting, advocating the precept of "extending *liangzhi*."[88] The term *liangzhi* originates in *Mencius*. Because of the complexity of its meaning, it is not easy to translate, and has been variously rendered as "primordial awareness," "innate knowledge," "conscientious wisdom," "intuitive knowledge of the good," "conscientious consciousness," or "good conscience."[89] Thus, *liangzhi*—being the essence of Yangming's teaching—can be perceived from a certain perspective to denote our conscience, which is simply our sense of right and wrong. There is a story that illustrates the *liangzhi* being already realized, meaning that *liangzhi* in us "is already perfect and so absolves us from the need of making efforts at spiritual cultivation":[90]

> A follower of Wang Yang-ming once caught a thief in his house at night, whereupon he gave him a lecture about *liang-chih* [*liangzhi*]. The thief laughed and asked: "Tell me, please, where is my *liang-chih*?" At that time the weather was hot, so the thief's captor invited him first to take off his jacket, then his shirt, and then continued: "It is still too hot. Why not take off your trousers too?" At this the thief hesitated and replied: "That does not seem to be

> quite right." Thereupon his captor shouted at him: "There is your *liang-chih*!"[91]

Feng Yu-lan believes the story "shows that every man possesses that intuitive knowledge [*liangzhi*] which is the manifestation of his original mind, and through which he immediately knows that right is right and wrong is wrong." Confucian spiritual masters are those who act in accordance with this *liangzhi*, which already exists within themselves. Therefore, "everyone, in his original nature, is a sage. That is why the followers of Wang Shou-jen [i.e., Yangming] were in the habit of saying that 'the streets are full of sages.'"[92]

For fear that the *liangzhi* being already realized would lead us to the misconception that Yangming's teaching is confined to conscience as the basis of moral behavior—and therefore bind it to the judgment that it is solely an ethical theory—we should hasten to add that *liangzhi* also has a strong spiritual dimension. In the final analysis, *liangzhi* should not be completely identified with our ordinary conscience. In fact, *liangzhi* as the manifestation of the original mind is identified by Yangming as the *tianli* (Heavenly Principle or Principle of Heaven).[93] *Tianli* is an ancient term found in the *Book of Rites*. Its literal meaning appears to remain unchanged for Yangming; but what is new in Yangming's thought is that he identified Principle of Heaven with *liangzhi*. This is predicated on the belief that *liangzhi* has its own dynamism and direction, and "if we learn to 'expand' our awareness [*liangzhi*] by extending its orbit of concern to an ever-enlarging circle of relationships (family, clan, village, nation, world, and beyond) [i.e., extending our *liangzhi*], we can experientially form one body with Heaven, Earth, and the myriad things."[94]

Yangming taught that one should be constantly aware of one's *liangzhi* in daily life. Despite this seemingly "simple and easy" method of self-cultivation, Yangming understood very well that to achieve a fruitful result of cultivation one should go through rigorous mental discipline through handling concrete affairs. Even Yangming himself had to admit that only through "a hundred deaths and a thousand hardships" could he acquire the wisdom of *liangzhi*. It took Yangming a number of years to discover the depths of the term, so that he could articulate its meaning as intuitive knowledge.[95]

A Modern Confucian Spiritual Master: Tang Junyi

The spirit of Confucianism was passed from the ancient sages to Confucius, and then to Song-Ming Neo-Confucians, such as Wang

Yangming. Entering the modern period, since the beginning of the twentieth century, Confucianism has been suffering from enormous setbacks in terms of its vitality and influence, and facing the crisis of modernization in China. In spite of this, Confucianism is still a living tradition. Tang Junyi (1909–1978) was one of the few Contemporary New Confucians who devoted his whole life to the revival of the spirit of Confucianism. He was a scholar and professor of philosophy. Throughout his academic career, apart from teaching and administrative duties, he was a prolific writer.[96] Tang might be labeled as a contemporary Confucian spiritual master, since his works show that he had profound experiential realization of the Confucian way, and many pupils were inspired by his teaching. Tang was among the few who could really capture the core values characteristic of Confucius's spirituality, and compare them with those of great spiritual masters in other of the world's religions—something that he succinctly expressed in his work:

> Jesus, Sakyamuni, Mohammed transcend all worldly spheres of scholars, entrepreneurs, geniuses, heroes, and men of courage and intelligence. Thus, all activities of life and culture, in their eyes, are just like clouds floating in the sky [that vanish easily and are illusive]. . . . In eradicating all worldly splendors to revert to the infinite spirit of the sages, is there anyone who can retain a little bit of splendor? However, while these sages eradicate all worldly splendors, thereby making their transcendence and divinity conspicuous, their transcendence and divinity enable them to manifest splendor in front of the common people. Confucius even eradicates this splendor [of transcendence and divinity], and everything [in him] becomes natural and ordinary. This is because the state of Confucius as a sage, on the one hand, transcends all spheres of scholars, entrepreneurs, geniuses, heroes and men of courage and intelligence; on the other hand . . . all activities of life and culture it affirms as real and not illusive; to all spirits of common people, scholars, entrepreneurs, geniuses, heroes, men of courage and intelligence and sages that have true values and are consistent with one another, it pays tribute and respect.[97]

Tang Junyi's words point clearly to the immanent or world-affirming character of Confucian spirituality, which is the spirit of respect, affirmation, and discovery of the spiritual values in all things in the universe. This characteristic of immanence and world-affirmation pervades Tang Junyi's philosophical system. In it, world philosophies are classified into various types, each finding a proper place. They are arranged in an evolutionary order from what is more superficial to what is deeper, and from what is narrower in scope to what is comprehensive and all-encompassing. Many sophisticated philosophical arguments for different positions were incorporated in the system, and each had been given a hearing to the best of Tang's knowledge.

Tang made effort to find a proper place for the insights of Indian and Western civilizations. But the world he admired most was still the world discovered in the Confucian philosophy of humanity and creativity. His aim was to deal with the existence of life as a whole and the spiritual worlds that open up to the human mind.[98] According to Tang, there are spiritual worlds that encompass different kinds of human activities. Each kind of human activity—such as, political, economic, social, military, cultural, and artistic—opens up a spiritual world to the human mind. Tang tied these activities into a philosophy of culture. In it, his philosophical reflection moves from abstract epistemological query to metaphysical realization, and then still farther to the development of history and culture bearing a religious dimension. Tang depicted an all-pervading, underlying moral consciousness as the foundation of the development of culture: this is the moral consciousness that drives us to affirm the existence of the world, and then to seek ways of spiritual ascendancy, eventually transcending the confines of time and space.[99] Given the synthetic character and the affirmation of culture in Tang's philosophy, it is no surprise that after Tang's death, his good friend Mou Zongsan (1909–1995), another Contemporary New Confucian, described Tang as "a giant in the universe of cultural consciousness."[100]

Not only in theory, but also in practice, Tang Junyi struggled to actualize his cultural ideal. This is shown in his founding, along, with other scholars the New Asia College in Hong Kong in the late 1940s. It was a time of hardship and poverty after World War II and the Civil War, during which Tang and his comrades, as homeless refugees, had to sleep in classrooms, with no other dwelling place. Many students who had lost their families lived in the college as well, and those who could not afford the tuition fee were welcomed on condition that they helped with cleaning the school.[101] In such a spirit of teaching and learning, coupled with the strong commitment of Tang and his companions to the Confucian ideal, the college later became a center for Contemporary Neo-Confucianism.[102] Thus, Tang, being a preacher of Confucianism as well as a person who lived it, did not set aside the concern for this world in his quest for transcendence. As William Yau-nang Ng writes:

> Tang's spirituality is thus not enveloped in the pursuit of inner life but points to concern for and participation in the struggle for the improvement of humanity. Viewed from this perspective, spirituality is not a merely personal matter; it is communal in character. In this regard, Tang's position reflects a continuation of the tradition of Confucian spirituality, which, as suggested by Julia Ching, "is a spirituality which unites inner sageliness and outer kingliness, a life of contemplation and a life of activity."[103]

Tang "shows a balance between pursuit of inner life and accomplishment in the world," and "reveals an affirmation of the complementarity of human and spiritual development."[104] This affirmation of the complementarity of human and spiritual development is exactly the characteristic of Confucian spirituality that is revealed in the spiritual masters of the tradition. No doubt, they make a significant contribution to the development of world spirituality today.

Notes

1. See Tu Weiming and Mary Evelyn Tucker, eds., *Confucian Spirituality*, 2 vols. (New York: Crossroad, 2003).

2. If we explain the term in a very broad sense, a spiritual master can refer also to a Confucian gentleman (or superior person, *junzi*) and virtuous person (or worthy person, *xian*). A gentleman is a person who has attained a high level of morality, whereas a virtuous person is even morally higher than a gentleman. They become sages in entering the perfect state of moral self-cultivation. Note: The convention in this chapter for rendering Chinese terms is that only proper names are capitalized. Relevant Chinese terms are added where deemed appropriate.

3. Xu shen and Duan Yucai, *Shuowen jiezi zhu* (An explanation of words and terms [by Xu shen in the Eastern Han], with a commentary [by Duan Yucai in the Qing dynasty (1644–1912)]) (Taipei: Hanjing wenhua shiye youxian gongsi, 1980), 598. See also Rodney L. Taylor, "Scripture and the Sage: On the Question of a Confucian Scripture," in *The Religious Dimensions of Confucianism* (Albany: State University of New York Press, 1990), 24.

4. Ibid.

5. Ibid. According to the *Shuowen jiezi*, *cheng* (meaning "manifest" or "disclose") serves as the phonetic and may have nothing to do with the

meaning of *sheng*. If we trace back to the oracle bone script, we find that the earliest graph form of *sheng* is the picture of an ear placed above a person. I am indebted to Professor Jingtao Sun for the information he provided for the Chinese character *sheng*.

6. See Julia Ching, "Who Were the Ancient Sages?" in *Sages and Filial Sons—Mythology and Archaeology in Ancient China,* ed. Julia Ching and R. W. L. Guisso (Hong Kong: The Chinese University Press, 1991), 16–17. That the sage hears the voice of spirits is suggested by Julia Ching; that the sage hears the Way of Heaven is suggested by Rodney Taylor (see Rodney L. Taylor, "Scripture and the Sage," 24).

7. Julia Ching, "Who Were the Ancient Sages?," 8.

8. *Yijing* (Book of Changes) in *Shisan jing zhushu* (commentaries to the thirteen classics), 8 vols. (Taipei: Yiwen yinshu guan, 1979), 1:17. Translation from Wing-tsit Chan, *A Source Book in Chinese Philosophy* (Princeton: Princeton University Press, 1963), 264. It is safe to consider the "great man" in the quotation as the sage. In a later text in the Eastern Han, the *Baihu tongyi,* similar statements are used to describe the sage. See Ban Gu, ed., *Baihu tongyi* (an explanation of the discussions of the White Tiger Hall), in *Huangqing jingjie xubian* (Supplement to the Classics of the Qing Dynasty) (repr., Taipei, 1968), chs. 1265–76; 276–81; see also Julia Ching, "Who Were the Ancient Sages?," 8, 19.

9. This is the saying of an important Ming Confucian, Wang Yangming (1472–1529); see his *Da xuewen* (inquiry on the *Great Learning*); translation from Wing-tsit Chan, *Source Book,* 659.

10. See Julia Ching, "Who Were the Ancient Sages?," 8–9.

11. D. C. Lau, trans., *Mencius* (London: Penguin Books, 1970), 6B.2, 172. Note: The convention in this chapter is not to give a page number of sources (e.g., *Analects* and *Mencius* translated by D. C. Lau) if the translation of passages is adopted from another book (e.g., Wing-tsit Chan, *Source Book*).

12. Wang Yangming, *Instructions for Practical Living and other Neo-Confucian Writings,* trans. with notes by Wing-tsit Chan (New York: Columbia University Press, 1962), 60; translation very slightly modified by the author.

13. The terms *Principle of Heaven, Mandate of Heaven,* and *Way of Heaven* that appear in various quotations are similar in meaning and may be conveniently regarded as equivalent terms in the context of this chapter—although they would have different connotations if discussed in detail. *Heaven* on many occasions is similar to these terms, except that it sometimes is used to convey a meaning synonymous with *shangdi,* the Lord on High. By contrast, the other terms, generally speaking, refer to the moral law or other aspects of Heaven.

14. For a longer list of ancient sages, see Julia Ching, "Who Were the Ancient Sages?," 1–22.

15. Ibid., 9–11.

16. D. C. Lau, trans., *Confucius: The Analects* (London: Penguin Books, 1979), 7.19, 88. Zilu was Confucius's disciple.

17. Ibid., 16.9, 140.

18. Ibid., 7.19, 88; see also Wing-tsit Chan, *Source Book,* 32.

19. Ibid., 7.24, 89.

20. Ibid., 7.22, 88.

21. Ibid., 6.28, 85.

22. Ibid., 7.21; see Wing-tsit Chan, *Source Book,* 32; translation modified by the author.

23. Ibid., 6.22; see Wing-tsit Chan, *Source Book,* 30; translation modified by the author.

24. Ibid., 11.22; see Wing-tsit Chan, *Source Book,* 36; translation modified by the author.

25. Ibid., 3.12, see Wing-tsit Chan, *Source Book,* 25; translation modified by the author.

26. See Fung Yu-lan [Feng Youlan], *A Short History of Chinese Philosophy* (New York: Free Press, 1966), 57.

27. See Shu-hsien Liu, *Understanding Confucian Philosophy: Classical and Sung-Ming* (Westport, CT: Greenwood Press, 1998), 23.

28. See Tu Weiming, "A Confucian Perspective in Learning to be Human," in *Confucian Thought: Selfhood as Creative Transformation* (Albany: State University of New York Press, 1985), 51.

29. Lau, *Analects,* 16.8; see Wing-tsit Chan, *Source Book,* 45; translation modified by the author.

30. Ibid., 14.35; see Wing-tsit Chan, *Source Book,* 42–43.

31. See Wing-tsit Chan, *Source Book,* 43.

32. Lau, *Analects,* 7.23; see Wing-tsit Chan, *Source Book,* 32.

33. Ibid., 9.5, 96.

34. Wing-tsit Chan, *Source Book,* 35.

35. Lau, *Analects,* 19.24; see Wing-tsit Chan, *Source Book,* 25; translation modified by the author.

36. Ibid., 19.24; see Wing-tsit Chan, *Source Book,* 48.

37. Ibid., 19.23, 156.

38. Ibid., 9.11, 97.

39. Ibid., 5.13; see Wing-tsit Chan, *Source Book,* 28.

40. Wing-tsit Chan, *Source Book,* 28.

41. H. H. Rowley, *Prophecy and Religion in Ancient China and Israel* (London: University of London, 1956), 125–26.

42. Hans Küng and Julia Ching, *Christianity and Chinese Religions* (New York: Doubleday, 1989), 111.

43. Lau, *Analects,* 17.19; see Wing-tsit Chan, *Source Book,* 47; translation modified by the author.

44. Shu-hsien Liu, *Understanding Confucian Philosophy,* 25–26.

45. Lau, *Analects,* 15.29; see Wing-tsit Chan, *Source Book,* 44.

46. Ibid., 7.34, 90–91.

47. Lau, *Mencius,* 2A. 2, 79.

48. Tu Weiming, "The Confucian Sage: Exemplar of Personal Knowledge," in *Saints and Virtues,* ed. John Stratton Hawley (Berkeley: University of California Press, 1987), 85.

49. Ibid., 85–86.

50. I am indebted to the insights of Professors Fung Yu-lan (1895–1990) and Tang Junyi (1909–1978) in my writing of the following sections of this essay. See Fung Yu-lan, *Short History*, 46–48; Tang Junyi, "Lun kongxue jingshen" (On the Spirit of the Learning of Confucius), in *Zhonghua renwen yu dangjin shijie bubian* (Supplementary Essays on Chinese Humanity and the Modern World), 2 vols. (Taipei: Xuesheng shuju, 1988), 1:234–41.

51. Lau, *Analects*, 2. 4; see Wing-tsit Chan, *Source Book*, 22.

52. Ibid., 7.6, 86; translation modified by the author.

53. Ibid., 4.8, 73; translation modified by the author.

54. See Fung Yu-lan, *Short History*, 46.

55. Lau, *Analects*, 8.8, 93; 20.3, 160.

56. Ibid., 9.30, 100; translation modified by the author.

57. Ibid., 9.26, 99; translation modified by the author.

58. Ibid., 13.27, 123; translation modified by the author.

59. Ibid., 5.11, 77–78.

60. Lau, *Mencius*, 3B.2; translation from Wing-tsit Chan, *Source Book*, 72.

61. Lau, *Analects*, 9.29, 100; translation modified by the author. A sage is a wise man, but a wise man may not be a sage. If we define spiritual master as *sheng* (which we translate as "sage") in Confucianism, then Confucius cannot be regarded as a spiritual master at the age of forty. If we broaden the definition of spiritual master in Confucianism (see note 2 above), then Confucius can be regarded as a spiritual master at thirty. Since "the man of wisdom has no perplexities" (*zhizhe bu huo*) is a well-known saying in Confucianism, and Confucius said clearly that he had no perplexities at forty, to say that he became a wise man at forty is justifiable and is widely accepted by scholars.

62. Zhu Xi, *Sishu jizhu* (Collected commentaries on the *Four Books*) (Hong Kong: Dazhong tushu gongsi, n.d.), 7, 61; translation by the author; Zhu Xi (1130–1200) was a prominent Confucian in the Southern Song dynasty (1127–1279) of China.

63. Lau, *Analects*, 12.10, 114; translation modified by the author.

64. Ibid., 12.21, 116; translation modified by the author.

65. Ibid., 4.3, 72.

66. See Fung Yu-lan, *Short History*, 46.

67. Ibid., 47.

68. Ibid.

69. Huang Zhongxi and Quan Zuwang, eds., *Song Yuan xuean* (Records of the Song and Yuan scholars), 3 vols. (Taipei: Shijie shuju, 1973), 1:441; translation by the author.

70. Lau, *Analects*, 6.27, 85.

71. Ibid., 9.2, 96.

72. Tu Weiming, "The Confucian Sage: Exemplar of Personal Knowledge," 77.

73. Taylor, "Scripture and the Sage," 25.

74. Ibid.

75. Lau, *Analects*, 2: 2, 63.

76. Taylor, "Scripture and the Sage," 26–27.

77. See Fung Yu-lan, *Short History,* 47–48.

78. Lau, *Mencius,* 5A.1–5, 138–44.

79. Ibid., 3A.4, 102; see also Ching, "Who Were the Ancient Sages?," 3–6.

80. Ching, "Who Were the Ancient Sages?," 2–3.

81. There may be two exceptions, Yan Yuan (the most outstanding disciple of Confucius) and Mencius (371–289 BCE?). Respectively, they were called *fusheng* (sage-returner) and *yasheng* (secondary sage). But it is obvious that they were regarded only as being close to the state of a sage.

82. *Instructions for Practical Living and Other Neo-Confucian Writings by Wang Yang-ming,* 249.

83. Wang Yangming, *WangYangming quanji* (complete works of Wang Yangming) (Taipei: Heluo tushu chuban she, 1978), 7.

84. "Nianpu" (chronological biography), in *Wang Yangming quanji,* 614–15.

85. *Wang Yangming quanji,* 655; translation from Julia Ching, *To Acquire Wisdom: The Way of Wang Yang-ming* (New York: Columbia University Press, 1976), 49–50; translation modified by the author.

86. Ibid., 382; translation from Ching, *To Acquire Wisdom,* 49–50; translation modified by the author. Zeng Dian was Confucius's disciple.

87. Ibid., 1, in Ching, *To Acquire Wisdom,* 51.

88. Ibid., 7.

89. See Tu Weiming, "Subjectivity and Ontological Reality—An Interpretation of Wang Yang-ming's Mode of Thinking," in *Humanity and Self-Cultivation: Essays in Confucian Thought* (Berkeley: Asian Humanities Press, 1979), 155, 160.

90. See Julia Ching, ed., *The Records of Ming Scholars* (Honolulu: University of Hawaii Press, 1987), 285.

91. Qtd. in Fung Yu-lan, *Short History,* 313; translation modified by the author.

92. Ibid.

93. See Tu Weiming, "Subjectivity and Ontological Reality," 155.

94. Tu Weiming, "Learning to Be Human: Spiritual Exercises from Zhu Xi and Wang Yangming to Liu Zongzhou," in *Confucian Spirituality,* 2:156–57.

95. "Nianpu," in *Wang Yangming quanji,* 648.

96. See Shu-hsien Liu, "The Spiritual Spheres of T'ang Chün-I [Tang Junyi]," in *Essentials of Contemporary Neo-Confucian Philosophy* (Westport, CT: Praeger, 2003), ch. 6, 89–90.

97. Tang Junyi, *Renwen jingshen zhi chongjian* (The Re-establishment of Humanistic Spirit) (Taipei: Xuesheng shuju, 1980), 227–28; translation by the author.

98. The description of Tang's philosophical system is borrowed from Shu-hsien Liu, *Essentials of Contemporary Neo-Confucian Philosophy,* 102.

99. Ibid., 93.

100. Ibid., 103.

101. William Yau-nang Ng, "Tang Junyi's Spirituality: Reflections on Its Foundation and Possible Contemporary Relevance," in *Confucian Spirituality,* 2:393.

102. According to Shu-hsien Liu, Contemporary New Confucianism refers to a large group of contemporary scholars who upheld Confucianism; whereas Contemporary Neo-Confucianism refers to a number of scholars within this large group, who emphasize the spiritual aspect and philosophical interpretation of Confucianism. The New Asia College is the center of this branch of Contemporary Neo-Confucianism. See Shu-hsien Liu, *Essentials of Contemporary Neo-Confucian Philosophy,* 21–40.

103. William Yau-nang Ng, "Tang Junyi's Spirituality," in *Confucian Spirituality,* 2:393; see also Julia Ching, "What is Confucian Spirituality?," in *Confucian Spirituality,* 1:94.

104. Ibid., 2:393–94.

8

Daoist Spiritual Masters

Eva Wong

The sage abides in non-action and practices the teachings without fanfare.
Although ten thousand myriad things arise, he is not the originator;
He acts in their interest but does not own them;
He accomplishes his tasks but does not brag about them.

—*Daodejing* [1]

The sages and wise ones
Carried the mystery and embraced the ultimate reality.
They covered their traces and hid from the world.
They conserved their energy and nourished the spirit.
Their tendons and bones were soft and strong.
They expelled all toxins from the body
And constantly preserved their internal energy.

> In time, their bodies were transformed and they became immortals.
>
> —*Triplex Unity*

> Does it really matter if someone is recognized as a sage or not? If you are truly honest, sincere, and upright in everything you do, do you need others to acknowledge your virtues to make you virtuous?
>
> —*Lieze*

Introduction

What is a spiritual master? How does one become a spiritual master of Daoism? Within Daoist tradition these are not easy questions to answer. In Chinese culture the concept "spiritual master" does not exist. There are master carpenters, master tailors, and master shipwrights—but strictly speaking, no masters in spirituality. Mastery implies acquiring a skill and becoming proficient in it. In Daoism, attaining enlightenment is not a matter of gaining expertise in a skill, but of cultivating a clear mind and nourishing a healthy body. It is said that Daoist spiritual practices are associated with "losing" rather than "gaining." We lose ego, aggression, desire, anxiety, pride, anger, and self-centeredness. And what do we gain? Nothing. If mind and body were cultivated with the intention to "gain" something, spirituality would have been defeated.

In the Daoist tradition, the closest equivalent that would help to define *spiritual master* is the sage—or the enlightened being. And if there is anything to be mastered, it is the egocentric mind and the lethargic body. Strictly speaking, however, the sage does not master body and mind, but transforms and tames them. In the process of spiritual cultivation, the sage transforms a weak, unhealthy body into a strong and energetic body, and tames a confused, egocentric mind into a clear and quiet mind that is free from desire and attachment. Daoism does not teach renunciation; thus, freedom from grasping does not mandate freedom from material things. Having material things in life is not an obstacle to enlightenment. The problem arises only when we become excessive. Likewise, thoughts are not negative, per se. The problem arises only when we use them to affirm a perspective of a world centered on ourselves. This view is echoed in Laozi's *Daodejing*:

> If you desire a lot, you're going to be extravagant. If you horde and hold on to your belongings, you're bound to lose them. Therefore, if you know contentment, you'll never run into trouble. If you know when to stop, you will not come to harm. As a result, you will live for a long time.[2]

The Path to Sagehood

How does one become a Daoist sage? The path to sagehood lies in cultivating mind and body. A quiet and empty mind is necessary for strengthening and nourishing the body, and a strong and healthy body facilitates clearing and stilling the mind.

Clearing and Stilling the Mind

The mind is intrinsically clear and still. However, for the typical person, clarity and stillness are clouded by desire, entrenched beliefs, and habitual illusions. In Daoism, the clear mind is the enlightened mind, and one who has an enlightened mind is a sage. The enlightened mind is likened to a full moon. Just as the moon can sometimes be hidden by clouds, the true nature of mind can often be obscured by desire and attachment. The enlightened mind is intrinsically clear and bright; it is not bright because we perceive it to be not bright.

How does the spiritual practitioner cultivate a clear mind? The key to cultivating a clear mind lies in entering and maintaining stillness, cultivating stillness, and merging with stillness.

The initial goal of Daoist meditation is to quiet the mind; thus, the first step is entering stillness. The ordinary mind is filled with thoughts, and to enter stillness is to stop internal chattering. If we are able to remove thoughts—mostly centered on the same theme, namely ourselves—we will find that there is very little thought left. Once we realize that most thoughts are "surplus," the mind will quiet down. As internal chatter diminishes, the mind enters stillness naturally. Thereafter, the practitioner will be able to maintain meditative stillness for long periods of time.

Once the practitioner is comfortable with entering and maintaining stillness, the next step is to cultivate stillness. In cultivating stillness, stillness is no longer limited to meditation or restful relaxation. Stillness becomes a part of every aspect of life. When stillness is cultivated, the mind will become clear. When mind is clear, it will be free from confusion and the tendency to indulge in egotistic pursuits.

The last step is merging with stillness. To merge with stillness is to embody stillness such that the dualities of subject and object, thinker and thought, actor and action, self and other, and internal and external are dissolved. In this state of stillness, we do not even have a concept of what it means to be still. We are stillness embodied.

A simple and contemplative lifestyle is conducive to clearing and stilling the mind. The sage adopts a simple lifestyle knowing that attachment to material things can lead to anxiety and worry. We are anxious that we do not have enough—and if we have enough, we are worried that we will lose it. Simplicity is not equivalent to renunciation. Rather, simplicity is living in moderation, in the spirit of what Laozi (sixth century BCE?) described as "rejecting the extreme, the excessive, and the extravagant."[3]

Daoist sages are not free from emotions. Neither do they suppress their feelings. Because Daoist spiritual masters are less affected and controlled by events in the world than are most people, they are less erratic in their thoughts and emotions. They are not excessively elated when things work out and are not depressed when things do not work out. Understanding the advice of Zhuangzi (ca. fourth century BCE) that grief, exaltation, and anger disrupt the peaceful mind, the sages see events as part of a larger scheme of things.

In interacting with the world, Daoist spiritual masters adopt an attitude of noninterference, humility, and simplicity. They do not inflate nor degrade achievements. In fact, sages are said to have no notion of what it means to achieve or attain. The *Daodejing* describes this characteristic of the sage: "His actions lead to results but he is not arrogant, nor does he dwell on their importance."[4] It is frequently misunderstood that sages do nothing. Far from doing nothing, they act according to what it is necessary. Sages respond to what is required rather than force things to go their way. This is what Laozi meant by "getting results by not using force."

Strengthening and Nourishing the Body

Sages strengthen and nourish the body not because they are attached to it. Rather, they know that a healthy and strong body is necessary for clearing the mind and developing the wisdom of enlightenment. The question posed by Laozi more than two thousand years ago is still pertinent today: "Fame or your body, which is more important for you? Your body or possessions—which is worth more?"

On one hand, the body is an obstacle to enlightenment."The reason why I am in trouble is because I have a body," Laozi said in the

Daodejing. The body is, indeed, the source of desire and attachment. Where there is birth, there will be suffering, illness, and death. Where there is a body, there will be desire. However, the body is also the avenue to enlightenment. It is through the body that we cultivate the mind. Strengthening the body helps us to clear the mind, and taming the mind helps us to nourish the body. The body is strengthened and nourished both externally and internally.

External strengthening of the body is concerned with nourishing the bones, muscles, tendons, and spine. Daoist practitioners use techniques of tendon-changing, marrow-washing, massage, kneading, and calisthenics to build external strength. They use techniques of breath regulation, circulation of internal energy, and meditation to build internal strength. It is no accident that *qigong* and martial arts such as *taijiquan* trace their origins to Daoism.

Internal strengthening is concerned with nourishing the internal organs, and preserving and cultivating generative, vital, and spirit energy. The preservation and cultivation of the three internal energies—generative, vital, and spirit—form the basis of Daoist spiritual training. Generative energy is conserved by regulating sexual activity and minimizing desire. Sages do not suppress sexual desire. Rather, the desires decrease naturally as Daoist spiritual masters understand that excessive sexual activity can harm the body. Vital energy is linked to breath, and is, therefore, cultivated through breath regulation. When breath is drawn into and expelled from the lower abdomen, the breath will be connected to the energy of life.

Zhuangzi described the breath of the enlightened being as "heavy, slow, and deep" as compared to the shallow breath of the ordinary person. With time, breath and life energy become intertwined, and internal energy is circulated in synchrony with each inhalation and exhalation. Spirit energy is nourished by stilling and clearing the mind. When the mind is free from desire and entrenched belief systems, spirit energy is conserved and nourished. When spirit energy is nourished, vital energy will be strong; and when vital energy is strong, generative energy will be plentiful.

The Sage's Balanced View of the World

Daoists believe that emotions are rooted in attitude, and that adopting a certain view of the world leads to experiencing specific kinds of emotions. If we believe that the world is a hostile place where we must be aggressive to survive, we are more likely to develop hostility, anger, greed, pride, and so forth. If we believe we are worthless and helpless, we will be more likely to develop sadness and despair. On the contrary, if we believe that every person is capable of attaining enlightenment and embracing the Dao, we will be more likely to develop kindness and compassion. Laozi said, "The sage accumulates nothing. He uses everything he has to help others. As a result, he ends up having more."[5]

The sage understands that mind and body must be cultivated simultaneously. A weak spine and tight tendons make sitting meditation difficult, and a wayward mind will dissipate life energy. Perhaps a quotation from Zhang Sanfeng's classic "Secret Taiji Method for Cultivating the Elixir" best illustrates how health of body and clarity of mind are closely related:

> Watch too long and the generative energy will be damaged.
> Listen too long and the vital energy (qi) will be damaged.
> Lie down too long and the meridians will be harmed.
> Stand too long and the bones will be damaged.
> Walk too much and the tendons will be damaged.
> Anger harms the liver.
> Scheming harms the spleen.
> Worrying harms the heart.
> Excessive sadness harms the lungs.
> Overeating harms the stomach.
> Excessive fear harms the kidneys.
> Too much laughing harms the abdomen.
> Too much talking harms the spinal fluid.
> Sleep too much and the saliva will lose its potency.
> Perspire too much and the yang energy will be harmed.
> Cry too often and the blood will be harmed.
> Too much sex will harm the marrow.[6]

Who Is a Sage?

Who is a sage? Who can become a sage? In the Daoist spiritual tradition, everyone has the potential to be enlightened. On one hand, a person does not have to be extraordinary or talented to become a sage. On the other hand, being intelligent or wealthy is not a liability. The history of Daoism is filled with role models of enlightened beings from every walk of life. Among the Daoist spiritual masters there are conventional and unconventional people, ordinary and extraordinary people, activists and hermits, aristocrats and beggars. Their disposition, demeanor, and lifestyle may differ, but all sages embody wisdom, compassion, and virtue.

The Conventional and the Unconventional

In Chinese history, no one was more honored than Confucius (551–479 BCE). He is the epitome of the sage and has become the model of all Confucian, Daoist, and Chinese Buddhist sages who lived after him. When we examine the life of Confucius, we find that he lived a rather conventional life within established society. A civil servant in early life and later a teacher, he married, raised children, and lived among family, friends, peers, and students. Why was Confucius regarded as a sage? It was not because he was an expert in ancient literature, rites and rituals, and history. It was not because the books he had written and compiled still form the core of the Chinese classics. And it was not because he had developed a philosophy that influenced the entire history of Chinese thought. Rather, he was remembered as a sage because of his wisdom.

It is said that Confucius was once asked if he was sage. In response, Confucius stated that he dared not claim to be one. He named other candidates, but never mentioned his own merits or achievements. Why? This is because Confucius understood that the moment one claimed to be a sage, he or she would no longer be one. If we are attached to the concept of sagehood, we will constantly be measuring ourselves against fixed standards. The wisdom of the sage is fathomless and cannot be measured by social standards or defined by public recognition. If we are truly virtuous, do we need others to acknowledge our virtues to make us virtuous?

It is said that the sage values skill, but delights in wisdom. The meaning of this statement is best illustrated in the following story about Confucius and his students: Zi Xia asked Confucius about the relative merits of the students Yan Hui, Zi Gong, Zi Lu, and Zi Zhang. Confucius said that Yan Hui surpasses him in compassion, Zi Gong debates better, Zi Lu is more courageous, and Zi Zhang is more graceful and dignified.[7] When Zi Xia asked Confucius why they followed him, Confucius replied that while each student had his merits, each also had shortcomings. He then added that he would not exchange their merits for his own.

Confucius understood that wisdom is not equivalent to competence in one or even many skills. Rather, wisdom is the ability to recognize strengths and weaknesses in ourselves and others. Sages know that although they may not surpass others in specific skills, they can help others become better individuals in their own ways. Confucius never boasted about his scholarship and wisdom or his merits as a teacher. He saw and respected the qualities of others and taught them according to their needs. Kind, generous, patient, and mild-mannered, Confucius taught people from all walks of life. More than two thousand years after his death, his teachings are still considered the highest wisdom to have come out of China.

Zhuangzi seems to have been the antithesis of Confucius. While Confucius lived a conventional life and taught that each person should cultivate virtue and be a responsible citizen, Zhuangzi cared nothing about social conventions. Learned and witty, Zhuangzi delighted in mocking the leisure class, the intellectuals, and the entrepreneurs. Not even the high-ranking politicians escaped Zhuangzi's satirical eye and sharp tongue. A story of Zhuangzi's encounter with the imperial messenger best illustrates his character:

> One time Zhuangzi was visited by an imperial messenger who carried the king's request for Zhuangzi to serve as an advisor in the court. Before the messenger would open his mouth, Zhuangzi said, "There was once a tortoise who was captured and put inside the imperial menagerie. The animal was decked out with jewels and given the best food, but all he did each day was brood inside a cage. Now, if you were a tortoise, would you want to sit in captivity and be covered with jewels or would you rather wag your tail and wallow in the mud?" Without a thought, the messenger replied, "Of course I would rather roll in the mud." Zhuangzi then said, "Tell the king that I too would rather wag my tail and wallow in the mud."[8]

Zhuangzi believed that noninterference and letting things be (Chinese: *wuwei*) are the highest virtues. Enlightened persons understand their place in the universe and know that they are not the prime movers. Therefore, they do not seek to control situations and bend things their way. When circumstances require action, the sage acts. When action is folly, the sage yields. Sages would force themselves to live in impossible circumstances no more than tropical plants would fight to live in arctic conditions. To quote the *Zhuangzi*: "The sage does not bring fortune and does not cause misfortune. He only responds when external circumstances call for it. He floats with life and rests with death."[9]

How can two starkly different individuals such as Confucius and Zhuangzi both be recognized as sages? If we carefully examine their views, we find that they are not that different—although one was conventional, and the other was unconventional.

Both men advocated harmony and tolerance. Confucius believed that a peaceful and prosperous society can be realized by practicing sacred rites and rituals, engaging in aesthetic and athletic pursuits, and living virtuously. Zhuangzi recommended that the same goal of a peaceful and prosperous society can be attained by practicing non-interference, and being nonattached to social conventions and niceties.

Both sages also believed that a quiet mind is the foundation of unbiased and clear thinking. Confucius asserted that a clear and quiet mind is cultivated by practicing virtues such as gratitude, harmony, dedication, honesty, propriety, integrity, and humility. Zhuangzi, on the other hand, recommended that emptying the mind of thoughts and desire, adopting a contemplative attitude, and living an unencumbered lifestyle are the foundation for realizing a bright and clear mind.

Both sages also understood that a strong and healthy body is integral to cultivating mental clarity. In this respect, Confucius advocated the practice of archery and horseback riding as techniques of physical strengthening, while Zhuangzi recommended practicing calisthenics, massage, and breath control.

While these two enlightened men lived differently, both believed that clearing the mind, strengthening the body, and living a peaceful, simple, and harmonious life are the keys to spiritual mastery or sagehood. A quote from the *Zhuangzi* describes the lives of Confucius and Zhuangzi most aptly:

> He does not worry and does not scheme. He is like a light that does not dazzle. Completely trustworthy, he does not need to make promises. His spirit is pure and his soul is not tired. In emptiness, nothingness, and simplicity, he is in harmony with the celestial way.[10]

The Ordinary and the Extraordinary

Tang Guanzhen was an ordinary woman in all respects. The daughter of an ordinary family of the Song dynasty (960–1279), she grew up, got married, and lived in the village where she was born. Not highly educated and having no special talents, the story of her life could have been that of any woman of her time—except that she encountered a Daoist immortal who cured her when she was severely ill. After Guangzhen recovered, she left home and began her spiritual training. Her progress surprised her teachers, and when they discovered that she was destined to attain immortality, they invited her to live in the celestial realm. Guangzhen, however, asked her teachers to delay the offer, explaining that she needed to return home to take care of her aging mother. Following this encounter with the immortals, Tang Guangzhen returned to her village and lived a quiet life caring for her mother. It was only after her mother passed away that she sought the immortals, and departed with them to the celestial realm.

Tang Guangzhen's life is the prime Daoist example that enlightenment is attainable by ordinary people, leading ordinary lives. Even after she had completed her spiritual training, and attained the ability of walking on the clouds and floating with the wind, Guangzhen did not seek to gain recognition in her community. She lived a simple life as she waited in the mortal realm to fulfill her filial duties. To Guangzhen, caring for her mother was as enlightened an activity as meditation. It was said that the only difference between her and other people in her village was that her face shone with an inner glow, and she was always rigorous and healthy.

Wei Huacun (251–334) was the opposite of Tang Guangzhen. Born into an aristocratic and artistic family, she was precocious and became highly educated. At age six, Huacun could read and understand the Daoist classics, and by age twelve she was acknowledged as an authority on major scriptures of Daoism. Culturally and intellectually sophisticated, her friends included famous artists, calligraphers, poets, and musicians. Moreover, because her parents were priests of the Celestial Teachers' School of Daoism, Huacun was introduced early in life to the rites, rituals, talismanic magic, and the arts of health and longevity. In her early twenties, she became a high-ranking priestess of Celestial Teachers' Daoism, a form of Daoism that emphasized the use of talismans to cure illness, and bring prosperity and fortune. However, Huacun soon became disappointed with a spiritual tradition that took advantage of common people's superstitions. She left the priesthood, and began to practice a meditation that focused on visualization of deities and mystical union with them. It was said that while in meditative trance, she received teachings from the immortals, which she recorded and titled "The Shangqing Scriptures." These teachings became known as the Shangqing School of Daoism, and Lady Wei Huacun was honored as the founder.

While Lady Wei attained the highest status that any woman or man could attain in her time, she was also a product of Chinese culture and tradition. When Huacun was in her twenties, her parents counseled her to get married. Although she had wished to devote her life to spiritual practice, Huacun—being a filial daughter—consented to the wishes of her parents. She gave birth to two sons, and took care of them until they came of age. Then, after making arrangements with her husband, she built a retreat in a remote area of the family estate and devoted her life to spiritual practice.

Lady Wei Huacun was regarded as an enlightened being and a sage not because she founded a lineage of Daoist teachings, but because of how she lived. Born into a family of Daoist priests, she could have stayed in a comfortable niche within the spiritual community familiar to her, but chose instead to bring new life to Daoist spirituality. Yet, Huacun was not so attached to her spiritual goals as to abandon her duties as a daughter and mother.

The Chinese social and cultural backgrounds of Tang Guangzhen and Wei Huacun stand in stark contrast to each other. Yet the two women had much in common. Both were filial daughters who did not consider family responsibility and spiritual practice to be conflicting. Tang Guangzhen and Wei Huacun are the ultimate examples of women who attained the highest levels of Daoist spirituality without compromising their responsibility and commitment to their families.

The Activist and the Hermit

Many people think that all Daoists are hermits. This is not true. In the history of Daoism, many sages were social and political activists who advised kings and nobles. Participation in political activity is not antithetical to Daoist practice. Even a casual reading of the *Daodejing* will reveal lengthy discussions on leadership and statecraft. The ideal ruler is a sage who governs without inducing fear, who is beyond praise or blame, and who leads the people without them knowing what it means to be led. The *Daodejing* also describes the sage as one who offers his skill for the welfare of the community, and retires when the work is completed. Being unattached to fame and recognition, and knowing when to withdraw, form the essence of Daoist social and political activism. Fan Li and his lover Xi Shi of the ancient Chinese Spring and Autumn period (ca. 771–403 BCE) are examples of activists who understood the meaning of these principles.

Fan Li was a minister during a time when China was plunged into civil war and social disorder. When the king was captured by the enemy in battle, Fan Li followed his lord into captivity. Seeing the king lulled by a rich and leisurely life under house arrest, the minister reminded his lord of the duty to free his people from bondage. With the help of Fan Li as military advisor and Xi Shi as spy, the king not only managed to escape captivity and recover his own fiefdom, but also conquered his former captor's lands. After defeating his enemy, the king asked Fan Li to serve as prime minister, and lavished him and Xi Shi with gifts of gold and land. However, Fan Li and Xi Shi knew that further involvement in politics would draw them into court intrigues and purges. So they took polite leave of the king and settled in lands far from the influence of their sovereign. As Fan Li and Xi Shi had expected, their former lord soon began a purge, executing and murdering ministers and generals who had helped him regain his kingdom. Knowing when and how to withdraw saved the lives of Fan Li and Xi Shi. Not attached to their accomplishments, they never talked about their deeds and achievements. Consequently, they left no trail for the king's assassins to follow. Not even their closest friends knew that the couple had been major players in the political world. Because they knew when and how to yield and withdraw, Fan Li and Xi Shi lived long lives in anonymity and contentment.

Just as there are Daoist spiritual masters who were activists, there are also those who never participated in public service. These sages are hermits by natural inclination. They lived in seclusion all their lives, and shunned the political and social world.

Sima Zhengzhen (646–735) was a hermit who declined offers from the emperor and queen mother to serve as the court's spiritual adviser. Trained as a scholar, and gifted as a poet and calligrapher, Zhengzhen lived a disciplined, yet carefree life. Often, he would hike the mountains or sail down rivers singing and writing poetry with like-minded friends. While not wandering, Sima Zhengzhen lived in seclusion on Mount Tiantai and practiced the arts of longevity. When asked why he chose to build his retreat on Tiantai instead of on Mount Zhongnan, Zhengzhen replied that he would rather live in a little-known region than in one that was crowded with so-called hermits wanting to attract imperial favor.

Sima Zhengzhen was one of the greatest sages in the history of Daoism. He developed and introduced Buddhist insight meditation into Daoist practice. Known also as internal gazing, this form of meditation focused on observing the rise and fall of thoughts in the mind to reach the understanding that thoughts are groundless and mind is intrinsically empty. More than a thousand years after his death, insight meditation is still widely practiced by Daoists today.

Retiring after serving the world, and never becoming involved with the world are both paths to the Dao. To quote the Daoist classic the *Mysteries of the Dao*:

> If they [the sages] choose to use their intelligence, they will serve the country; if not, they will live as a hermit in the

> mountains and forests. In positions of wealth and power, they are not proud; when impoverished they do not blame others. Advancing and retreating according to the situation, they balance movement and stillness.[11]

Fan Li and Xi Shi tasted power and withdrew when it was timely. Sima Zhengzhen saw power and shunned it from the beginning. These sages all understood the meaning of yielding, but each acted according to his or her natural inclination. To force the natural activist to be a hermit, or force the natural hermit to be an activist would be to interfere with the natural way of things. Interfering with the natural way is not the path of the Dao.

The Aristocrat and the Beggar

Perhaps no two sages differed so much in social standing and lifestyle as Liu An (179?–122 BCE), who was an aristocrat, and Zhou Dian, who was a mad beggar of the early Ming dynasty (1368–1644).

Liu An was a prince who was not interested in political power. Although a cousin of the emperor, he distanced himself from politics and chose to live without the luxuries that were granted to a royal relative. Known for compiling the Daoist classic *Huainanzi,* a definitive collection of the teachings of early Daoism, Liu An did not fraternize with members of the royal family or participate in the pursuits of the nobility such as hunting and chariot racing. Delighting in music, poetry, and the arts of longevity, the prince enjoyed the company of Daoist scholars, sages, diviners, and alchemists. Legends tell us that Liu An was visited by Daoist immortals who offered to teach him a skill of his choice: commanding the weather and the elements, taming wild beasts, summoning ghosts and spirits, hiding the movement of armies, mastery in the weapons and martial arts, or divination and the arts of longevity.

Liu An chose the last skill, explaining that he had no interest in feats of power. It was this choice that saved Liu An's life. Although Liu An never wanted to be involved in politics, fate had it that he would become its victim. Liu An's son was accidentally killed by the son of the emperor's secretary during sword practice. Fearing revenge, the secretary told the emperor that Liu An was plotting a rebellion. When the imperial troops arrived at Liu An's home to arrest him, the prince, having a premonition of the upcoming disaster, had swallowed the pill of immortality and disappeared into the immortal realm. The art of longevity and divination saved Liu An's life.

Zhou Dian was the antithesis of Liu An. While Liu An was a culturally sophisticated aristocrat who embraced the Daoist arts and abhorred politics, Zhou Dian was an uncouth and mad beggar who not only got involved in politics, but also played an important role in putting an emperor of a new dynasty on the throne. It was said that when Dian met Zhu Yuanzhang, he foretold that Yuanzhang would defeat the Mongols and become emperor. Throughout his campaigns against the Mongols and other contenders to the throne, Yuanzhang was assisted by Zhou Dian, who predicted the movements of the enemy forces. Zhu Yuanzhang eventually became emperor and restored peace and prosperity to his kingdom. However, toward the end of his life, the emperor lost his sanity. Convinced that his ministers and generals were plotting rebellion, he began to kill his former advisers, the mad beggar included. Zhou Dian was arrested and thrown into a cauldron of boiling water, but the beggar was oblivious to the fire and heat. The emperor then tried to restrain him by locking him in a cell in a monastery. Zhou Dian escaped and wreaked havoc in the monastery's shrines with his mad antics. Finally, the emperor released Zhou Dian, realizing that the mad beggar was not a political threat. After escaping from the clutches of the emperor, Zhou Dian disappeared into mountains and was never heard of again. The other advisors of Zhu Yuanzhang were not so fortunate. Many remained as ministers and generals out of blind loyalty or greed, and all but a few were murdered.

While one shunned politics and the other embraced it, the aristocrat Liu An and the mad beggar Zhou Dian both saw through the illusions of temporal power, and both escaped with their lives. Each lived because he understood the meaning of this statement from the *Daodejing*: "Pride with wealth and power bring disaster." Liu An's noninvolvement in politics gave him the time to study divination and the arts of longevity, which eventually helped him escape treachery and death. Zhou Dian's understanding of the timeliness of leaving the political scene and his skillful way of making an exit allowed him to escape the paranoia of an aging king.

Conclusions

Sagehood, enlightenment—and, for that matter, spiritual mastery—is a state of mind and body. There are tales of enlightened beings walking through fire and floating with the wind. However, these abilities per se do not make one person more enlightened than another. They are simply by-products of spiritual training. Equanimity, good health, clarity of mind, and a peaceful disposition form the essence of sagehood. The enlightened mind is the ordinary mind, which is not mysterious, extraordinary, or unnatural; and the indestructible body is the healthy body. Knowing this, the Daoist spiritual master does not make a fuss about being enlightened. If we consider enlightenment to be an extraordinary achievement, we would have missed its meaning. Consider the story of a man named Lungshu told in the *Lieze* (ca. fifth century BCE).

Lungshu claimed that he was ill, and challenged the best doctors to cure him. This was how he described his illness:

> "When I am praised by others, I do not feel pride. When others speak badly about me, I do not feel disgraced. When I gain something, I am not happy. When I lose, I am not sad. Life and death, riches and poverty, fortune and misfortune are the same to me. As a matter of fact, I can see people as pigs and see myself as other people. When I'm at home, I feel I am wandering around. When I'm in my country, I feel like I am among foreigners. Since I got this illness, I have lost all interest in becoming rich and famous. I don't care about titles, land, and renown. I don't think much about rules and regulations and I am not affected by the emotions of people around me." The doctor, who happened to be a friend of Lungshu's, responded by saying, "I can see that your mind is empty and you are close to being a sage. You have only one problem left, and I believe that this is the cause of your illness. Your illness is seeing wisdom as a strange disease. I am afraid you are the only one who can cure yourself."[12]

Lungshu had gotten rid of all his attachments except one. He still retained a conception of what it meant to be enlightened. Comparing enlightenment to a strange illness, Lungshu made it mysterious, extraordinary, and unnatural.

Enlightenment is a normal experience attainable by everyone. Sagehood is not something spectacular—and there is nothing to master in spiritual mastery. The best description of a sage is found in the *Daodejing*:

> He blocks up his orifices, closes the door, softens the gaze, becomes one with the dust, files down sharpness, and straightens out the tangles.[13]

The best illustration of sagehood or spiritual mastery is found in this record of Lieze's life: Lieze lived a simple life at home, cooked for his wife, and did the housework. He took care of the pigs, and was kind to everyone and everything. He distanced himself from worldly matters, and freed himself from the entanglement of truths and lies. He was no longer a piece of carved jade, but an unadorned block of wood. In the midst of the muddy world, he remained true to himself; and in simplicity and stillness, he spent the rest of his life.

If the Daoist sage had a motto in life, it would be "Live simply so that others may simply live." This quote could have come from a Daoist classic, but the words are actually Mahatma Gandhi's.[14]

Notes

1. All quotes from Daoist texts are my translations. The *Daodejing* (*Tao-te Ching*) is also known as the *Laozi*. Excerpts from the *Daodejing*, the *Zhuangzi*, and the "Secret Taiji Method for Cultivating the Elixir" can be found in my *Teachings of the Tao* (1997). The *Lieze* is translated in full in my *Lieh-tzu: A Taoist Guide to Practical Living* (2001). "The Mysteries of the Tao" is translated in full in my *Nourishing the Essence of Life* (2004). More information on the lives of the Daoist immortals can be found in my *Tales of the Taoist Immortals* (2004). All books are published by Shambhala Publications, Boston.

2. *Daodejing*, ch. 44.

3. Ibid., ch. 29.

4. Ibid., ch. 30.

5. Ibid., ch. 8.

6. Eva Wong, trans., *Teachings of the Tao* (Boston: Shambhala Publications, 1997), 152; see the book for my full translation of "Secret Taiji Method for Cultivating the Elixir."

7. This statement is a paraphrase of my translation in *Lieh-tzu: A Taoist Guide to Practical Living* (Boston: Shambhala, 2001), 37.

8. This story is from the *Zhuangzi*, ch 17.

9. This is from ibid., ch. 15; the translation is from my *Teachings of the Tao*, 38.

10. This is from ibid., ch. 15; the translation is from my *Teachings of the Tao*, 38.

11. The translation is from my *Nourishing the Essence of Life* (Boston: Shambhala, 2004), 48.

12. The translation is from my *Lieh-tzu*, 40.

13. *Daodejing*, ch 56; my translation.

14. This is said to be a famous saying of Gandhiji's when he was in living in South Africa.

Concluding Remarks

Arvind Sharma

Exotericism

The preceding chapters provided an overview of the place of the spiritual master in Judaic, Christian, Islamic, Hindu, Sikh, Buddhist, Confucian, and Daoist traditions. One striking fact emerging from this survey is that the role of the spiritual master tends to involve both esoteric and exoteric dimensions of religion. This conclusion is somewhat counterintuitive because one might, at first blush, be inclined to think that the spiritual master is likely to be concerned with the esoteric dimension alone. However, as Victoria Kennick signaled in the opening chapter, the social impact of the spiritual master cannot be overlooked. Some spiritual masters, with the active participation of the public, founded traditions and institutions that have lasted for centuries. In this respect, it is difficult not to be impressed by the sheer longevity of the Buddhist *saṃgha,* which has a history of almost two thousand five hundred years behind it. It started as an exoteric movement, although it developed esoteric dimensions in the course of its history. The Buddha famously stated in the *Mahāparinibbāna Sutta* that "there was no esoteric doctrine in his teaching, nothing hidden in the 'closed-fist of the teacher' (*ācariya-muṭṭhi*), or to put it in other words, there never was anything 'up his sleeve.'"[1] This farewell sermon of his is worth citing in some detail:

> Ānanda, what does the Order of the Sangha expect from me? I have taught the *Dhamma* (Truth) without making any distinction as exoteric and esoteric. With regard to the truth, the Tathāgata has nothing like the closed fist of a teacher (*ācariya-muṭṭhi*). Surely, Ānanda, if there is anyone who thinks that he will lead the Sangha, and that the Sangha should depend on him, let him set down his instructions. But the Tathāgata has no such idea. Why should he then leave instructions concerning the Sangha? I am now old, Ānanda, eighty years old. As a worn-out cart has to be kept going by repairs, so, it seems to me, the body of the Tathāgata can only be kept going by repairs. *Therefore, Ānanda, dwell making yourselves your island (support), making yourselves, not anyone else, your refuge; making the Dhamma your island (support), the Dhamma your refuge, nothing else your refuge.*[2]

It is therefore a matter of some significance that esoteric traditions emerged within Buddhism, in which even the confessions at the fortnightly gatherings by the monks are made in public. That is, they confessed in an assembly of monks rather than to an individual. We shall examine the significance of the esoteric developments within Buddhism later in these concluding remarks. At this point, what needs to be recognized is that the exoteric dimension of the figure of the spiritual master, in a sense, provides a reality check to the esoteric dimension. Victoria Kennick refers to cases of spiritual masters who mislead their followers, sometimes to their death; and it is on the basis of such negative social impact that one is able to make judgments about them. The biblical dictum *ye shall know them by their fruits* applies with illuminating force in such cases.

> Ye shall know them by their fruits. Do men gather grapes of thorns, or figs of thistles?
> Even so, every good tree bringeth forth good fruit, but a corrupt tree bringeth forth evil fruit.
> A good tree cannot bring forth evil fruit, neither *can* a corrupt tree bring forth good fruit.

> Every tree that bringeth not forth good fruit is hewn down,
> and cast in fire.
> Wherefore by their fruits ye shall know them.[3]

This recognition of the exoteric dimension to the work of spiritual master is salutary because it can help distinguish, at least retrospectively, between good and bad spiritual masters. Moreover, it can signal proactively when an esoteric tradition *begins* to display signs of bearing bad fruit. After all, traditions founded by spiritual masters that are sound to begin with may take a turn for the worse.

Esotericism

We must now deal with the fact that religious traditions founded in an explicitly exoteric way also seem to develop an esoteric dimension as they grow. This is obvious in the transformation of Buddhist tradition from Theravāda Buddhism to Mahāyāna Buddhism—and even more so in its transformation into Vajrayāna Buddhism. It is perhaps a little less obvious, but equally true within Islamic tradition, which does not even contain a monastic tradition, in accord with the *ḥadīth*: "There is no monasticism in Islam." That such a religion also evolved a tradition of religious masters espousing an esoteric dimension is striking. One needs to examine why such should be the case, including its persistence in modern times, especially given the tendency in certain circles of modern Islam to marginalize or even eliminate the Ṣūfī component.

It seems, at bottom, to have to do with the place of individuality in a religious tradition, and the fact that the needs of individuals sometimes must be met individually rather than more generally. Perhaps it might be useful to distinguish here between what an individual might need *in general,* and a person's individual needs. Every individual needs food and this need can be met by supplying food in general. But if someone has individual dietetic needs, as we notice during plane flights, the person has to be served a special meal. Thus, what an individual might need in general can be met exoterically; *but a person's individual needs require a more esoteric approach, as it were.*

Such personal needs arise both in the case of religious traditions that work with a cafeteria approach and in those that favor a set menu approach to reality, though for slightly different reasons. In the case of Hindu tradition, for instance, which allows everyone to choose one's deity to worship in accord with its doctrine of *iṣṭadevatā,* the need arises because of the wide range of choice. Indeed, its variety may require someone who can tell us where to go, just as we need the help of the staff in the supermarket to find the right place to look for what we need. The spiritual master, in this case, helps determine which part of the tradition—in terms of its gods, scriptures, practices, and so on—may be relevant for someone. The polycentrism[4] of Hindu tradition, thus, sheds light on the role of the *gurū*, or spiritual master in it.

This description of the cafeteria approach could probably be extended to cover other non-Abrahamic traditions as well. On the other hand, Abrahamic traditions, with their set menus, also meet the individual's needs. However, the individual's needs are met by spiritual masters in these traditions in a slightly different way—by evolving a separate dietetic supplement for the nourishment of the individual in addition to the main menu. Thus, in both cases, spiritual masters cater to individual's needs, but according to a different approach.

Individuality and Spirituality

From the individual to the personal is but a step. The moment one is not satisfied with experiencing only the communal dimension of religion—but wants to know more about the truth on the basis of which the community is founded and to experience it for oneself—the texture of religious life changes. This transition is articulated these days in the frequently encountered statement: "I'm not religious, I am spiritual." On the basis of various opinion surveys, the statement can be parsed as follows: I do not believe in following institutionalized or communal religion; I want to experience religion on my own. This is the course that some great spiritual masters who founded well-known religions followed (although all attempts to strike out on one's own are not admittedly always that spectacular). The reason why the individual holds the key in this respect was well articulated by the major figure of the Protestant movement, Martin Luther, when he said: "Everyone must do his own believing as he will have to do his own dying."[5] The individual is now groping for spirituality, but what is spirituality?

Spirituality

The word *spirituality* is best understood in the light of two other words, *physicality* and *mentality*. All three words have a large and ambiguous semantic provenance, so it would be good to identify the sense in which they are being employed here. We are all conscious that we possess a physical body. Then, we can use the word *physicality* to denote such body-consciousness. When we eat, or when we feel pain or drowsiness, we are operating in the realm of physicality. There are also times when we lose physicality, or body-consciousness. When we are watching an engrossing movie on TV, for instance, we lose awareness of our body. We do not lose the body, but we do lose an awareness of it. We are then operating in the realm of *mentality,* or mind-consciousness, as distinguished from body-consciousness. To reiterate, it is possible to transcend body-consciousness or physicality. Still, we must clarify that we do not transcend the body as such, for it is still there, and we can easily be recalled to it by mere touch. Nonetheless, we do transcend body-consciousness in moments of intense mental absorption.

Our life, as it usually is lived, consists of our experiences in the realms of body-consciousness and mind-consciousness, or what we have called physicality and mentality. Now if mentality can transcend physicality—that is, if mental consciousness can supervene over physical consciousness—without involving the loss of body, then is it possible that one could transcend *both* body-consciousness and mind-consciousness without involving loss of mind? The significance of this possibility would lie in the fact that if the transcendence of bodily consciousness lifts us into a realm of the mind where we can have enriching experiences that we could not have without transcending body-consciousness, could there also exist a spiritual realm similarly offering its own range of life-enriching experiences that we cannot have until we transcend both body-consciousness and mind-consciousness? Leaving mind-consciousness behind may no more constitute loss of mind, than leaving body-consciousness behind involves losing the body. What would happen if the mind, like the body, fell out of the ambit of our consciousness?

Spirituality, in order to be experienced, involves transcendence of both physicality and mentality. In connection with this transcendence of body-consciousness and mind-consciousness, three questions immediately arise: Is there such a beyond? Even if it is there, is it worth exploring or just something like a dead planet? and How do we get there, if it is worth experiencing? Spiritual masters who teach about these matters answer unequivocally that there is such a beyond, that it is worth experiencing, and that there are ways of doing so. They promise that a new mental world opens up when we rise above body-consciousness; and the more we rise above it, the more clearly and rewardingly it opens up. Similarly, when we rise above mind-consciousness or the scattered thoughts we experience most of the time, a new spiritual world opens up before us; and the more we rise above mind-consciousness, the more clearly and rewardingly it opens up.

This foray into spirituality from physicality and mentality does not mean that body and mind are destroyed in spiritual experiences. Rather, it indicates that they are transcended. In fact, they remain capable of interfering with our spiritual consciousness, just as hunger may intrude on our mentality. The more completely the body-mind is transcended, or the longer the period of such transcendence, the greater the extent to which spiritual realms of worthwhile experiences can open up. They are as different from our mental experiences as mental experiences are from physical experiences. Of course, spirituality, too, will have to be accomplished within a state of consciousness. In fact, we transcend both body and mind every day when we enjoy deep sleep; in doing, so we lose normal consciousness, but still retain a state of consciousness.

The Role of the Spiritual Master

In order to gain access to spiritual realms, one may need a master. The word *master*—which would have gone rhetorically unnoticed in culturally hierarchical times—can raise an eyebrow in our more egalitarian age, however. If our age is thus harder on the word *master,* it is softer on the word *spiritual*! As noted earlier, ours is an age in which people are chary of describing themselves as "religious," and cheerfully identify themselves as "spiritual." Therefore, the expression "spiritual master" is likely to be greeted with mixed emotions by the reader, with the word *spiritual* winning a measure of wholehearted approval that may not be extended to the word *master*.

It is a matter of daily, even casual, experience that a master is required whenever a hierarchy of knowledge is involved. We need a master to instruct us in the alphabet of a new script as soon as we decide to learn one; we learn the rudiments of running our car from the person who teaches us how to drive a car; and we even learn how to run our computer sometimes from our children, without any loss of a sense of security and self-confidence. In fact, we are happy to learn. Then why might one not feel the same way toward a spiritual master? If we are prepared to learn from our physics teacher about the nature of matter, why should we feel less certain about the arrangement when it comes to learning about matters metaphysical from a spiritual master? After all, we need an instructor to teach and guide us in even trivially mundane matters. Is it any surprise, then, that one should need a spiritual master for traversing the more treacherous terrain of spiritual life? It should, therefore, not be a matter of surprise that a spiritual master has a role to play in almost all of the world's religions.

The Privilege of Interiority

This argument shirks a key point—namely, that our spiritual life has to do with our interiority. The need for a teacher is demonstrably manifest in our outer life, but does the same hold for our inner life? The argument can be carried even further if we substitute the words *public and private life* with *our outer and inner life*. It is true that we feel the need of an instructor to negotiate the public realm, but what about our inner life of feelings and emotions? We choose the people we consult in these matters very carefully or not at all! And if we take the more intimate area of sex into account, then the parallel becomes telling. There is a saying in Bengali that a child seeks instructions from his parents in all matters—except this one!

This point is capable of being extended into the metaphysical realm as well. Just as we do not need instruction in sex because it is instinctual in us, could not the spiritual dimension of life be similarly intuitive—so that having an instructor invites the allegation of superfluity? But we do hear of sex therapists in this age of self-help books. So perhaps there are things for which we do not seem to need help at the outset, but for which we may need instruction to bring them to a successful conclusion. Thus, the distinction between the outer and the inner domain may be useful in refining the argument that we need to be instructed in the simplest of tasks, so why should it be different with the case of the loftiest of undertakings.

The Problem of Ego

It may be helpful to try to identify the real cause of discomfort that such a need for a "master" generates in us, and the situation can be explained as follows. Almost all spiritual paths require that we reconfigure our sense of the self—of who we are—significantly. In fact, this sense of self, or "ego," is said to be the main obstacle we need to overcome to progress on the spiritual path. It becomes the duty of the spiritual master to dilute our ego, if we approach a master on the spiritual path instead of going our own way. This is highly problematical. There is, of course, the natural tendency to remain who we are. We are all inclined to resist any effort to change the status quo. But the point cuts deeper.

Several mystical paths call upon one to surrender one's ego to the spiritual master. At the very least, the spiritual master tries to attenuate the ego, as should be clear from the following story of Junayd of Baghdād:

> Shiblî was a pupil of the famous theosophist Junayd of Baghdâd. On his conversion, he came to Junayd, saying: "They tell me that you possess the pearl of divine knowledge: either give it me or sell it." Junayd answered: "I cannot sell it, for you have not the price thereof; and if I give it you, you will have gained it cheaply. You do not know its value. Cast yourself headlong, like me, into this ocean, in order that you may win the pearl by waiting patiently."
>
> Shiblî asked what he must do.
>
> "Go," said Junayd, "and sell sulphur."
>
> At the end of a year he said to Shiblî:
>
> "This trading makes you well known. Become a dervish and occupy yourself solely with begging."
>
> During a whole year Shiblî wandered through the streets of Baghdâd, begging of the passers-by, but no one heeded him. Then he returned to Junayd, who exclaimed:
>
> "See now! You are nothing in people's eyes. Never set your mind on them or take any account of them at all. For some time" (he continued) "you were a chamberlain and acted as governor of a province. Go to that country and ask pardon of all those whom you have wronged."
>
> Shiblî obeyed and spent four years in going from door to door, until he had obtained an acquittance from every person except one, whom he failed to trace. On his return, Junayd said to him:
>
> "You still have some regard to reputation. Go and be a beggar for one year more."
>
> Every day Shiblî used to bring the alms that were given him to Junayd, who bestowed them on the poor and kept Shiblî without food until the next morning. When a year had passed in this way Junayd accepted him as one of his disciples on condition that he should perform the duties of a servant to the others. After a year's service, Junayd asked him:

> "What think you of yourself now?" Shiblî replied:
> "I deem myself the meanest of God's creatures."
> "Now," said the master, "your faith is firm."[6]

Parallels from others of the world's religions are not difficult to identify, though their comparability remains a vexed issue. Marpa treated Milarepa so harshly that Marpa's wife even helped forge a letter to enable Milarepa to escape Marpa's tutelage temporarily; and Ramakrishna is known to have put Vivekananda through a similar test.

The blandishments on the ego can take even subtler forms. There is the famous Zen anecdote of the senior and the junior monk who were returning to the monastery when they had to cross a rivulet that was now swollen with water. A young maiden was wondering whether she could venture across when they arrived on the spot. The elder monk just lifted her with his hands and carried her across, resuming the journey. This happened in the afternoon. That night the junior monk said to the senior monk, "You should not have done that!" "What shouldn't I have done," asked the senior monk. "You should not have carried the maiden across because it is against the rules of the order." Thereupon the senior monk replied, "I left her at the bank in the afternoon and you are still carrying her!" There is a similar account of a junior and a senior monk who arrive at a river to find that a woman was in danger of drowning. The senior monk dives in and carries her to safety. This happens during the day. Come night, the senior monk is challenged on his rescue operation by the junior monk, and the senior monk retorts, "I laid her down on the bank in the morning and you are still hugging her."

True, the monks at the river were not master and disciple, but senior and junior monk. Yet the point holds, and is more explicit in the following Ṣūfī account: A particular disciple of a *shaykh* had a handsome beard of which he was rather proud. One day the master told him, "You are much attached to your beard." The disciple took this as a mark of masterly disapproval, and when the *shaykh* passed by the next day he saw the disciple removing this beard hair by hair. At this the *shaykh* remarked to him, "You are even more attached to your beard today than you were yesterday!"

The Irony of Interiority

Stories of spiritual masters and their work of ego degratification point up a curious irony. While the fact that spirituality involves interiority may make the need for a master less relevant, ironically, the fact that our interiority is involved may make the need for one more relevant. This is because it is so difficult to be objective about oneself.

> At a game of chess the on-lookers can tell what the correct move is, better than the players themselves. Men of the world think that they are very clever, but they are attached to the things of the world—money, honours, sense-pleasures, etc. As they are actually engaged in the play, it is hard for them to hit upon the right move. Holy men who have given up the world are not attached to worldly objects. They are like the on-lookers at a game of chess. They see things in their true light and can judge better than the men of the world. Hence, in living the holy life, one must put faith only in the words of those who meditate upon God and who have realized Him. If you seek legal advice, will you not consult lawyers who are in the profession? Surely you will not take the advice of the man in the street.[7]

The psychodynamics of the spiritual path might render the disciple particularly vulnerable. An unscrupulous master could well stoop to exploit it, hence the emphasis on the need for a *proper* spiritual master. Small wonder some Hindu texts insist that one's chosen master should be without an ego of his own—for it is obviously dangerous to put oneself at the disposal of a *gurū* who still has one. Yet the need for a spiritual master is widely felt. The exceptions of people who attain the ultimate spiritual goal without a visible master only prove the general rule that one is required.

It is also an interesting point that the spiritual master does not reveal all—but only what is necessary for the spiritual development of the disciple. For example, at one point the Buddha picked up a handful of leaves from the forest floor, and asked his disciples which were more numerous, the leaves in the hand or those in the surrounding forest. When they replied, "Very few in your hand, lord; many more in the grove," he said:

> Exactly. So you see friends, the things that I know and have not revealed are more than the truths I know and have revealed. And why have I not revealed them? Because, friends, there is no profit in them; because they are not helpful to holiness.[8]

Moreover, one has sometimes to be ready to receive the truth. As Jesus himself is reported to have said, "I still have many things to say to you, but you cannot bear them now. When the spirit of truth comes, he will guide you into all the truth" (Jn 16:12).[9]

The Absence of Superfluous Masters

One still needs to interrogate this need for a spiritual master further—for it would be fatal to take at face value the argument that just as one needs a teacher to learn mundane things, one needs a master to learn about spiritual things. What brings the two situations together is the desire to learn something. Thus, the crucial element without which the whole picture is incomplete in the spiritual sphere is that of *spiritual yearning*. It is a point well established in mystical literature across the world's religions that often a spiritual breakthrough appears at the point of extreme psychological and spiritual despair—and that breakdown often leads to breakthrough. Accounts abound that connect the appearance of the spiritual master in one's life to the depth of this spiritual yearning. In this sense, there are no superfluous spiritual masters! The great message, then, of the world's religions is that we will get the spiritual experience we seek if we want it badly enough, and the spiritual master one needs for this to happen will appear as an outcome of this longing. This insight is celebrated in a famous parable—not attested in any accessible Christian source—that Ramakrishna (1836–1886) attributes to Jesus Christ:

> Jesus Christ was one day walking along the seashore when a devotee approached him and asked him, "Lord, how can one attain God?" Jesus directly walked into the sea with the enquirer and immersed him in the water. After a short time he released him, and raising him by the arm, asked him, "How did you feel?" The devotee replied, "I felt as though my last moment had come—the condition was desperate." Upon this Jesus said, "You shall see the Father when your heart pants for Him as it has panted for a breath of air just now."[10]

Back to the Exoteric Realm

What we have done so far is to explore the basics of approaching the esoteric realm to which spiritual masters claim to guide us. It is instructive, however, to revert to the exoteric realm once again. In the interest of a balanced conclusion, we draw attention to an area of study for the future, which relates to the issue of conflict among spiritual masters. One does not have in mind here the conflicting truth claims that spiritual masters may make (an issue with which the philosophy of religion is familiar),[11] but rather conflict between religious masters themselves. A life of Swami Vivekananda (1863–1902) contains the following account:

> During these days also, the Swami had an experience of a disquieting nature. Alluding to it he spoke [of it] later as "a crisis in his life." A disciple of a Mohammedan Fakir used to come to him occasionally, attracted by his personality. Hearing one day that he was suffering from fever and severe headache, the Swami out of compassion touched him on the head with his fingers and, to his great surprise, the man's ailments left him. After that he became very much devoted to the Swami, and came to him oftener than before. But the man's Guru, the Fakir, when he heard of this, became bitterly jealous of the Swami, and afraid lest his disciple forsake him, spoke ill of the Swami and warned his disciple not to see him. Finding that his words had no effect, the man was irate and abused the Swami to his disciple. And actuated by a spirit of revenge, as also, perhaps, to convince him of his greater psychic power, he threatened to use charms against the Swami and prophesied that he would vomit and feel giddy before he left Kashmir. This actually came about and the Swami was precipitated into great perplexity of mind and furious wrath, not against the Fakir but against himself and his Master. He thought: "What good is Shri Ramakrishna to me?—What good are all my realisations and preaching of Vedânta and the omnipotence of the Soul within, when I myself could not save myself from the diabolical powers of a black magician?" This experience exercised his mind so much that even when he reached Calcutta three weeks later, it continued to agitate him, and he told the Holy Mother, who happened to be there at the time, all about it.[12]

It should not be taken for granted that if the world becomes more "spiritual," peace will automatically descend on earth. Apart from the conflicting claims in the realm of truth, there could also develop conflict in terms of power as the legacy of the spiritual masters works itself out among their followers. But if the spiritual masters in this may turn out to be a problem, they could also be part of the solution, for the causes of such conflicts are the very forces they enjoin their followers to transcend.

Notes

1. Walpola Rahula, *What the Buddha Taught* (1959; repr., New York: Grove Press, 1974), 2.

2. Ibid., 61; emphasis by Walpola Rahula.

3. Mt 7:16–20 (KJV).

4. See Julius Lipner, *Hindus: Their Religious Beliefs and Practices,* 2nd ed. (Abingdon: Routledge, 2010).

5. Cited in Huston Smith, *World's Religions* (San Francisco: Harper, 1991), 357.

6. Reynold A. Nicholson, *The Mystics of Islam* (1914; repr., Bloomington, IN: World Wisdom, 2002), 25–26.

7. Ramakrishna, *Sayings of Sri Ramakrishna* (Madras: Sri Ramakrishna Math, 1987), 186.

8. Mary Pat Fisher, *Living Religions,* 7th ed. (Upper Saddle River, NJ: Prentice-Hall, 2008), 147.

9. See Smith, *World's Religions,* 361.

10. Ramakrishna, *Sayings,* 166. Here is another version: "'The master said, My child, if you desire after God, God shall come to you.' The disciple did not understand his master fully. One day both went to bathe in a river, and the master said, 'Plunge in', and the boy did so. In a moment the master was upon him, holding him down. He would not let the boy come up. When the boy struggled and was exhausted, he let him go. 'Yes, my child, how did you feel there?' 'Oh, the desire for a breath of air!' 'Do you have that kind of desire for God?' 'No, sir.' 'Have that kind of desire for God, and you shall have God.'" Swami Vivekananda, *Ramakrishna and His Message* (Almora: Advaita Ashrama, 1972), 32.

11. See John H. Hick, *Philosophy of Religion,* 4th ed. (Englewood Cliffs, NJ: Prentice-Hall, 1990), ch. 9.

12. *Life of Swami Vivekananda, by His Eastern and Western Disciples* (Calcutta: Advaita Ashrama, 1965), 600. For an account of conflict between two religious masters in Indonesia, see the doctoral dissertation of Julia Day Howell, *Vehicles for the Kalki Avatar: The Experiments of a Javanese Guru in Rationalizing Ecstatic Religion* (Department of Anthropology, Stanford University, September 1976).

List of Contributors

Osman Bakar, formerly Malaysia Chair of Southeast Asian Islam at the Prince al-Waleed Center for Muslim-Christian Understanding at Georgetown University in Washington, D.C., is Deputy CEO of International Institute of Advanced Islamic Studies (IAIS) Malaysia. He is also Emeritus Professor of Philosophy of Science at the University of Malaya and Consultant at the university's Center for Civilizational Dialogue, as well as a visiting research fellow, Center for Interdisciplinary Studies of Monotheistic Religions (CISMOR) at Doshisha University in Kyoto. He has written seventeen books and nearly three hundred articles on Islamic thought and civilization, particularly focused on Islamic science and philosophy, and Islam in Southeast Asia.

Mary Pat Fisher is the director of international correspondence at the Gobind Sadan Institute for Advanced Studies in Comparative Religion, New Delhi. She wrote the widely used world's religions textbook, *Living Religions,* now in its eighth edition (2010), and co-authored an accompanying anthology, among other works. She is engaged with interreligious dialogue, contributing to the work initiated by Baba Virsa Singh.

Harold Kasimow is the George Drake Professor Emeritus of Religious Studies at Grinnell College in Iowa. He is co-editor, with Byron L. Sherwin, of *No Religion Is an Island: Abraham Joshua Heschel and Interreligious Dialogue* (1991) and *John Paul II and Interreligious Dialogue* (1999). His latest co-edited book is *Beside Still Waters: Jews Christians and the Way of the Buddha* (2005). His *The Search Will Make You Free: A Jewish Dialogue with World Religions* (2006) is published in an English and Polish bilingual edition by Wydawnictwo Wam, the Jesuit publishing house in Krakow, Poland. He serves on the editorial boards of several scholarly journals, and his articles on interfaith dialogue and on Abraham Joshua Heschel have been published in the United States, Poland, England, Belgium, India, China and Japan.

Victoria Kennick (Urubshurow) is professor of humanities at the University of Maryland University College. From the University of Chicago she earned a BA in philosophical psychology, MAs in humanities and public policy, and a PhD in history of culture. She wrote *The Complete Idiot's Guide to the Life of Buddha* (2007) and *Introducing World Religions* (2008). In various articles, she explored problems of interreligious dialogue, interpreting religious symbols, and reading spiritual biography (hierophanic history).

Arvind Sharma, formerly of the Indian Administrative Service, received his Masters in Theological Studies (1974) from Harvard Divinity School and his PhD in Sanskrit and Indian Studies (1978) from Harvard University. He commenced his teaching career in Australia, where he taught for ten years, first at the University of Queensland, Brisbane, and then at the University of Sydney. He is presently the Birks Professor of Comparative Religion in the Faculty of Religious Studies at McGill University, which he joined in 1987. He has also taught at Temple University, Boston University, Northeastern University, and Harvard University in the United States and has published extensively in the field of Indology and comparative religion.

James A. Wiseman, OSB was on the faculty of the School of Theology and Religious Studies at the Catholic University of America from 1985 until 2011, teaching courses primarily on Christian spirituality. In June 2011 he was elected abbot of St. Anselm's Abbey, his monastic community in Washington, DC. He has long been active in interreligious dialogue, and co-edited two volumes emanating from Buddhist-Christian dialogues held at the Abbey of Gethsemani. He also wrote *Theology and Modern Science* (2002), and *Spirituality and Mysticism: A Global View* (2006).

Eva Wong follows the Xiantianwujimen and Quanzhen lineages of Daoism. As a member of the hermit tradition of Daoism, she does not advertise herself or talk much about what she does. She has written and translated more than fifteen books on Daoism, including: *Cultivating Stillness* (1992), *Harmonizing Yin and Yang* (1997), *Cultivating the Energy of Life* (1998), *The Tao of Health, Longevity, and Immortality* (2000), *A Master Course in Feng-shui* (2001), *Seven Taoist Masters: A Folk Novel of China* (2004), *Nourishing the Essence of Life* (2004), *Tales of the Taoist*

Immortals (2004), *Holding Yin, Embracing Yang* (2005), and *Tales of the Dancing Dragon: Stories of the Tao* (2007).

Simon Man Ho Wong earned a BA and MA in Chinese culture from National Taiwan University, and a PhD in East Asian Studies from the University of Toronto. He taught religion and culture at Wilfrid Laurier University of Ontario, and is now an associate professor in the Division of Humanities at the Hong Kong University of Science and Technology. Based on research on Confucianism, Neo-Confucianism, Daoism, and Chinese Buddhism, he published articles on Chinese philosophy and religion, and a book on Liu Tsung-chou (Liu Zongzhou) (1578–1645), the Confucian philosopher: *Liu Tsung-chou ji qi shen-du zhe-xue* (*Liu Tsung-chou and His Doctrine of Vigilance in Solitude*) (2001).

Index

Abba Apollos, 81
ʿAbd al-Qādir, Amīr, 92
abstinence, 59, 61, 69n25
Abū Bakr, 101
ācārya, 112
Ādi Granth, 151. *See also* Gurū Granth Sāhib
aesthetic shock, 167, 168, 169, 185n36. *See also* encounter dialogues (*kien mondō*)
afterlife, 106
ahiṃsā, 62
ʿAlī ibn Abī Ṭālib, 101
Amar Dās, Gurū, 132, 145, 146, 147, 148, 149
Analects, 192, 199, 201, 203
  quotations on: ancestral spirits and death, 194; being unbending, 203; the gentleman (benevolent man), 194, 204, 208; Heaven, 195, 199; King Wen and culture (*wen*), 195; man and the Way, 200; the *Odes* in, 209; the Mandate of Heaven (*tianming*), 194–95; perplexity, 203–4; Shen Ch'eng (Shen Cheng), 203; standing in awe, 194–95; the Way (*dao*), 196, 202; the Way of Heaven (*tiandao*), 198
  See also Confucius: self-reflections on his
Aṇgad, Gurū, 131, 132, 144–45, 146–47, 148
anger, 140, 143, 204, 226, 228, 229–30
Antony of Egypt, Saint, 87
Arab Spring, 49, 178, 186n59
arhat, 50n2
Arjan Dev, Gurū; Arjun Dev, 132, 136, 140, 141, 148, 149
Arjuna, 23, 45, 116
Āryadeva, 165, 184n29
ascetics. *See* Antony of Egypt, Saint; Augustine of Hippo, Saint; Nānak, Gurū; Siddhārtha
asceticism
  Christian, 87
  Jewish attitudes towards, 57–58, 60, 62
  See also *saṃgha*
Augustine of Hippo, Saint, 81–82, 85, 88

Baal Shem Tov, 36, 56–57, 58, 67
Bābā Balak Singh, 134
Bābā Srī Chand, 135, 138
Baba Virsa Singh, 134–38
  Fisher (M. P.), contributing to work initiated by, 255
  on Gurū Granth Sāhib as Eternal Gurū, 142
  on spiritual transformation, the pain of, 144
  Surendra Nath on, 137

Baba Virsa Singh *(continued)*
visionary appearances to, of: Bābā Srī Chand, 135; Gurū Gobind Singh, 135
Bahá'u'lláh, 43
Bāhva, 113
Baoxi, 211
barakah, 92, 100, 102, 106
barakah muḥammadīyah, 38, 103
Bāṣkali, 113
bay'ah, 103
benevolence, 62, 192, 200, 202
Bhadda Kuṇḍalakesa, 161–62
Bhagavadgītā, 23, 45, 133
Bhago. *See* Mai Bhago; Mālik Bhago
Bhāī Buddha, 147, 148
Bhāī Gurdās, 131
Bhāī Makhan Singh, 148
bhikkhuni, 183n16, 187n63. *See also* Bhikshuni, *bhikṣuṇī*
Bhikshuni, *bhikṣuṇī*, 161, 163, 177, 178–79. See also *bhikkhuni*; *saṃgha*: *bhikṣuṇī*
bias, 1, 45–46
Bible, 133. *See also* Hebrew Bible (Old Testament); New Testament
bla-ma
as doorway to teachings, 167
as fourth "Jewel" in Buddhist Refuge, 166, 184n33
guidance to disciple of, 169–70
Milarepa on, 164
obedience to, 165
spiritual bond with, 170
tantric visualization of, 171, 172
yearning for, 167, 170
See also lama
bliss, 60, 143, 182n7
Bodhidharma, 174
Bodhisattva, *bodhisattva*, 50n2, 169
Book of Changes (*Yijing*), 191, 211
Book of History (*Shujing*), 190, 190–91, 209
Book of Odes (*Book of Poetry*) (*Shijing*), 209, 210
Book of Music (*Classic of Music*) (*Yuejing*), 209
Book of Rites (*Liji*), 190, 209, 215
Brahma, Brahmā (creator), 26, 111, 166
Brahmā Sahampati, 159
Brahman, *brahman* (ultimate reality), 111, 113, 114, 117, 124
brāhmaṇa (priest), 160, 182n7. *See also* Brahmin, brahmin
Brahmin, brahmin, 25, 128, 159. See also *brāhmaṇa* (priest)
breath
control of, 233
of life, 3
panting for, 251, 253n10
regulation of, 229
spirare and, 74
vital energy and, 229
Buddha (Gautama). *See* Gautama, Gautama Buddha; Sakyamuni; Siddhārtha, Prince; see also *Siddhartha* (Hermann Hesse)
Buddha, buddha, generic term, 50n2
bodies (*kāyas*) of, 171, 183n12
Dharma and Dhamma vs., 171–72, 177 *(see also* Buddhadharma, *buddha-dharma*)
and disciples, 155, 160, 167–68, 174
dog vs., 173–74
Gautama as a newly realized, 158, 161
limited powers of, 157
-mind, 174
as spiritual master: one who cannot "teach," 157; teacher, 48, 159; Guru, *gurū*, 169, 170, 171, 172
among the Three Jewels, 159, 166, 184n33 (*see also* Three Jewels)
(buddha) vision, 159
word (*vacana*) of, 163
Buddhadharma, *buddha-dharma*
Buddhist tradition as, 39
books on, by Ayya Khema, 178

Brahmā Sahampati asks Gautama to teach, 159
as embodiment of: Chan spiritual master, 174; Gautama Buddha, 171–72, 174
equal opportunity of, 178–79, 180–81
explanation of, as skillfull means (*upāya*), 164
Gautama's determination to follow, in previous lifetime, 181–82n1
Gautama's reverence for, 159, 168, 177
hearing, thinking, and meditating on, 157–58
investigation of, recommended to Buddhists, 48, 160
mixing the mind with, 157–58, 179
nonduality of, 173, 177
spiritual yearning for, by: Huineng, 177; Milarepa, 167; Sadaprarudita, 167
Therī as having realized, 161
transmission of, 163
as ultimate spiritual master, 167
buddha-kāyas, 183n12
buddhavacana. See under Buddha, buddha, generic term
buddha vision, 159
Buddhist tradition, overview, 155–87
Confucian values and, 175–77
egalitarian ethos of, 161, 178, 180
esoteric teachings in, 242
gurū in: 47, 164, 166, 168–69, 170
history: 241–42, 243
religious practices: confession, 242; refuge in the lama and Three Jewels, 159, 166, 184–85n33; visualization, 171, 172
spiritual masters: definition of, 181; qualities of, 163–65, 183n23 183–84n24; recognition of, 169–70 (*see also* Buddhadharma, *buddha-dharma*); as role models, 175–77
teaching stories and accounts: Ayya Khema, 177–78; Baddha Kuṇḍalakesa, 161–62; Buddha (Gautama), 157, 158–59, 160, 182–83n7250; Huineng, 176–77; Joshu and the monk, 173–741 Mahāprajāpatī, 161; Milarepa, 167, 168, 169–71; Nāropa and Tilopa, 168–69; Prince Siddhārtha, 155–56, 166; Sadaprarudita, 167; Tenzin Gyatso, (Dalai Lama), 178; Therī Dhammadinna, 163; Thich Nhat Hanh, 179
women in, 161–63, 177–78, 178–79, 180, 186–87n63

cakra, 171
Capernaum, 76
Carmelite nuns and Carmelites, 77, 88
Catuḥśataka, 165
celestial realm, 234
Celestial Teachers' Daoism, Celestial Teachers' School of Daoism, 234
charity, 80, 131
China
ancient sages of: Yao, Shun, Yu, Tang, King Wen, King Wu, and Duke of Wu as, 192; 211, 215, 219n6, 219n14
dynasties of: Eastern Han, 190; Han, 210; Jin, 191; Ming, 191, 212, 215, 237; Northern Song, 205; Qing, 218n3; Song, 173, 191, 215, 233; Southern Song, 221n62; Wei, 191
legendary figures of: Yao and Shun, 192, 211; Yellow Emperor, 211
literature of, *see* Confucian classics; *and specific titles*
periods: Spring and Autumn, 235; Warring States, 211
See also Confucian tradition, overview; Daoist tradition, overview

Ching, Julia, 190, 211, 218
Christ. *See* Jesus, Jesus Christ, and Jesus of Nazareth
Christian tradition, overview, 73–90
  God: graciousness and mercy of, 77; and Jesus, 10, 76; the need of a call from, 88 (*see also* Holy Spirit)
  history: early monastic movement (third century), 79
  religious practices: cleanness (spiritual), 59, 61, 62, 144
  spiritual master: definition of, 74; etymology of, 73–74
  spiritual masters: criteria for, 88; Jesus as demonstrating qualities of, 76–86
  teaching stories and accounts: Antony of Egypt, Saint, 87; Apollos and the young monk, 80–81; Augustine of Hippo, Saint, 82; Jesus, 75, 76, 78–79, 83, 251, 253n10; Merton, Thomas, 85–87; Nouwen, Henri, 84–85; Pachomius, Saint, 83–84; Thérèse of Lisieux, Saint, 77–78
Clinton, Bill, President, 44
compassion
  master of personal relationships, for living beings, 35
  discussion of, in, tradition: Buddhist, 164, 175; Confucian, 231; Daoist, 230; Hindu, 252; Jewish, 62; Sikh 150
  discernment with, 80
  guidance with, 127
  motivation with, 184
  problems with lack of, 48, 80, 164
  See also loving-kindness
Confucian classics
  Five Classics, Taylor (Rodney L.) on, 209
  Six Classics, 209–10
  See specific titles, e.g., Book of Changes (Yijing)
Confucian tradition, overview, 189–223
  Contemporary New Confucians, 216–17, 223n102
  God in: 189, 198
  Neo-Confucians: Contemporary New Confucians vs., 223n102; concept of heart (*xin*) of Heaven and Earth among, 206; Song and Ming thought of, 191, 215–16
  religious practices: attending to *liangzhi* in daily life, 214–15; overcoming perplexity, 203–4, 205
  sage (*sheng*) in: characteristics and qualities of, 192–97, 200, 211–12, 19n6, 219n8; Confucian ideal of, as political leader, 210–11; Confucian lineage of, 211, 215–16; Confucius as exemplar of, 207–10; Confucius's reluctance to claim status as, 200; contributions of, 206–7; criteria of being, 205–6; definition of, 190–92, 202, 207, 212, 218n2, 221n6; difficulty of becoming, 201, 222n81; Israelite prophet vs., 198–99; mission of, 198; Tang Junyi on, 216 (*see also* sagehood, Chinese; Wang Yangming)
  spiritual masters, definition of, 190, 218n2, 221n61
  teaching stories and accounts: Confucius, 193–94, 195–96, 201, 231; Tang Junyi, 216–17; Wang Yangming, 212–13; Wang (Yangming) Yang-ming's follower, 214–15
Confucius, 43
  ancient sages, relationship to, 215
  challenge to status quo of, 32
  characteristics of, 192–97
  contemporary scholarship on: H. H. Rowley, 198–99; Hans Küng, 199
  four criteria of sagehood met by, 207–11

on Heaven (*tian*), 194–96
as model of all Confucian, Daoist, and Buddhist sages, 231
on perplexity, 203–4, 205
as sage: final Chinese, 212; preeminent Chinese, 192; *zhisheng xianshi* (greatest sage, foremost teacher), 208
self-reflections of, on his: demeanor and habits, 193, 200, 201; relationship with Heaven, 195, 196; silence and Heaven (*tian*), 199
spiritual evolution of, 201–5, 221n61
and students: Yan Hui, 231; Zeng Dian (Tseng Tien), 231, 222n80; Zigong (Zi Gong), 195–98, 200, 231; Zi Lu, 231; Zi Xia, 231; Zi Zhang, 231
unity of Heaven and man in, 197–201
Yangming vs., 213
Yao and Shun, admiration for, 211
Zhuangzi vs., 232–33
Zigong (Zi Gong) on, 196–97
See also *Analects*
Contemporary New Confucians. *See under* Confucian tradition
contributors, to this book
list of, 255–57
references to: Bakar (Osman), 2, 39, 41, 47; Fisher (Mary Pat), 3, 13; Kasimow (Harold), 2, 35; Kennick (Victoria Urubshurow), 3, 241, 242; Sharma (Arvind), 2, 15, 34, 41, 42, 47, 49; Wiseman (James, A.), 2, 3, 41; Wong (Eva), 3; Wong (Simon Man Ho), 3
task of, 2
councils, Christian: Chalcedon, Ephesus, Nicea (first), 37
Cousins, Ewert, 5–6
Creator deity, 189
Hindu notions of, 166 (*see also* Brahma, Brahmā)
Jewish notions of, 58, 60, 61, 62, 63
Sikh notions of, 129
See also God
crusades. *See* First Crusade

Dalai Lama. *See* Gyatso, Tenzin
dalai lama, institution of, 12
Dao, Way, 35, 202, 230, 236, 237. *See also* Heaven (*tian*): Way of (*tiandao*)
Daodejing
quotations from: 225, 226–27, 228, 228–29, 238, 239
sage, concept of, in, 235
See also *Laozi*, text
Daoist tradition, overview, 225–40
religious practices: clearing and stilling the mind, 227–28; internal gazing of Sima Zhengzhen (Buddhist influence), 236; strengthening and nourishing the body, 228–29; visualization and mystical union, 234
sages: activist vs. hermit, 235–37; aristocrat vs. beggar, 237–38; Confucius, 231–32, 233; Confucius vs. Zhuangzi, 232–33; conventional vs. unconventional, 231–33; ordinary vs. extraordinary, 233–35; Zhuangzi, 232–33
spiritual master (enlightened person, sage): body of, 228–29, 230; characteristics of, 225–26, 231, 235; definition of, 226; mind of, 227–28, 229, 230; motto of, 240; path to becoming, 227–30; as role model, 230
teaching stories and accounts: Fan Li, 235–36; Lieze, 240; Liu An, 237; Lungshu, 239; Sima Zhengzhen, 236; Tang Guanzhen, 233–34; Wei Huacun, 234–35; Zhou Dian, 238; Zhuangzi, 232

Dātū (son of Gurū Aṅgad), 147
Day, Dorothy, 43
Dayananda Sarasvati, 120
Devadatta, 43
Devībhāgavata Purāṇa, 111
Dhamma, 158. *See* Dharma; *dharma*
Dhammadinna (therī), 163
Dharma, *dharma*
  Buddhist, 159, 166, 170, 172, 173, 174, 184n33
  Hindu, 23
  See also Dhamma
dharma encounter, 162
dharma-kāya, 171, 183n2
Dharma-nature, 171–72
dhikr, 105. *See also* Muslim tradition: religious practices
didaskalē, 50n2, 75
dīkṣā, 41, 122
disciples
  anecdotes about: Buddhist, 160, 166, 167, 175, 249; Christian, 75, 253n10; Confucian, 195–97, 199; Hindu, 15, 23, 23–24, 26, 114–15, 115–16; Jain, 31; Sikh, 130–31, 136–37; Ṣūfī, 248–49, 252 (*see also* teaching stories)
  antiauthoritarianism of, 49; Buddha's advice to, on 35, 48, 156–57, 160, 172
  benefits to, from spiritual masters, 36, 103, 140–41, 143–45
  and categories of religious perception of, 22, 24–26, 32
  comments on, in connection with, tradition: Buddhist, 155, 161–63, 179; Christian, 87; Confucian, 192, 193, 214, 219n16, 222n81, 222n86; Jewish, 56, 64, 65, 70n34; Muslim, 95, 97, 98, 101, 104–5; Sikh, 117, 127–28
  and confidence in leaders: loss of, 11, 18; gaining of, 41
  and emulation of spiritual masters, 93 (*see also* spiritual masters: as role models)
  esoteric, hidden experience of spiritual masters by, 21, 31, 41, 117, 122, 125n13, 133, 146, 168, 170
  and existential meaning, sources of, 20–21, 40
  exploitation of, 116, 250
  and faith, 47, 49, 117
  and inanimate or not human spiritual masters, 47
  initiation of, 100, 103–4, 160, 248–49
  lineage inheritance of, 35, 101–2, 113, 169
  and need for spiritual master, 120–21
  and perception of spiritual masters, 149: causality regarding, 47, 168–69
  qualifications and qualities of, 47; Buddhist, 165–66, 169, 175–76, 181, 184n29, 184n32; Hindu, 113, 118; Ṣūfī, 102
  and relationship with spiritual master, nature of, 53n41; Buddhist, 157, 164, 166–71, 175, 176, 250; Christian, 75, 79, 250–51; Confucian, 213–14; Hindu, 49, 115–16, 122–23; Sikh, 136, 141–42, 144, 149–50; Ṣūfī, 103, 106, 248–49
  responsibilities of, 47, 101, 103–4, 106, 157–58, 160, 163–64, 166, 181, 183n23
  ritual activities of: Buddhist, 159, 160, 166; Sikh, 143, 144, 148; Ṣūfī, 104–6; outgrowing of, 114 (*see also under specific traditions, e.g., Muslim tradition, overview: religious practices*)
  as role models, 166
  and surrender to spiritual masters, religious leaders: benefits of, 47–48, 104, 124, 144, 248–49; cautions of, 48, 49, 165; harm of, 48–49, 164

and ultimate lack of spiritual masters or identity, nonduality between, 49, 117, 121–22, 123–24, 125n23, 169, 172–74
uncritical, 33, 165–66, 184n32, 249
divine eye, 23
Divine Name *Allāh*, 104. *See also* Muslim tradition: religious practices
docēre, 77
Doctrine of the Mean, 191
Dresner, Samuel, Rabbi, 65
Duke Ling of Wei, 193
Duke of Zhou, 192
Durgā, Goddess, 131

ego
degratification of, 249
lack of, in *gurū*, 250
as obstacle to progress on the spiritual path, 47, 247
problem of, 247–49
removed from zeal yields purity, 62
spiritual masters and, 49, 123
surrender or loss of, 144, 226, 248
Egypt. *See* Christian tradition: early monastic movement (third century)
Ehi passiko and *ehi paśya*, 160, 161
Einstein, vii
Eliade, Mircea, 4–5, 50n5, 53n32
Elijah ben Solomon of Vilna, 56, 68n5
Elimelech of Lizensk, 57, 68n6
encounter dialogues (*kien mondō*), 172, 173, 174, 175, 185n49. *See also* aesthetic shock
enlightenment and awakening
animals and, 186n49
Buddhist: of Buddha, activities immeditately after, 159, 182–83n7; Buddhist spiritual mastery, as standard for, 39; and Dharma, 172; of Huineng, 176–77, 186n58; path to, 178; in *Siddhartha* (Hermann Hesse), 155–56; in Zen, 173–75
Daoist: as potential for all, 230, 234; as state of mind and body, 226, 228–29
Confucian: of Wang Yangming, 212–13
Sikh: Gurūs chosen through vision of, 146; Gurūs as having, 127, 131, 134, 148; as *gyan* (wisdom of the Word), 142, 148
epistata, 50n2, 75
esoteric, 29, 37
category, dimension of religious perception, 41; in Gold (D.), 20–22, 26, 29, 35; lack of, in Weber (M.), 19–20
dimension of inner life, 39, 41; checked by exoteric dimension, 242–43; function of, 243; in Gold (D.), 16, 21; lack of, in Weber (M.), 18; in Sufism, 94–95, 243; as *ṭarīqah*, 96
and exoteric, 29, 34, 35, 243, 251; in Buddhist history, 241–42; in Gold's model, 16, 20–21, 25–26, 52n26, 52n31; in Sufism, 39, 41, 95–96, 108n16
means of teaching, help, communication by: Confucius in *Spring and Autumn Annals*, 210; foci of the divine (various, in Gold), 23, 25, 52n31; Hindu *gurū*, 41; Jesus, 41; spiritual masters, 34, 241; story of Nāropa, 184n32
spiritual substance, function: of Prophet (Muḥammad), 91, 93, 98
evils
ideas on dealing with: Buddhist, 156, 167, 170; Christian, 80, 84; Jewish, 58, 60–62, 64; Sikh, 133, 140, 143–44

evils *(continued)*
good and: Confucian sage's fortunes of, 191; Confucius's indifference to, 205
fruit of, from corrupt tree, 242

Falwell, Jerry, 43
Fan Li, 235–36, 237
faqīr, 100, 102, 105, 106, 130
Feng Yu-lan, 215
filial piety, 175–76, 211, 234–35
First Crusade, 43
Five Beloved Ones. *See* Pañj Piāre
Fraade, Steven D., 58
friendliness that is careless, 86
Fuxi (Fu-hsi), 211

gadol ḥador, 50n2, 56
Gandhi, Mahatma, 119, 240, 240n14
ga'on, 50n2, 56
Gaon of Vilna, 57, 58, 59, 64, 67
Gautama, Gautama Buddha, 43
advice to disciples, 48, 156, 157, 160–61, 172
birth and death dates of, 182n2
decision to teach of, 158–59
ethos of: egalitarian, 180; nonauthoritarian, 156, 158, 160, 172, 181
female disciples of, 161–63
first seven weeks after awakening of, 182–83n7
as the future, 155, 166, 181n1
language spoken by, 182n5
lineage of, 174, 175, 183
as *mahāpuruṣa*, 30
as master of contemplation, 35
as role models, 39, 40
spiritual lineage of, 38, 183n13
as spiritual master par excellence, 156
symbolic body of, 30, 31
symbolic conduct of, 32
Rahula (Walpola) on, 156–57
Sadaprarudita vs., 167
as savior, 157
as singular personality, 24
Smith (H.) on, 123
teachings of: as egalitarian, 178–79; Jewish teachings vs., 70n34; as nonauthoritarian, 160, 181, 242
worship of, at Gobind Sadan (India), 137
See also *buddha-dharma*; *Jātakas*; Sakyamuni; *Siddhartha* (Hermann Hesse), Siddhārtha, Prince; Tathagata, Tathāgata; teaching stories and accounts: Buddhist
Gobind Sadan: in India, 136, 137, 255; in New York, 152
Gobind Singh, Gurū
in Bābā Virsa Singh's vision, 135
Khālsā established by, 133, 143
as final human Sikh *gurū*, 117, 133
and Gurū Granth Sāhib: names, as successor, 133, 134, 142, 151; presence of, emanating from, 152
heroism of, in battle, 150
Light (*jot*) of Nānak, view of, 131–32
miracle of, 146
nonsectarian mission of, 136
sacrifices of, for God's mission, 140
writings of, 131–32, 138–39
God
Christian notions of: graciousness and mercy of, 77; and Jesus, 10, 37, 76; spiritual master in need of call by, 88 (*see also* Holy Spirit)
Confucian notions of: 189, 198
Hindu notions of (*see under* gods; *gurū*)
incarnations of, 37
Jewish notions of: communion with (*devekut*), 64, 68n4; love of, 35–36, 56, 62; saint's attitude toward, 59–60; service to, 59; submission to will of, 63; rejecting

concept of supernatural, in Reconstructionist Movement, 69n15 (see also *tzaddik*; Jewish tradition, overview: religious practices)
love of, by master of personal relationships, 35
Muslim (Islamic) notions of, 104, 105, 106, 107; journey to, 103; life dedicated to, 92; major prophets sent by, 102; in six articles of faith and five pillars, 108n10 (see also *dhikr Allāh; ṭarīqah*)
Sikh notions of: devotion to, 132; faith in, 127, 136; and Gurū, 138–39, 144, 145, 149; intimate relationship with, 137; the name of, 140; path to, 131, 138; remembrance of, 133, 134; as *sant*, 134; as *Satgurū*, 142–43 (see also *Nām*; Nānak, Gurū: relationship with God)
See also Creator deity; gods; *and specific authors and texts*
godling, 19 (*see also* gods)
gods
Buddhist notions of (*see* Brahmā Sahampati)
Confucian notions of: sages as like, 190–91; disinterest of Confucius in, 193–94
Hindu notions of, 111, 244; non-worship of, 26
See also godling
Gold, Daniel
and categories of religious perception: 15, 16, 18–22, 28
epistemological turn of, 18–19
on four immanent foci of the divine, 16, 52n31; *gurū* as, 22–26
on grammar of religious perception, 16
method of, impacting Kennick's definition of *spiritual master*, 16–17, 52n26
morphological frame, in work of: as nonhierarchical, 16, 17, 21, 22, 28, 52n26; and typology, 18, 19, 22, 27, 52–53n32
Weber, methods of, vs., 7–8, 15–20, 45, 51n21, 51–52n24, 52–53n32, 53n41
Gongxi Hua [Kung-hsi Hua], 200
grace
charisma and, 4, 36, 50n3, 51n21, 51n24, 53n42
Christ, as anointed with, 30
of God, 147, 198
Gold (D.) and concept of, 17, 21, 24
of Hindu guru, *gurū*, 24, 41, 122
of Jewish *tzaddik*, 57, 68n6
of the Lord, 80
as *mysterium fascinans*, 32
of Prophet Muḥammad (see *barakah muḥammadīyah*)
of Sikh Gurū, 130, 136, 140, 141, 145
of Ṣūfī master (see *barakah*)
Gurmukh, 132, 149
Gurūs, *gurūs*, 50n2
Buddhist notions of, 47, 164, 166, 168–69, 170
Hindu notions of: 34, 111; danger of egoistic, 250; *gurūdakṣiṇā*, 116; *gurū-siśya*, 117; relation to God 15, 112; 117–18, 121, 123–24 (*see also* grace; Hindu tradition: history of *gurūs* in)
Sikh notions of: as key symbol of 3; as lineage office in, 12; lineage transmission of, 26–27; 127, 128, 131–32, 142; as Nānak, 14; qualities of, 138–43; recognizing the, 146–49; relationship of, with disciples, 134–35, 149–50; role of, 143–46; and routinization, 37; scripture as, 12–15, 18, 26–27, 151–52; succession, crisis of, 147–48 (*see also* Gurū Granth Sāhib; Sikh tradition, overview; *Wāhe Gurū*)

Gurūs, *gurūs* *(continued)*
in theory (*see* Gold, Daniel: on four immanent foci of the divine; Weber, Max: on charismatic individuals)
See also grace
Gurū Granth Sāhib
book survives fire at Gobind Sadan (NY), 152
contents of, 133, 134, 138, 142, 144, 152–53n3
as embodiment of the Gurū, 127, 133, 134, 152
as Eternal Gurū and eternal teacher, 142, 152
and Gold's model, 18, 24, 27
and Hukam, 151
and hymns of *bhagat*s in, 134
non-Sikhs, little known among, 152
quotations from: Gurū Amar Dās, 132, 149; Gurū Angad, 145; Gurū Arjun Dev, 136, 140, 141–42, 149; Gurū Gobind Singh, 143 (*see also* Gobind Singh, Gurū: writings of); Gurū Nānak, 129, 129–30, 139, 140, 141, 144; Gurū Rām Dās, 138, 140, 145, 145–46; Kabīr, 133
ritual treatment of, 137, 151–52
as Sikh Gurū, final, 133, 134, 142, 151
and Weber's model, 12–15, 24, 27, 38
Gyatso, Tenzin (dalai lama), 157, 158, 164, 165, 178, 179, 183n23, 186n63

ḥadīths, 37, 92, 94, 96, 103, 108n11, 243
ḥakham (pl. *ḥakhamim*), 36, 50n2, 56, 57
Hargobind, Gurū, 132, 148
Hari Rāi, Gurū; Hari Rai, 132
Harkrishan, Gurū; Hari Krishan, 132–33, 147–48
ḥasid, *Ḥasid*, Ḥasid, and *Ḥasidim* (pl.), 50n2, 57, 58, 64, 68n6. *See also* Baal Shem Tov; Elimelech of Lizensk; Mendel of Kodzk, Rabbi
havan, 137
heaven
Christian notions of, 31; treasures of, 82
Jewish notions of, 57, 62
Muslim notions of: access to the royal assembly of, 106; Will of, 102
See also Heaven (*tian*)
Heaven (*tian*), 219n13
heart (*xin*) for, and Earth, 206
Lord on High (Shangdi) as, 197, 199
Mandate of (*tianming*), 194–96, 200, 201, 204, 206, 210, 212
Principle of (*tianli*), 192, 215
sage as coequal with, 191
unity of, and man (*tian ren heyi*), 197
Way of (*tiandao*), 197, 198, 200, 205, 207, 209, 212, 219n6, 219n13
See also *Analects*: quotations from; Confucius: on Heaven (*tian*)
Hebrew Bible (Old Testament), quotations from
Deuteronomy (Deut), 35, 56
Exodus (Ex), 55
Isaiah (Is), 30, 58
Leviticus (Lev), 55, 56
Proverbs (Prv), 58
Psalms (Ps), 30
See also Bible
Herrschaft. *See* Weber, Max
Heschel, Abraham Joshua, 43
as Jewish saint, 65–67
on Rabbi Mendel of Kotzk and the Gaon of Vilna, 57–58
on the three paths to God, 65–66

as philosopher of wonder, 65
as prophet, 70n40
Sherwin, Byron, as disciple of, 65, 68n6
thought of, compared to Luzzatto's, 66–67
wonder in, 65
writings of: *A Passion for Truth*, 57; *God in Search of Man*, 65
Hesse, Hermann, views of, 155, 156, 158
Hindu tradition, overview, 111–25
gurū: 34, 111; *gurūdakṣiṇā*, 116; *gurū-siśya*, 117; relation to God 15, 112; 117–18, 121, 123–24 (*see also* grace)
history of *gurūs*, 112; classical, 114–17; medieval, 117–18; modern, 118–23; Vedic, 112–14
religious practices: devotion to the name of God, 117; faith in *gurū*, 117; fervent exaltation of the *gurū*, 118
spiritual masters: qualifications of, 112–13, 114–17; warnings, hesitations about, 118, 119
teaching stories and accounts: Bāhava and Bāṣkali, 113; Droṇācārya and Ekalavya, 116; Mahatma Gandhi, 119; Ramakrishna and Naren (Vivekananda), 119–20; Ramana Maharshi, 120–22; Rāmānuja, 115–16; Ṛbhu and Nidāgha, 114–15; Satyakāma Jābāla, 113–14; Swami Vivekananda, 252
See also Creator deity
history of religions, academic discipline, 2
Eliade (M.) as founding scholar of, 4, 50n5
Gold (D.) and, 16, 20, 22, 27–28, 51n21, 53n41, 50n5
method of, 5, 16, 27; and question of truth claims of, 6; religionist and reductionist balance as important to, 7, 43; religionist vs. reductionist views in, 4, 7, 14–15, 28, 43, 53n41; two-pronged, 5
and reductionist approach: as corrective to religionist approach, 6, 28, 43, 50n5; definition of, 4; and sociology, 53n41; and Weber, 7;
and religionist approach: of Cousins (Ewert), 5–6; definition of, 4; of Eliade (M.), 4–5; reductionist critique of, 6; *religious meaning* and, 16; theology vs., 6, 50n5
sociological methods of Weber (M.) vs., 12, 14, 27–28
and value judgments, 45–46
Holbrooke, Richard, 44
holiness
Gautama Buddha's view of what is helpful to, 250
in Jewish thought, 67n1, 56, 58; Luzzatto's path to, 59–65
Holy Spirit, 64, 74, 76
Hongren (Hung-jen), 176
Huainanzi, 237
Huineng (Hui-neng), 175–77, 186n58
Hujwīrī, Abū al-Ḥasan al-, 98, 99
Hukam Nath, 146
Hukam, 136, 151

Ibn al-ʿArabī, Muḥammad, 102, 109n19
ʿilm, 105
immortals, 226, 234, 237, 240n1
internal strength, 229
interiority, 47; irony of, 249–51; privilege of, 247
International Thomas Merton Society, 88
Islamic tradition, overview. *See* Muslim tradition, overview
Israel, 65, 68n6. *See also* prophets

Jabālā, 114
Jacobs, Louis, 57, 68n6
Jain practitioners, 31, 40, 161, 162
Jātakas, 165, 166
Jeremiah, 32
Jesus, Jesus Christ, and Jesus of Nazareth, 43
  characteristics of, as: incarnation, 36, 37; initiator of spiritual lineage, 38; preeminent Christian spiritual master, 74–76; prophet, 9–10; sage, 216; servant of others, 81; singular personality, 24; Son of God, 37; spiritual healer, 78–79
  charisma of, 33
  discernment of, 82–83, 250–51
  on disciples not being rabbis (teachers), 75
  empathy of, 84
  five qualities of, 75–87
  Jewish thought of, 67n2
  mystic experience of, reported by Thérèse of Lisieux, 41, 78
  opposition to, 76
  and Pharisees, 75, 78
  self-authenticating nature of words and deeds of, 76
  symbolic body of, 29–30, 31
  symbolic conduct of, 32, 33
  teacher-disciple relationship parallel to Hindu, 125n13
  teaching with authority, 76–77
  tempations in the desert of, 87
  worshipped at Gobind Sadan (India), 137
Jewish tradition, overview, 55–71
  God in: communion with (*devekut*), 64, 68n4; love of, 35–36, 56, 62; saint's attitude toward, 59–60; service to, 59; submission to will of, 63; rejecting concept of supernatural, in Reconstructionist Movement, 69n15
  religious practices: *devekut* (communion with God), 64; ethical self-perfection, 64 (*see also* Musar movement); immersion in everyday life, 58; meditation on death, 70n34; the path of watchfulness, zeal, cleanness, abstinence, purity, saintliness, humility, fear of sin, and holiness, 59–65; the path of wonder, approaching the Bible with one's whole being, and sensing God's presence in sacred deeds, 65–66; sanctification of food and drink, 59; separating from the world, 58; studying Torah, 58, 65
  Sages, sages (*ḥakhamim*): *ḥasid* vs., 57; Luzzatto (M. H.), on, 61, 62; as *talmid ḥakhamim*, masters of Torah, 56
  spiritual master (saint): definition of, 56; Mithnagdic vs. Ḥasidic conceptions of, 59; as *talmid ḥakham, tzaddik, ḥasid, ga'on,* and *gadol ḥador*
  teaching stories and accounts: Jewish: Baal Shem Tov, 56, 58; Vilna Gaon, 57–58
  See also Creator deity; *and specific thinkers, e.g. Heschel, Abraham Joshua*
John Paul II, Pope (Karol Jósef Wojtyla), 43, 45, 77, 255
Jones, James Warren (Jim Jones), 43, 44
Justin Martyr, 30
Just War, theory, 45

Kabīr, 133, 134, 153
kalām, 108n13
Kalamas, 160
karmas, 145, 169
Katz, Dov, Rabbi, 64
Kaur, 143
khalīfah, 101–2

Khālsā, 133, 143
King Wen, 192, 195
King Wu, 192
King, Martin Luther, Jr., 67, 70n40
kīrtan, 132, 151
kleśa, 164, 184n24
Kṛṣṇa, Lord 23, 37, 43, 45, 133
Kulārṇavatantra, 118
Küng, Hans, 198, 199
kyriē, 50n2, 75

Laden, Osama bin, 43
  as false prophet, 44
  hostility toward presumed supporters of, 152
  hypothetical meeting with Thich Nhat Hanh, 180
lama, 48, 164, 168, 170, 171, 183n23. See also *bla-ma*
Laozi, sage. See *Daodejing*; *Laozi*, text
Laozi, text, 225 240n1. See also *Daodejing*
Lehna (Gurū Aṉgad), 131
liangzhi (*liang-chih*), 214–15 (*see also* Wang Yangming)
Lieze, sage, 240
Lieze, text, 226, 239
Lincoln, Bruce, 6–7, 36, 42. *See also* moral exhaustion
Liṅga Purāṇa, 118
Lithuania, 64, 70n34; 70n37
Liu An, 237–38
Lotus Sūtra, 167
loving-kindness, 31, 43, 62
Luke, Gospel of, 75, 78, 89n8. *See also* New Testament: quotations from
Luzzatto, Moses Hayyim
  ascetic strain of, 58, 69n25
  Jewish path to holiness of, 59–64; Heschel's path vs., 65, 66–67
  original sin, idea rejected by, 69n24
  Phinehas ben Yair vs., 59–60

Manmukh, 149
Mahābhārata, 116, 124n2
Mahāprajāpatī, 161
Mahāyānasūtrālaṃkāra, 164
Mai Bhago, 150
Maimonides, Moses, 57
majlis, 105–6
Mālik Bhago, 130–31
mantra, 115–16, 149. *See also* Mūl Maṃtar; *Nām*
Manusmṛti, 111–12
Mark, Gospel of, 76, 81. *See also* New Testament
Marpa, 48, 168, 169, 170, 171, 249
Marx, Karl, 74
meditation. *See specific traditions, e.g., Daoist tradition: meditation in*
Megasthenes, 161
Mendel of Kotzk, 57
Merton, Thomas, 85–87, 88
Mesillat Yesharim, 59, 64, 65, 69n15, 69n24, 70n36
Milarepa
  on the spiritual teacher, *bla-ma*, lama, 48, 164
  as disciple, prime exemplar of Tibetan Buddhist, 166–71
  meditations on his *bla-ma*, lama, 170–71, 172
  relationship with Marpa, of, 249
  Sadaprarudita of the *Lotus Sūtra*, as resembling, 167, 177
  See also Marpa; *rnam-thars*
Mithnagdim, 58, 64
mitzvot, 56, 60, 62, 66
Mongols, 238
Montaldo, Jonathan, 88
Mool Mantra. *See* Mūl Maṃtar
moral exhaustion, 28, 42–43. *See also* Bruce Lincoln
Mourides, 95, 108n8
Mou Zongsan, 217
Muḥammad, Prophet, 43
  auspicious marks between shoulder blades of, 30
  as first Ṣūfī, 99

Muḥammad, Prophet *(continued)*
two functions of, as major prophet, 102
mysterium fascinans of, 32
as role model, 38–39, 91, 93
as spiritual master par excellence, 37
spiritual succession of, 102–3, 108n12
Ṣūfī love for, and his family, 96
See also *barakah muḥammadīyah*; *silsilah*
Mughals, 148
Muktsar, 150
Mūl Maṃtar, 129–30
Muṇḍaka Upaniṣad, 112
murād, 92, 107n2. See also *shaykh*s
murshid, 50n2, 92, 102, 107n2. See also *shaykh*s: and disciples
Musar movement, 64–65, 70n37. *See also* Luzzatto, Moses Hayyim; Salanter, Israel
Muslim tradition, overview, 91–109
God in: 104, 105, 106, 107; journey to, 103; life dedicated to, 92; major prophets sent by, 102; in six articles of faith and five pillars, 108n10 (see also *dhikr Allāh*, *ṭarīqah*)
history, 92, 95, 97–98, 99, 243
Qur'ān and *ḥadīth*s: on deviation from orthodox interpretations of, 94–96
religious practices: *dhikr Allāh*, 104–5; immersion in traditional culture, 94; emulation of Prophet Muḥammad, 94, 98; participation in the spiritual assembly (*majlis*), with spiritual concert (*samā'*), 105–6; performance of the five pillars, 108n10
Ṣūfī master: criterion for legitimacy of, 100–1; definiton of: 91–92; succession process of, 101–3; as *shaykh*, *pīr*, *murshid*, *murād*, *tuan gurū*, 92
teaching stories and accounts: Junayd of Baghdād, 248–49; *Mantiq-ut-tayr* (conference of the birds), 185n41

Nām, 132, 138, 142, 143, 144, 145. See also *dhikr*; Muslim tradition, overview: religious practices
Nāmdharis, 134
Nānak, Gurū, 128–32
appearance in a mystic vision, 138
ascetic companions of, Hindu and Muslim, 128
and God, relationship with, 128, 129, 130, 141
the *jot* (Light) of, 131–32, 134, 151
and the Mūl Maṃtar, 129–30
as name of all Sikh *gurū*(s), 14
and the *sant* tradition, 153–54n8
and the Sikh lineage, 26, 27, 117, 128, 132, 146, 147, 148
stories of, 130–31, 140–41, 152n2
teachings of, 139, 144
and Udāsīs, 135
Naqshbandīyah Order, 101
Naren, 119–20. *See also* Vivekananda, Swami
Nasr, Seyyed Hossein
as a contemporary Ṣūfī teacher, 106, 107n4
as spokesperson for Sufism, 95, 96, 97, 99, 100, 108n9, 108n13
on Ṣūfī *shaykh*s and disciples, 102, 103–4, 105–6
on the Ṣūfī Path (*ṭarīqah*), 105
on Ṣūfī traditional forms and symbols, 93
Neo-Confucians. *See* Confucian tradition: Neo-Confucians; Wang Yangming
New Testament, 74, 77, 78
quotations from: Gospel of John (Jn), 83, 84, 251; Gospel of Luke (Lk), 75, 79; Gospel of Mark (Mk), 31, 67n2, 75, 76, 78, 81;

Gospel of Matthew (Mt), 75, 83, 342–43; Paul, 2 Corinthians, 87
See also Bible; Luke, Gospel of; Mark, Gospel of
Newton, Isaac, vii
Ng, William Yau-nang, 218
Niebuhr, Reinhold, 70n40
Nirvana, *nirvāṇa*, 157, 163
nonauthoritarian: Confucius as, 193; Gautama (Buddha) as, 158, 181
nonduality, 172–73, 177
Nouwen, Henri, 84–85, 88

obligation of obedience
and authoritarian political leaders, 49
authority and, 34, 35; charismatic, 8–10, 21, 27, 39, 43; legal, 8
and categories of religious perception, dependence on, 47
and control, personal and social, 31, 33, 43; resisting of, 45, 46–48
diminution of, 19; through routinization, 10–12
existential meaning and, 16
legitimacy of domination, rule, authority, and, 8, 17, 18, 21, 27, 42
owed to Sikh scripture and human Gurūs, 14
spiritual master as garnering, 10, 27, 36
surrender and, 7, 48–49
vitality of inner life and, 19
Osama bin Laden. *See* Laden, Osama bin
Old Testament. *See* Hebrew Bible (Old Testament)

pabbajita, 161
Pachomius, Saint, 83–84
Pañj Piāre, 143
paradox and conundrum
of the Buddhist spiritual master, 156, 172
of the Hindu *gurū*, 117, 120
in Zen: as embedded in *Mu!*, 173; as seed of nondual identity, 172–75; of "there is no north and south in Buddha nature," 177
Paul, Saint, 87, 125n13. *See also* New Testament: quotations from
perplexity: Buddhist, 160; Confucian, 203–4, 205; Hindu, 252 Jewish, 2
pīr, 50n2, 92, 107n2, 140–41
pīr-murīd, 117
Platform Sūtra, 173, 175–77, 186n58
Procrustes, 1
prophets
belief in, as article of faith in Islam, 108n10
Confucian sages vs., of Israel, 198
dual functions of, in Islam, 102–3
as saints in Islam, 102
Sikh celebration of, at Gobind Sadan (India), 137
as Sikh role models, 138
spiritual masters, prime exemplars of, 37
See also Heschel, Abraham Joshua: as prophet; Jeremiah; Jesus: as prophet; Laden, Osama bin: as false prophet; Muḥammad, Prophet; Prophet of Islam; Weber, Max: on charismatic individuals
Prophet of Islam, 30, 38

qigong, 229
qi, 230
Qur'an, Qurʾān, 133
and *ḥadīths*, 37, 96
and Islamic Law, 96 (see also *sharīʿah*)
and the Prophet, 99
Ṣūfī adherence to, 92, 94, 96, 104

rabbi, 2
Radhasoami, meaning of term and movement, 134
Ramana Maharshi, 15, 47, 120, 121, 123, 124, 125n23

Rām Dās, Gurū, 132, 138, 140, 145, 145–46, 149
Rāma, Rām, 24, 25, 27, 37
Rāmānuja, 115–16; 116–17
Rāmāyaṇa, 24, 25, 27
Refuge, refuge, 156, 159, 171, 182–83n7, 242. *See also* Buddhist tradition: religious practices; Three Jewels
religion: institutional, communal vs. individual spirituality, 244
religionist issues. *See* history of religions, academic discipline; *see also* Cousins, Ewert; Eliade, Mircea; Gold, Daniel
reductionist issues. *See* history of religions, academic discipline; sociology, academic discipline; *see also* Lincoln, Bruce; Weber, Max
religions of faith vs. religions of experience, 63
religious leaders, 137
  charisma of, 29, 49 (*see also* Weber, Max: on charisma)
  evaluation of, 43–46, 49
  spiritual masters vs., 48, 53n41
  spiritual master as subcategory of, 3
  disqualified as spiritual master, 7, 31, 47 (*see also* spiritual master: qualifications and qualities of)
  and the obligation of obedience, 16, 33, 42–43, 47, 48, 49
  and power or authority: abuse of, 4, 7, 42; social, 16
ren, 192, 202
renunciation, 40, 137, 226, 228
rnam-thars, 168, 184n32. *See also* Marpa; Milarepa
Roy, Dilip Kumar, 120–21
Roy, Rammohun, 119

Sabbath, 59, 76
Sacks, Jonathan, Rabbi, on Maimonides, 57
Sadaprarudita, 167, 177
sagehood, Chinese
  Confucius and Zhuanzi as having attained, 233
  Confucius as claiming an inabilty to attain, 200–1, 231
  Confucius's life as showing path to attainment of, 201–5
  nature of, 191, 201, 227, 233, 238–40
  Wang Yangming as having attained, 214
  See also Sages, sages
Sages, sages
  Chinese (*sheng*), 3
  Chinese Buddhist, 231
  Confucian: characteristics and qualities of, 192–97, 200, 211–12, 19n6, 219n8; Confucian ideal of, as political leader, 210–11; Confucian lineage of, 211, 215–16; Confucius as exemplar of, 207–10; Confucius's reluctance to claim status as, 200; contributions of, 206–7; criteria of being, 205–6; definition of, 190–92, 202, 207, 212, 218n2, 221n6; difficulty of becoming, 201, 222n81; Israelite prophet vs., 198–99; mission of, 198; Tang Junyi on, 216
  Daoist: activist vs. hermit, 235–37; aristocrat vs. beggar, 237–38; body of, 228–29, 230; characteristics of, 225–26, 231, 235; Confucius as, 231–32, 233; Confucius vs. Zhuangzi as, 232–33; conventional vs. unconventional, 231–33; definition of, 226; mind of, 227–28, 229, 230; motto of, 240; ordinary vs. extraordinary, 233–35; path to becoming a, 227–30; as role model, 230; Zhuangzi as, 232–33

Jewish: *ḥasid* vs., 57; Luzzatto (Moses Hayyim) on, 61, 62; as *talmid ḥakhamim*, master of Torah, 56
See also Confucian tradition, overview; Daoist tradition, overview; Jewish tradition, overview
sage-kings, 209, 211, 212, 218
Sakyamuni, 216. *See also* Gautama, Gautama Buddha; *Jātakas*; *Siddhartha* (Hermann Hesse), Siddhārtha, Prince
Salafists, 98
Salanter, Israel, 64, 67, 70n34
salvation
in Gold's model, 21, 24, 52n31
Jewish notions of, 60
Buddhist notions of, 155, 156, 158, 172, 182
*samā*ʿ, 105
sambhoga-kāya, 171, 183n12
saṃgha
bhikṣu and bhikkhu, Bhikkhu, 161, 179, 186–87n63
bhikṣuṇī and bhikkhuni, Bhikkhuni, 161–63, 178–79, 180, 186–87n63
controversy over ordination of women among males in, 186–87n63
fourfold, of monks, nuns, laymen, and laywomen, 180
Gautama Buddha, running of the, 160, 161–63
longevity of, 241–42
among the Three Jewels, 159, 166, 184–85n33
samyaksambuddha, 50n2
Śaṅkara, 113
Sāriputta, 162
Satyakāma, 113–14
Secret Taiji Method for Cultivating the Elixir (Zhang Sanfeng), 230
Sen, Keshub Chunder, 119
sexual activity
abstaining from, 161
excessive, as harmful, 230
instruction in, as helpful, 247
regulating, 229
revulsion over pleasures in, 58
Shabbatai Tsevi, 43
Shādhilī, Abū al-Ḥasan al-, 105
Shādhilīyah Order, 105
Shangqing School of Daoism, 234
Shangqing Scriptures, 234
sharīʿah, Islamic Law, and religious law (in Islam)
bringing of, as function of major prophets, 102
exoteric, vs. esoteric *ṭarīqah*, 95–96
institutionalization of, vs. institutionalization of Sufism, 96–97
necessity of, in Sufism, 96–97
Ṣūfī beliefs and practices disapproved in, 94–95
and *taṣawwuf*, 99, 108n13
shaykhs
definition of, 50n2, 92, 107n2
and disciples: as *muqaddams* and *khalīfahs*, 101–2; relationship with, 48, 104–6, 249
spiritual lineage of, 101–2
as title, 101–2
See also *barakah*; Muslim tradition, overview: teaching stories and accounts; *silsilah*, Ṣūfīs: masters
Shiv Dayal Singh, 134
Shuowen jiezi, 190, 218–19n5
Siddhartha (Hermann Hesse), 155
Siddhārtha. Prince, 155, 158, 161, 166. *See also* Gautama, Gautama Buddha; *Jātakas*; Sakyamuni; *Siddhartha* (Hermann Hesse)
Sikh tradition, overview, 127–54
egalitarian ethos of, 136–37, 143
God in: devotion to, 132; faith in, 127, 136; and Gurū, 138–39, 144, 145, 149; intimate relationship with, 137; the name of, 140;

Sikh tradition *(continued)*
path to, 131, 138; remembrance of, 133, 134; as *sant*, 134; as *Satgurū*, 142–43 (see also *Nām*; Nānak, Gurū: relationship with God)
Gurūs, *gurūs*: as key symbol of 3; as lineage office in, 12; lineage transmission of, 26–27; 127, 128, 131–32, 142; as Nānak, 14; qualities of, 138–43; recognizing the, 146–49; relationship of, with disciples, 134–35, 149–50; role of, 143–46; and routinization, 37; scripture as, 12–15, 18, 26–27, 151–52
religious practices: *kīrtan*, 132, 151; Hukam, 151; recitation of Mūl Maṃtar, 129–30
teaching stories and accounts: Baba Virsa Singh, 134–36; Gurū Amar Dās, 146–47; Gurū Aṉgad, 144–45; Gurū Gobind Singh, 133, 143, 146, 150; Gurū Har Rāi, 132; Gurū Harkrishan, 132, 147–48; Gurū Nānak, 128–31, 140–41; Gurū Teg Bahādur, 147–48
See also Creator deity; Gurū Granth Sāhib; Gurūs, *gurūs*
silsilahs, 101, 108n16
Sima Zhengzhen, 236–37
simplicity, Daoist, 202, 228, 233, 240
Singh
Khālsā members named, 143
See also Bābā Balak Singh; Bābā Virsa Singh; Bhāī Makhan Singh; Gobind Singh, Gurū; Shiv Dayal Singh
Śiva, 111, 118
Smith, Huston, 42, 76, 122
sociology, academic discipline
method of Gold (D.) vs., 20
and reductionist approach, 4, 16
as a value-free discipline, 45–46
and Weber (M.), 15–16, 19, 26–28, 42, 50–51n9, 51n21, 63n41
See also history of religions, academic discipline; Weber, Max
solitude, 58, 60, 62, 87, 170
spirituality, vii; understood in light of physicality and mentality, 244–46
spiritual masters
and abuse of authority, 116 (*see also* religious leaders)
authenticity of, 2; assessed by quality of disciples, 102
as authoritative teacher of traditions, 3–4, 7, 28–29, 33–38, 39, 43, 44, 54n46
as charismatic mediator, 3–4, 7, 17, 28–33, 36, 38, 39, 43, 44, 54n46
as category of religious perception: 22, 28, 29, 32, 35, 41, 47, 53n41 (*see also* Gurū, *gurū*); lacking in Weberian model, 19
communication of: across a time gap, 41; by thought, look, or touch, 41 (*see also* disciples: esoteric, hidden experience of spiritual masters by)
conflict between, 147–48, 252–53 253n12
and disciples: advice to, 35, 48, 75, 79–80, 179, 193–94; responsibility for, 40, 41, 48, 75, 97, 103–4, 105, 114–15; role in relation to, 92, 100, 103, 106, 124, 144, 157, 164, 167, 169, 183–84n24; role reversal in relation to, 115–16 (*see also* teaching stories and accounts)
as egalitarian, 143, 148–49, 213
as false, 44, 118, 146
as healers, 78
inanimate or not human, 12–15, 29, 47
and moral authority, 34, 35, 36–37, 38, 42, 45: loss of, 42
as nonauthoritarian, 193 (*see also* disciples: antiauthoritarianism of)

obligation of obedience, inspiring an, 27, 35
as personally supporting religious vitality, 3–4, 7, 28–29, 34, 38–43, 44, 45, 47, 53n41, 54n46
political restrictions on, 95
presumed lack of, among: Confucians, 3, 189; Jews, 2, 55
qualifications and qualities of, 2, 34; as authoritative, 10, 12, 43, 76, 88 (*see also* Jesus: five qualities of); Buddhist teachings on, 163–65, 183–84n24; as charismatic, 9–10, 11, 13, 29, 33 (*see also* Weber, Max: on charisma); Confucius's teachings on, 192–93, 197, 200; as esoteric, 21; as exceptional, 29, 33; as exemplary, 9; hierarchy of (Luzzatto, M. H.), 59; Hindu teachings on, 112–17; as lacking ego, 250; as *mysterium fascinans* and *mysterium tremendum*, 32–33; as numinous (Otto, R.) 33; as revolutionary, 32; Sikh teachings on the, 138–43; Wang Yangming's teachings on, 212
religionist vs. reductionist views of, 7, 28
revolutionary impact of, 36
as role models, 45, 93, 122–23, 144, 200
shadow side of, 42, 123
social functions, contributions of, 103, 123, 143, 157
succession of, 113, 131–34, 142, 146–48
See also Gold, Daniel; Gurūs, *gurūs*; *pīr*; Prophet of Islam; prophets; religious leaders; sagehood, Chinese; Sages, sages; *shaykhs*; *spiritual master*, definition; Ṣūfīs: masters; Weber, Max; *and specific traditions*
spiritual master, definition, vii, 1, 3, 7, 15–16, 28–43, 53n41
distortion in, 1
efforts to define, by contributors, 2
etymology of, Latin words pertaining to: *magister*, 3, 4, 73; *magister navis*, 73; *magister populi*, 73; *magnus*, 3, 73; *spirare*, 3, 4, 47, 74; *spiritualis*, 3, 4, 50n4, 74
as "fabrication," two senses of, 1–2
and Gold (D.), relationship to concepts in works of: *gurū*, 16–17, 27; holy man, 17
master in: as denoting more than masculine gender, 3; as problematical, 246; *spiritual* vs., 246
and procrustian bed, 1–2
religionist and reductionist perspectives, accommodated, 28
spiritual in: as problematical, 3
testing the, 43–45
as trope, 2, 3, 17
Venn diagram as clarifying, 28
and Weber (M.), relationship to concepts of: charismatic individuals, 8–12, 14, 16, 27; the person, 12–15; routinization of charismatic authority, 14, 15
See also religious leaders; *and specific traditions, e.g., Christian tradition*
spiritual surgery and pain of transformation, 144, 169–70, 248–49
spiritual yearning, 167, 170, 177, 251
Spring and Autumn Annals, Chunqiu (*Ch'un-Ch'iu*), 209, 210
Śrī Aurobindo, 15, 119, 120, 122
śrotriya, 34, 113, 116
śruti, 113
Ṣūfīs
activities in the *zāwiyahs*, *khānagāhs*, 105

Ṣūfīs *(continued)*
critique of modern, 99
doctrines drawn from Qur'ān and *ḥadīths*, 96
garb, 38–39, 148
master-disciple relationship, 47–48, 92, 104 (*see also* disciples)
masters: charismatic attraction of, 103; legitimacy of, 100–1, 102; Prophet Muḥammad, relationship to, 101, 102 (see also *barakah muḥammadīyah;*); spiritual duties of, 92; as "traditional man" par excellence, 9; in the West, 97 (see also *shaykh*)
orthodox Islam and: *arkan al-'islām* and *arkan al-īmān*, adherence to, 96; loyalty to, 94
Prophet Muḥammad, emulation of, 38, 91
ritual activities of, 104–5
spiritual lineages, 38 (see also *silsilah*s)
teachings, 185n41, 249
traditionalism, 93, 106
See also Muslim tradition, overview; Sufism
Sufism
accusations against, as not orthodox Islam, 93–96
critique of, 98–100; as "a reality without a name," 98, 99; as "a name without a reality," 98
exoteric dimension, importance of, 41
fight for survival of, 2
illegality of, 95
initiation into, 103–4
institutionalization of, 108n12
interaction with Hindu tradition of, 117
marginalized in modern Islam, 243
orders, global nature of, 97–98, 101 (see also *turuq*; and *specific orders;*)
as perennial, timeless, 93, 107
"perpetual tension" between, and *sharī'ah*, 96–98
See also Muslim tradition, overview; Ṣūfī(s); *taṣawwuf*
Ṣūfī tradition, overview. *See* Muslim tradition, overview; Ṣūfīs; Sufism
sunnah, 98
śunyatā, 164
surrender
danger of, 48 (*see also* obligation of obedience)
of disciple to spiritual master, 47–48, 104, 124, 144, 151, 248–49
uncritical, to authority, 7, 49
Śvetāśvatara Upaniṣad, 112, 118
synagogue, 68, 75, 76
Syria, 79. *See also* John of Damascus; Prophet of Islam

tafakkur, 105
Tagore, Debendranath, 119
Tagore, Rabindranath, 119
taijiquan, 229
talmid ḥakham, talmid ḥakhamim (pl.), 36, 50n2, 56
Talmud, 64, 67–68n3, 69n25
Tang Guanzhen, 233–34, 235
Tang Junyi, 215–18
ṭarīqah, 41, 91, 95–96, 100, 103, 108n16
taṣawwuf, 92, 93, 98, 99. *See also* Sufism
Tathagata, Tathāgata, 157, 160, 242. *See also* Gautama, Gautama Buddha; *Jātakas*; *Siddhartha* (Hermann Hesse), Siddhārtha, Prince
TATVAMASI, 124
teaching stories and accounts
Abba Apollos and the young monk, 80–81
Amar Dās, Gurū, 146–47
Aṉgad, Gurū, 144–45
Antony of Egypt, Saint, 87
Augustine of Hippo, Saint, 82
Ayya Khema, 177–78

Baal Shem Tov, 56, 58
Baba Virsa Singh, 134–36
Baddha Kuṇḍalakesa, 161–62
Bāhava and Bāṣkali, 113
Buddha (Gautama), 157, 158–59, 160, 182–83n7250
Confucius, 193–94, 195–96, 201, 231
Dhammadinna, Therī, 163
Droṇācārya and Ekalavya, 116
Fan Li, 235–36
Gandhi, Mahatma, 119
Gobind Singh, Gurū, 133, 143, 146, 150
Har Rāi, Gurū, 132
Harkrishan, Gurū, 132–33, 147–48
Huineng, 176–77
Jesus, 75, 76, 78–79, 83, 251, 253n10
Joshu and the monk, 173–74
Junayd of Baghdād, 248–49
Lieze, 240
Liu An, 237
Lungshu, 239
Mahāprajāpatī, 161
Mantiq-ut-tayr (conference of the birds), 185n41
Merton, Thomas, 85–87
Milarepa, 167, 168, 169–71
Nānak, Gurū, 128–31, 140–41
Nāropa and Tilopa, 168–69
Nouwen, Henri, 84–85
Pachomius, Saint, 83–84
Ramakrishna and Naren (Vivekananda), 119–20
Ramana Maharshi, 120–22
Rāmānuja, 115–16
Ṛbhu and Nidāgha, 114–15
Sadaprarudita, 167
Satyakāma Jābāla, 113–14
Siddhārtha, Prince, 155–56, 166
Sima Zhengzhen, 236
Tang Guanzhen, 233–34
Tang Junyi, 216–17
Teg Bahādur, Gurū, 147–48
Tenzin Gyatso, (Dalai Lama), 178
Thérèse of Lisieux, Saint, 77–78
Thich Nhat Hanh, 179
Vilna Gaon, 57–58
Vivekananda, Swami, 252
Wang (Yangming) Yang-ming's follower, 214–15
Wang Yangming, 212–13
Wei Huacun, 234–35
Zhou Dian, 238
Zhuangzi, 232
See also specific traditions, e.g., Daoist tradition, overview: teaching stories and accounts
Teg Bahādur, Gurū, 132, 133, 148
Thérèse of Lisieux, 41, 77–78, 88
Therī, 161, 163, 183
Three Jewels (Buddhist), 159–60, 184n33
Tirumālai Aṇṭān, 116
Torah, 133
gadol ḥador as, leader of the generation, 56
Heschel (A. J.) on, 66
Jesus and, 67n2
and Luzzatto (M. H.): complying with, 69n25; on path to holiness of, 60, 62
Phinehas ben Yair on, 59
study of: and asceticism, 57, 62; to avoid evil inclinations, 57, 62; as *mitzvah*, 59; prayer vs., 56, 64; worldly involvement vs., 57, 58
talmid hakhamim as sage who mastered, 56
words of, as special, 56, 68n4
See also Hebrew Bible (Old Testament)
Toynbee, Arnold, Dr., 136
Tracy, David, on finding God through "the beloved Son," 76–77
trope, 112. See also *spiritual master*: as trope
tuan gurū, 50n8, 92, 107
turuq, 92, 97, 108n12. *See also* Sufism: orders, global nature of
tzaddik, 50n2, 56, 57, 68n6

Udāsīs, 135
'ulamā', 94, 95, 96

ultimate reality, vii, 6
  Daoist notions of, 225
  Hindu notions of, 114; as Brahman, 111; and *brahmaniṣṭha*, 34–35, 113, 116
upādhyāya, 50n2, 112
upaniṣads. See *specific titles*
Urban II, Pope, 45

Vedas, 35, 112, 113, 133
Virājānanda, Swami, 120
Viṣṇu, 26, 37, 111
Vivekananda, Swami, 119, 249, 252. *See also* Naren

Wāhe Gurū (*Srī Wāhe Gurū*), 138, 142
walāyah, 93, 100, 102, 107n6
Wang Shou-jen. *See* Wang Yangming, Yangming
Wang Yangming, Yangming
  aspiration to become a sage, 212
  on *gewu*, the "investigation of things," 213
  on *liangzhi* (*liang-chih*), 214–15
  poems of, 213
  on sages, 191–92, 212, 213, 215
  Xi Ai on, 213–14
  on *zhizhi*, the "extension of knowledge," 213
Ware, Kallistos, Bishop, 87
Way. See *Dao*, Way of Heaven (*tiandao*)
Weber, Max, 8–15
  on charisma: definition of, 9, 15, 29, 36, 50n3, 50–51n8, 51n21, 51n24, 53n41, 53n42; in Gold's model, 17, 20; Jesus and, 10, 33; loss of, 12–13; moral authority conveyed through, 38; and the obligation of obedience, 10–12, 14, 18, 19, 27; transmission of, 37
  on charismatic individuals, 9–10; magicians, priests, and prophets as, 8, 9, 11, 12, 14, 16, 18, 19; *spiritual master* defined as, 9–10
  Herrschaft typology of, 8, 10, 12–14, 50n3, 51–52n24, 53n41
  on routinization of charismatic authority, 10–12, 17–18, 20, 27, 38, 53n32; Gurū Granth Sāhib as challenge to theory of, 12–15; withstanding the process of, 12, 14, 18–19, 36, 37
  See also *spiritual master*, definition: and Weber (M.)
Wei Huacun, 234–35
wisdom
  Buddhist notions of, 163, 172
  and charisma (Weber), 9
  Confucian notions of, 190, 200, 203–4, 211, 221n61, 231–32 (see also *liangzhi*)
  Daoist notions of, 228, 239
  and eternal heritage (Gold), 17, 23, 52n31
  Luzzatto (M. H.), stress on, 62
  portrayal of, by religious authorities, 7, 28
  of Saint Thérèse of Lisieux, 77
  Sikh notions of, 127, 130, 134, 140, 142, 145, 148
wonder, and standing in awe, 65, 194–95

Xi Shi, 235–36, 237

Yao and Shun, 192, 211

zaddik hador, 65. See also *tzaddik*
zeal, 59, 60–62
Zhang Zai
  on contributions of a sage, 206
  as an important Neo-Confucian, 205
Zhou Dian, 237–38
Zhu Yuanzhang, 238
Zhuangzi, sage, 228, 229, 232–33
Zhuangzi, text, quotations from, 232, 233

www.ingramcontent.com/pod-product-compliance
Lightning Source LLC
Chambersburg PA
CBHW030528230426
43665CB00010B/812
9781438444987